Table of Contents

Sponsor

Discover the Future of API Analysis

API Insights isn't just another tool; it's a game-changer in API schema analysis. We delve deep into three critical aspects of your API - Performance, Design, and Security - providing you with invaluable insights and a comprehensive evaluation.

1. Security, Your Top Priority

Our proprietary tests go beyond the surface to unearth potential security risks. We identify vulnerabilities like API Key Exposure, Cyclical ID Attack Risks, and IDOR Risks. With API Insights, you not only have a tool to help ensure the security of your API but also safeguard the data it handles.

2. Performance Excellence

A high-performing API leads to satisfied customers. We evaluate your API's performance using cutting-edge techniques. From inspecting headers in a single GET request, we are assessing Caching, CDN Usage, and HTTP/2 or HTTP/3 utilization, we leave no stone unturned. Expect a faster and more stable API if you implement our insights.

3. Design Matters

Good design is at the heart of every successful API. API Insights evaluates how well your schema serves developers' needs and how effectively your API is designed. We scrutinize aspects such as error code handling, Personally Identifiable Information (PII) risks, language consistency, and parameter and endpoint descriptions.

Ready to revolutionize your API Schema experience? Visit apiinsights.io today to harness the full potential of this 100% free tool.

Introduction

Hey!

My name is Ash Allen, and I'm a freelance Laravel web developer based in the United Kingdom.

Over the past five years, I've worked on many projects that range from websites for small, local businesses to large-scale enterprise applications for large companies.

During this time, I've been lucky enough to work with fantastic people and companies and learned a lot from them. I've also worked on interesting projects and seen how different teams tackle different problems.

If there's one thing I've noticed during this time, it's that most web applications eventually integrate with an external API. Whether this is for simple things such as sending emails or more complex things such as integrating with a third-party payment gateway, being able to lean on external systems to do the heavy lifting for you can significantly benefit your application. It can allow you to focus on the core features of your application and let external companies handle things you don't need to (and don't want to) worry about. For example, instead of building a payment system for your new web application, you can use Stripe to handle payments. This lets you focus more on building cool new features and have Stripe worry about payment processing.

I've worked with many different APIs, including Stripe, Mailgun, Twilio, Marketo, Zapier, Twitter, Vonage, GitHub, and many more. While working with these APIs, I've noticed common patterns and best practices that I (or the team I'm working with) have been able to use. I've also seen mistakes and oversights that came back to bite us later on.

In this book, we will cover the techniques I've learned and give you a better understanding of how to consume APIs directly from your Laravel application.

We'll start by covering what APIs are, the benefits they provide, the different types of APIs that you might come across, and how to authenticate with them. We'll then cover code techniques I use to make consuming APIs easier. We'll discuss things like `final` classes, `readonly` classes and properties, composition over inheritance, interfaces, data transfer objects, and more.

After this, we'll cover how to consume an API from your Laravel application using Saloon. We'll discuss things like making requests, OAuth2, caching responses, error handling, and testing your API integrations.

Finally, we'll move on to cover webhooks. We'll discuss what they are, how to set them up, and how to securely handle them in your Laravel application.

By the end of this book, you should have an excellent understanding of how to consume APIs directly from your Laravel application using maintainable, testable, and extensible code. You should be confident in your ability to integrate with third-party APIs and able to do so in a secure and robust way.

About APIs

Before writing any code, we must understand some things about APIs. This chapter will cover what APIs are, the different types of APIs you might come across, and the benefits and drawbacks of consuming APIs in your web applications. We'll also cover common data formats you'll encounter in APIs. We'll then cover different types of authentication and API integration security best practices. By the end of this chapter, you should understand how APIs can be used in your Laravel applications and have a good foundation for the rest of the book.

What is an API?

Essentially, APIs (application programming interfaces) are a way for systems to communicate with each other. They allow you to build integrations with systems and services to offer your users more features.

They are typically used to send and receive data without needing to know a system's inner workings. This allows you to focus on building the core of your system and letting other people build specialized features. For example, you might use a third-party payment system such as Stripe to handle payments. This means you don't need to worry about many of the complexities of handling payments, such as PCI (payment card industry) compliance, because they handle storing card details.

Another example of using an API in your application may be using HubSpot to manage your clients. You could use the HubSpot API to create a new contact in HubSpot when a user signs up for your website's newsletter or fills out a contact form. This would allow you to keep your client data in one place and make them easier to manage.

You may also use an API as part of your application's authentication and authorization process. For example, you can allow users to sign in to your application using their Google account. To do this, you could use the Google API to authenticate the user and retrieve their details (such as their name, email address, profile picture, etc.). You've likely seen this before when signing into an application and being presented with options such as "Sign in with Google" or "Sign in with Facebook".

The following diagram shows the high-level flow of how you can send API requests to an external system and receive a response:

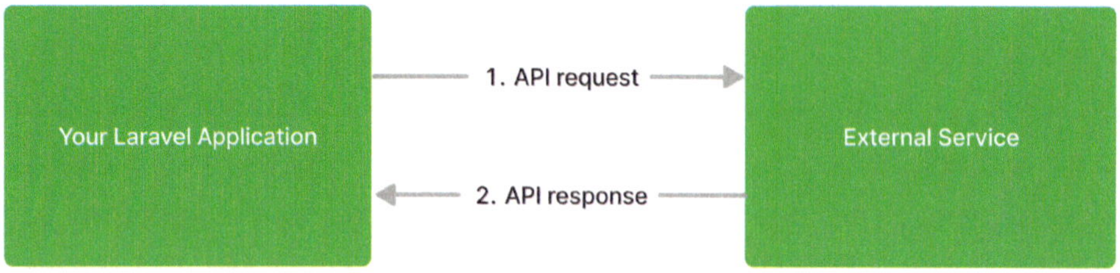

Depending on the types of Laravel projects you work on, you may have already interacted with external APIs without realizing it. Here are some common APIs that you may have already worked with and possible use cases for them:

- **Stripe** - Payment processing
- **Mailgun** - Sending emails
- **Mailchimp** - Email marketing
- **Twilio** - SMS messaging
- **Vonage** - SMS messaging
- **Facebook** - Social media post scheduling
- **Twitter** - Social sign in
- **Instagram** - Social sign in
- **Google** - Social sign in and cloud storage (Google Drive)
- **GitHub** - Accessing repositories and user data
- **AWS**- Cloud storage (S3)

As well as using APIs to communicate with external systems, they can be used to communicate between internal systems. For example, imagine you have an e-commerce website that is split into two separate applications:

- A customer-facing website for viewing products and placing orders.
- An admin panel for employees to manage the stock and orders.

Your admin panel may display some statistics from the customer-facing website. To do this, you could create an API on the customer-facing website that returns the statistics. The admin panel could then make a request to the website's API to retrieve the statistics and display them. This means the admin panel doesn't need to know how the customer-facing website works; it just needs to know how to make a request to the API. This allows you to keep the two systems separate and makes it easier to maintain them. If you were to change how the customer-facing website works, you wouldn't need to change the admin panel because it only interacts with the API. This is a great example of how APIs can be used to communicate between internal systems while abstracting away the system's inner workings. You may also not want the customer-facing website's API publicly accessible, so you could make it private and only allow requests from the admin panel.

The following diagram shows the high-level flow of how you can send API requests between the two systems:

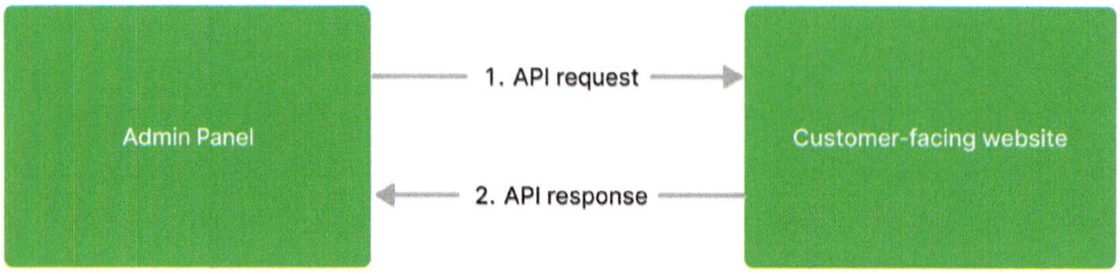

Data Formats: JSON vs. XML

This book will focus on consuming APIs that accept JSON as the request body and return JSON as the response body. However, it's important to be aware that there are other types of data formats that can be used, such as XML. Although you'll most likely work with APIs in your Laravel applications that use JSON, you may sometimes need to consume XML APIs.

Let's look at the difference between JSON and XML and the pros and cons of each.

Data Format: JSON

JavaScript Object Notation (JSON) is a lightweight format that can be used for structuring data. Generally, it can be easy to read and write in PHP, so it's a format you'll often come across. In your Laravel applications, you may see JSON being used for things such as:

- API response bodies (whether the response is sent from or to your application).
- API request bodies (whether the response is sent from or to your application).
- Storing translations in your application (e.g., `resources/lang/en.json`).

JSON supports a limited amount of data types, such as strings, numbers, booleans, arrays, and objects. Let's take a look at an example of some JSON data that makes use of each of these data types:

```json
{
    "name": "John Doe",
    "email": "john.doe@example.com",
    "phone": "555-123-4567",
    "approved": true,
    "age": 27,
    "hobbies": [
        "golf",
        "tennis",
        "football"
    ],
    "address": {
        "street": "123 Main Street",
        "city": "New York",
        "state": "NY",
        "zip": "10001"
    }
}
```

Let's break down the JSON structure above:

- At the top level of the object, the `name`, `email`, and `phone` fields are all strings.
- The `approved` field is a boolean.
- The `age` field is a number.
- The `hobbies` field is an array of strings.
- The `address` field is an object that contains the `street`, `city`, `state`, and `zip` strings fields.

Advantages of JSON

Now that we understand what JSON is, let's look at some of the benefits of using JSON.

Easy to Read and Write

Although data structures like JSON are usually intended to be written and read programmatically, you'll often find that you'll need to read them yourself. You may want to do this to inspect the structure of an API response or to add a new field to a config file.

Due to JSON's simple syntax and format, it's generally human-friendly and can be easy to read and write. This can make it easier to work with than other data formats, such as XML.

Smaller Request, Response and File Sizes

As a result of JSON's lightweight format, it can often result in smaller request, response, and file sizes when compared to other formats, such as XML. Request and response sizes may not be important for smaller applications, but they can become a problem for larger applications that handle a lot of traffic and need to be efficient. Keeping the response sizes as small as possible reduces the chance of exceeding bandwidth limits and improves response times.

Native Support in JavaScript

A huge benefit of using JSON is that JavaScript natively supports it and can be easily parsed by it. This makes it easy to pass data from your Laravel Blade views straight into your JavaScript code or make API requests to external services from your JavaScript files, among other things.

Widely Adopted

JSON is a widely adopted format, which means you'll come across it quite often. As a result, it can be easy to find documentation and examples of how to work with it. This can make it easier to start using the format and consuming APIs that use it because the syntax is something you'll be familiar with.

Disadvantages of JSON

Although JSON is a great format, it has some disadvantages that you should be aware of.

No Support for Comments

As JSON objects grow in size and complexity, you may want to add comments to explain what a particular field is used for. You may particularly want to do this if you're using JSON to define a config file for your application.

However, JSON does not support comments, so this can't be done. This can make it harder to maintain JSON files as they grow and may result in you using a different data format, such as YAML or a PHP array instead, depending on your use case.

Cannot Be Validated Against a Schema

Unlike XML, JSON does not support the concept of a schema. In XML, you can define a schema that specifies the intended structure of an XML document. This can be useful for validating that the XML document is structured correctly and contains the correct fields. In the context of APIs, this is a handy feature because you can validate the XML request body before sending the API request and have confidence that the API will accept it, knowing that the same schema will be used on the API side to validate the request's structure.

Since JSON has no native support for this type of schema, it's not as straightforward to ensure that you have the correct structure.

Data Format: XML

Extensible Markup Language (XML) is another data format that can be used for structuring data. In your Laravel applications, you may have encountered XML files such as the `phpunit.xml` file used to configure PHPUnit in your project's root directory.

It has a similar structure and appearance to HTML, so simple objects can feel quite familiar to work with. However, due to its verboseness, it sometimes becomes overwhelming to read and write as the complexity of the data structure increases.

Let's take a look at how we could represent our previous JSON structure as XML:

```xml
<person>
    <name>John Doe</name>
    <email>john.doe@example.com</email>
    <phone>555-123-4567</phone>
    <approved>true</approved>
    <age>27</age>
    <hobbies>
        <hobby>golf</hobby>
        <hobby>tennis</hobby>
        <hobby>football</hobby>
    </hobbies>
    <address>
        <street>123 Main Street</street>
        <city>New York</city>
        <state>NY</state>
        <zip>10001</zip>
    </address>
</person>
```

In the XML object above, the structure is relatively simple to read.

Adding attributes to XML elements to provide extra information is also possible. As an example, let's remove the `<approved>` element and add it as an attribute to the `<person>` element instead:

```xml
<person approved="true">
    <name>John Doe</name>
    <email>john.doe@example.com</email>
    <phone>555-123-4567</phone>
    <age>27</age>
    <hobbies>
        <hobby>golf</hobby>
        <hobby>tennis</hobby>
        <hobby>football</hobby>
    </hobbies>
    <address>
        <street>123 Main Street</street>
        <city>New York</city>
        <state>NY</state>
        <zip>10001</zip>
    </address>
</person>
```

Advantages of XML

Now that we understand what XML is, let's look at some of the benefits of using XML.

Self Describing

Due to XML's verbose nature, a well-structured XML document can often be easy to understand. This is because the structure of the document can be self-describing as a result of the tags and attributes that are used.

Can Be Validated Against a Schema

XML provides the functionality for a schema to be defined for a document. This can ensure the document's structure is as expected and can be used as part of the validation process to ensure it contains the correct fields and attributes.

Imagine we want to validate that a `<person>` object contains a `<name>` field, an `<email>` field, and an `<age>` field. We could define a schema for this object that looks like this:

```
<person>
    <name>John Doe</name>
    <email>john.doe@example.com</email>
    <age>27</age>
</person>
```

To ensure the object is valid, we could define a schema for the XML. A few formats can be used to define an XML schema, but the most common is XML Schema Definition (XSD). For our example, an XSD might look like this:

```xml
<xs:schema elementFormDefault="qualified"
           xmlns:xs="http://www.w3.org/2001/XMLSchema"
>
  <xs:element name="person">
    <xs:complexType>
      <xs:sequence>
        <xs:element type="xs:string" name="name"/>
        <xs:element type="xs:string" name="email"/>
        <xs:element type="xs:integer" name="age"/>
      </xs:sequence>
    </xs:complexType>
  </xs:element>
</xs:schema>
```

As you can see in the schema above, we've defined that the `<age>` field should be an integer. Thus, if we were to create a `<person>` object with a string value for the `<age>` field, the schema would not validate, and the object would be invalid.

The XML schema can be used to validate the object programmatically before using the object. For example, you can validate your XML document before sending it as a request body to an external API. Or, the API may want to validate the XML document when it is received before processing it.

Similarly, if you are building the XML document manually (such as in a config file), your integrated development environment (IDE) would be able to validate the object against the schema and display error messages if the object does not match the schema. To do this, we could update the XML document like so (assuming that the schema file is located at `https://example.com/my-person-schema.xsd`):

```xml
<person
    xmlns:xsi="http://www.w3.org/2001/XMLSchema-instance"
    xsi:noNamespaceSchemaLocation="https://example.com/my-person-schema.xsd"
>
    <name>John Doe</name>
    <email>john.doe@example.com</email>
    <age>27</age>
</person>
```

Supports comments

An advantage of using XML over JSON is that it supports comments. This can be useful when you want to provide additional information about the structure or contents of the document.

XML comments are defined the same way you would define comments in HTML. For example, let's add a comment to the XML document above:

```xml
<!-- This is a comment -->
<person>
    <name>John Doe</name>
</person>
```

Disadvantages of XML

Although XML has some advantages, it also has some disadvantages that you should be aware of.

Verbose

Due to the verbose nature of XML and its support for elements and attributes, XML documents can become difficult to read as they grow in complexity and size.

More Difficult to Parse in PHP and JavaScript

Compared to JSON, XML can be more difficult to parse in PHP and JavaScript. Although you can read XML documents in both these languages, it's not always as straightforward as running something like `json_encode()` or `json_decode()` in PHP when working with JSON.

Thus, working with XML documents can add extra complexity to your code.

HTTP Message Structure

During this book, we'll look at many examples of HTTP messages sent as API requests and responses. These examples will follow a standardized structure to help you understand the different parts of the message.

To familiarize yourself with this structure, let's look at an example API request and response.

Example HTTP Request Message

Imagine we want to send a request to an API endpoint that will create a new user. To do this, we'll need to send a `POST` request to the `/users` endpoint. We'll also need to include an `Authentication` header that contains an API key that we can use to authenticate the request. We will also need to include the `Content-Type` and `Accept` headers that tell the API that we are sending the request body in JSON format and want to receive the response in JSON format.

The HTTP message for the request may look something like this:

```
POST /users HTTP/3
Host: example.com
Content-Type: application/json
Accept: application/json
Authorization: Bearer 1234567890

{
    "name": "John Smith",
    "email": "john@example.com",
    "password": "secret"
}
```

The message above can be broken down into three separate parts:

- Start line
- Headers
- Body

The start line and headers are separated from the body by a blank line.

The start line is the first part of the message:

```
POST /users HTTP/3
```

The start line specifies that we want to send a `POST` request using the HTTP version 3 protocol to the `/users` endpoint.

We then have the headers for the request. Headers contain information about the request, such as the HTTP method, the URL, authentication details, and so on.

```
Host: example.com
Content-Type: application/json
Accept: application/json
```

In our example, we've specified that we want to send the request to the host available via the `example.com` domain (meaning the request will be sent to `https://example.com/users`). We've also specified that we want to send the request body in JSON format and that we want to receive the response in JSON format.

The final part of the message is the request body:

```
{
  "name": "John Smith",
  "email": "john@example.com",
  "password": "secret"
}
```

The request body is in JSON format and contains the data that we want to send to the API. In this case, we're sending the name, email, and password of the user that we want to create.

Example HTTP Response Message

Continuing with our example of creating a user via an API request, let's now look at the HTTP message response we might receive from the API.

The HTTP message for the response may look something like this:

```
HTTP/3 201 Created
Content-Type: application/json

{
    "id": 1,
    "name": "John Smith",
    "email": "john@example.com"
}
```

You may have noticed that the structure of the response is very similar to the structure of the request in that it contains a start line, headers and a body.

The start line and headers of the message form the first part of the response:

```
HTTP/3 201 Created
Content-Type: application/json
```

We can see that the response is returned using the HTTP version 3 protocol and that the response body is in JSON format. The response also contains the status code `201 Created` to indicate that the request was successful and that a new resource was created.

The body of the response is the second part of the message:

```
{
    "id": 1,
    "name": "John Smith",
    "email": "john@example.com"
}
```

The response body then contains some information about the newly created user. Depending on the API you're interacting with, this response may contain more information about the newly created user. On the other hand, some APIs may only return the ID of the newly created resource.

Let's take a quick look at several other common HTTP response messages you may encounter when working with APIs.

You'll likely come across HTTP `404 Not Found` responses that indicate that the resource you're trying to access does not exist:

```
HTTP/3 404 Not Found
Content-Type: application/json

{
  "status": 404,
  "error": "Not Found",
  "message": "The requested resource could not be found."
}
```

Another common response that you may come across is the HTTP `401 Unauthorized` response, which typically indicates that your API keys are invalid:

```
HTTP/3 401 Unauthorized
Content-Type: application/json

{
  "status": 401,
  "error": "Unauthorized",
  "message": "Invalid API key."
}
```

One more common response you may encounter is the HTTP `422 Unprocessable Entity` response, which typically indicates that the request body contains invalid data. You'll likely come across this when trying to create or update a resource via an API request:

```
HTTP/3 422 Unprocessable Entity
Content-Type: application/json

{
  "status": 422,
  "error": "Unprocessable Entity",
  "message": "The given data was invalid.",
  "errors": {
    "name": [
      "The name field is required."
    ],
    "email": [
      "The email field is required."
    ]
  }
}
```

Now that we've briefly covered the structure of HTTP messages, this should help you understand the examples we'll be looking at throughout the rest of the book.

Types of Web APIs

This book focuses on REST APIs that use JSON, which is likely the most common type of API you will come across when building Laravel applications. However, it's important to be aware of other types of APIs (such as GraphQL, RPC, and SOAP) you may come across and what they are used for. You'll generally consume REST APIs in your apps using JSON, but you may sometimes need to work with these other types. For this reason, we'll delve into REST APIs more than the other types, but we'll still have a quick look at the other types.

REST APIs

Representational State Transfer (REST) APIs are the type you will usually come across when building Laravel applications. REST is an architectural style for building APIs and provides a set of constraints (think of these as guidelines or rules) that developers can follow.

Generally, you communicate with REST APIs using the Hypertext Transfer Protocol Secure (HTTPS) protocol. This means you can use the HTTP methods (such as `GET`, `POST`, `PUT`, `PATCH`, and `DELETE`) to perform create, read, update, and delete (CRUD) operations on resources. Typically, REST APIs can use either XML or JSON to send and receive data.

The REST constraints encourage a simple and standardized approach to API communication. This makes it easier for developers to understand and use the API. Let's take a look at the constraints that REST APIs follow:

1. Client-Server Constraint

The REST architecture is based on a client-server model.

The term "client" refers to the application or machine consuming the API. The client would typically be responsible for handling the user interface and user input. The term "server" refers to the application or machine that provides the API. The server would typically accept API requests, handle business logic, and send responses back to the client.

This constraint means that the client and server can exist independently, and this separation means that either side can be updated without impacting the other.

2. Stateless Constraint

The REST architecture specifies that all requests to the API should be stateless. This means that the server should not store any state about requests and that each request should be independent of the previous request. Thus, a REST API should not use things like cookies, sessions, or URL parameters to store state.

Instead, the client should send all the information the server needs to process the request in the request itself. This approach encourages isolation, making it easier to scale the API, as the server does not need to store any state between requests.

3. Cacheable Constraint

The REST architecture specifies that clients must be able to cache responses sent from the server, so responses must include information that tells clients whether the response can be cached and for how long.

Allowing clients to cache responses can reduce the number of API requests a client may need to make. This can improve the client application's performance and reduce server load. This is particularly useful when a large number of clients are using the API.

Suppose you're sending a request to an API that provides exchange rate information between two currencies on a given date. You may want to cache the response for a given date so that you don't need to make the same request again in the future (since the exchange rate for a given date won't change). This means that future requests for the same date could be served from the cache or storage (such as Redis or the database) rather than needing to make a request to the API.

4. Uniform Interface Constraint

The REST architecture specifies that the API should have a uniform interface. This means the API should have a standardized way of communicating with it. This makes it easier for developers to understand and use the API.

This constraint is broken down into four sub-constraints:

4.1. Resource Identification in Requests

This sub-constraint specifies that a resource can be identified in the request. This means the request should specify the resource it wants to interact with, typically by passing a resource identifier in the request's uniform resource identifier (URI).

For example, if you want to get a list of all the users in your application, you may send a `GET` request to the `/users` URI. This URI would identify the resource you want to interact with (in this case, the "users" resource). Similarly, if you want to get details of a specific user with an ID of `1`, you may send a `GET` request to the `/users/1` URI. This URI identifies the resource you want to interact with.

4.2. Resource Manipulation Through Representations

This sub-constraint specifies that a client should be able to manipulate (create, update, and delete) resources by passing representations of the resource in the request's body. This representation should contain all the information that the server needs to perform the action on the resource.

For example, if you want to create a new user, you may send a `POST` request to the `/users` URI. This URI would identify the resource you want to interact with (in this case, the "users" resource). The request body would also contain a representation of the user that you want to create. If the request body was in JSON format, a simple example may look something like this:

```
{
    "name": "John Smith",
    "email": "john@example.com",
    "password": "secret"
}
```

The JSON example contains all the information the server needs to create a new user. Likewise, if we wanted to update the user, we could send another request with the updated representation of the user to the API.

4.3. Self-Descriptive Messages

This sub-constraint specifies that the API should use self-descriptive messages for both the request and response, so all the necessary information needed by the server and client to understand the request or response should be included in the request or response. Thus, the request or response should not rely on external information for the client or server to understand them.

The various HTTP methods can indicate the action the request wants to perform on the resource, making the messages self-descriptive. The following HTTP methods are typically used:

- `GET` - Retrieve a resource. This is typically a read-only operation and should not change the resource's state.
- `POST` - Create a new resource. It's not idempotent, meaning that sending the same request multiple times may create multiple resources.
- `PUT` - Update an existing resource or create one if it doesn't already exist. This is idempotent, so sending the same request multiple times will typically only create or update one resource.
- `DELETE` - Delete an existing resource. Like `PUT`, this is idempotent such that the resource will stay deleted.
- `PATCH` - Update an existing resource (typically only making partial updates to a resource). This is not idempotent; the resource may be updated multiple times if the same request is sent multiple times.

You may also come across other HTTP methods, such as the following:

- `HEAD` - Retrieve the headers for a resource. This is similar to `GET` but doesn't return the response body. This is useful for fetching metadata about a resource without needing to fetch the entire resource and can be used to check if a resource exists.
- `OPTIONS` - Retrieve information about the communication options available for a resource. This is useful for determining what HTTP methods are supported by a resource.

In addition to using the HTTP method to indicate the action, headers in a request can provide additional information that the server can use. For example, the request headers may contain authentication tokens; the response headers may contain information about rate limiting, the payload data type, and information about caching. For instance, the `Content-Type` header can be passed in the request or response to specify what data type the request or response body is in. For example, if the request body is in JSON format, the `Content-Type` header would be set to `application/json`. If the request body is in XML format, the `Content-Type` header would be set to `application/xml`. This allows the server to know how to parse the request body.

The client can also pass an `Accept` header in the request to specify the data type the response should return. Similar to the `Content-Type` header, this allows the client to know how to parse the response body. For example, if the client wants the response in JSON format, the `Accept` header would be set to `application/json`. If the client wants the response to be in XML format, the `Accept` header would be set to `application/xml`.

To further assist the client, the API can also use HTTP status codes to indicate the status of the request. For example, if the request was successful, the API could return a `200 OK` status code. If the resource in the request couldn't be found, the API could return a `404 Not Found` status code. The following are some of the most common codes indicating the status of requests:

Success Codes (2xx) indicate that the request was received, understood, and accepted.

- `200 OK` - Request successful
- `201 Created` - New resource created
- `202 Accepted` - Accepted but not yet completed (e.g., action queued)
- `204 No Content` - Successful, but no content to return

Client Error Codes (4xx) indicate the request was unsuccessful because the client made an error.

- `400 Bad Request` - Error in the request (e.g., malformed URL, missing headers, etc.)
- `401 Unauthorized` - Client is not authenticated
- `403 Forbidden` - Client is not authorized to access the resource
- `404 Not Found` - The resource could not be found
- `405 Method Not Allowed` - The HTTP method (`GET`, `POST`, etc.) is not allowed on the resource
- `422 Unprocessable Entity` - The request body contains invalid data (e.g., fields in the request body failed validation when creating or updating a resource)

Server Errors (5xx) indicate something wrong with the server.

- `500 Internal Server Error` - Unsuccessful due to an error on the server

As a result of using the payload, HTTP methods, headers and status codes, the request and response can be self-descriptive and contain all the information needed by the server and client to understand the request or response. These principles can help the API follow the "Stateless Constraint" by removing the need to rely on any external information to understand the request or response.

To provide some context, let's briefly refer back to our examples from the "HTTP Message Structure" section, where we send a request to create a new user, as they are examples of self-describing messages. The request may look something like this:

```
POST /users HTTP/3
Host: example.com
Content-Type: application/json
Accept: application/json

{
    "name": "John Smith",
    "email": "john@example.com",
    "password": "secret"
}
```

The example request specifies that a `POST` request should be sent using the HTTP version 3 protocol to the `/users` URI on the `example.com` domain (meaning the request will be sent to `https://example.com/users`). The request also specifies that the request body is in JSON format and that the response should also be in JSON format. The request body contains the information the server needs to create a new user.

Assuming that the request was successful and that the server was able to create the new user, the response may look something like this:

```
HTTP/3 201 Created
Content-Type: application/json

{
    "id": 1,
    "name": "John Smith",
    "email": "john@example.com"
}
```

In the example response, we can see that the response is returned using the HTTP version 3 protocol and that the response body is in JSON format. The response also contains the status code `201 Created` to indicate that the request was successful and that a new resource was created. The response body then contains some information about the newly created user.

4.4. Hypermedia as the Engine of Application State (HATEOAS)

Another sub-constraint of the REST architecture is the "Hypermedia as the Engine of Application State" (HATEOAS) constraint. This constraint states that the API should provide links to related resources in the response.

This can allow the client to navigate the API without knowing the URLs of the related resources. For example, imagine we want to retrieve a user from the API and then retrieve their blog posts. In a REST API, this would typically be done in two separate requests. The first request would be to retrieve the user, and the second would be to retrieve the user's blog posts. If the API does not implement HATEOAS, the response body of the first request may look something like so:

```json
{
    "id": 1,
    "name": "John Smith",
    "email": "john@example.com"
}
```

As you can see, the response body only contains information about the user. If we want to retrieve the user's blog posts, we need to find the URL of the blog posts resource (presumably from the API documentation) and then build the URL in our code to send the request. This URL may be something like `users/1/posts`. However, if the API implements HATEOAS, the response body of the first request may look something like so:

```json
{
    "id": 1,
    "name": "John Smith",
    "email": "john@example.com",
    "links": [
        {
            "rel": "posts",
            "href": "/users/1/posts"
        }
    ]
}
```

As we can see in the JSON response, there is now a `links` property, which contains an array of links to the related resources. In this case, we can use the `rel` property of the link to determine which link we need to use to retrieve the user's blog posts. Thus, when we make our second request to fetch the posts, we don't need to know the URL and instead can programmatically get the URL directly from the first response.

It's worth noting that there is no standardized way of implementing HATEOAS in an API. As a result, the `links` property may be named something else, such as `related` or `resources`. The `rel` property may also be named something else, such as `type` or `name`. Similarly, the `links` property may not be in the response body. Instead, the links may be returned in the response headers. For example, the `Link` header may return links to related resources. You should be aware of this when working with different APIs, so you must check the API documentation.

5. Layered System Constraint

The layered system constraint states that the client should not be able to tell whether it is connected directly to the server or an intermediary (such as a proxy server, load balancer, or gateway). As a result of doing this, the client doesn't need to know how the server is implemented or how the request is routed to the server. Instead, they can be treated almost as a black box and the client can just send a request to the server and receive a response.

Implementing this constraint means that the server can have the flexibility to change its infrastructure and request handling without the client needing any changes to its code. For example, imagine an API service was updated to use a load balancer (that routed to multiple application servers). In that case, clients using the API wouldn't need to make any changes to their code because they're making requests to the API as a whole rather than a specific machine. An API implementing the layered system constraint could also be updated to have additional security measures or caching mechanisms without the client's knowledge.

6. Code-on-Demand Constraint (Optional)

The final constraint, which isn't used very often, of the REST architecture is the "Code-on-Demand" constraint. This constraint is optional, so an API can still be considered RESTful if it does not implement this.

The constraint states that the server can return executable code to the client that can be used to extend the client's functionality. This is typically JavaScript code that can be executed in the browser. For example, the server may return some JavaScript code that can be used to render a UI component.

This constraint is optional because returning executable code is not always necessary. It should always be used with caution as it can introduce security vulnerabilities by allowing code to be executed on the client you haven't written yourself.

Advantages of REST APIs

REST APIs can provide a range of advantages over other types of APIs. Let's take a look at some of them.

Simplicity

Compared to other types of APIs (such as GraphQL and SOAP), REST APIs are generally much simpler to use. This is due to the fact there is a smaller learning curve to understanding the overall architecture and how to use it. This makes it easier for developers to use the API and be onboarded to a project using it.

Scalability

Because REST APIs implement the "layered system constraint", the API can be scaled to handle increased loads if needed. For example, if a specific part of the API receives more traffic than the other parts, it could be scaled independently of the other parts of the API — this may be by moving the specific part to another server or adding caching mechanisms to the specific part. This can all be done without the client's knowledge and without the client needing to make any changes to their code.

Performance

REST APIs can be faster than other types of APIs (such as SOAP) because they can use smaller payloads. For example, SOAP APIs require the payload to use an "envelope" (covered later), which can significantly increase the payload size and the time it takes to process the request on the server. However, REST APIs typically use JSON as the data format for the request and response payloads, which is much smaller than XML and doesn't require an envelope.

Caching

Another advantage of REST APIs is that their responses can be cached. As a result of this, it means that developers consuming the API can improve the performance of their application by storing the response. This is also extremely useful for avoiding rate limits imposed by the API provider.

Disadvantages of REST APIs

Although REST APIs provide a range of advantages, they also have some disadvantages that you should be aware of. Let's take a look at some of them.

Lack of Standardization

Although the flexibility of REST APIs can be seen as an advantage, this can result in a lack of standardization. Different APIs may implement REST principles in different ways, so getting used to the "quirks" of a specific API can be difficult.

For example, as we've already briefly covered, if a REST API implements HATEOAS, the related resource links may be added via a `links`, `related`, or `resources` property in the response body or via a response header. This means you usually need to read the API documentation to understand how the API has been implemented.

Over-Fetching and Under-Fetching

One of the disadvantages of REST APIs is that they can suffer from "over-fetching" and "under-fetching". Over-fetching is when the API returns more data than you need, and under-fetching is when the API doesn't return enough data, and you need to make additional requests to get the data you need.

To demonstrate these points, imagine you want to make an API request to retrieve a user's name from an API endpoint. If the API returns the user's name but also the user's email address, phone number, and address, this would be an example of over-fetching. This is because you only need the user's name, but the API returns more data than you need. This can result in slower performance and larger payloads, especially when interacting with the API at scale.

Conversely, imagine you want to retrieve a user's name and a list of their blog posts. Because REST API requests are typically made for a single resource, you'd need to make two separate requests to the API — one to retrieve the user's name and another to retrieve the list of blog posts. This is an example of under-fetching because you need multiple requests to the API to get the data you need.

These points are both solved by GraphQL APIs, which we'll cover later in this section. GraphQL APIs allow you to specify exactly what data you need in a single request, avoiding over-fetching and under-fetching.

Versioning

Typically, REST APIs are versioned by adding a version number to the URL of the API. For example, if the API is currently on version 1, the URL may look something like this:

```
https://api.example.com/v1/users
```

Whereas if the API is on version 2, the URL may look something like this:

```
https://api.example.com/v2/users
```

Adding version control to the URL means that the API can be updated without breaking existing clients using an older version of the API. Although this can be advantageous, it can also be a disadvantage because it can result in the API having multiple versions that need to be maintained by the API provider.

From an API consumer perspective, it can sometimes also be troublesome because you may need to update your integration to use the newer version of the API so you can still have access to the latest features. Because many breaking changes are usually bundled into a new API version, this can sometimes be a time-consuming process affecting many parts of your API integration.

This issue doesn't typically exist in GraphQL APIs because they are usually version-less. Instead, GraphQL APIs are usually updated by adding new fields to the schema. This means that existing clients can still use the API without making any code changes. However, if the client wants to use the new fields, they can update their integration to use the new fields. They can also deprecate existing fields to indicate to the consumer that the field should no longer be used. Thus, API integrations can be updated incrementally and at a pace that suits the consumer rather than updating all of the integration at once.

GraphQL APIs

GraphQL is a query language for APIs as well as a runtime that can be used to serve the queries.

To understand GraphQL, it's useful to have a brief glimpse into the history of how it came to be and the issues it aims to solve. In 2012, Facebook started rebuilding their native iOS application to prepare it for an ever-growing native mobile app market. The original API that powered the "news feed" in the app returned HTML, so it was difficult to make changes, and the API was tightly coupled with the mobile app. Facebook decided to hire some additional iOS app developers and attempted to migrate the app over to using a newer RESTful API. Using this approach, data could be returned to the app from the API, and then the app could handle building and displaying the news feed as needed.

However, the developers started to experience some problems that made them question whether a RESTful API would be the most suitable for rebuilding the app. They ran into several problems:

- **Under-fetching and over-fetching** - As we've already covered, RESTful APIs are prone to under-fetching and over-fetching. For some applications, this isn't usually a problem. However, for a website as large as Facebook that has a large number of users, this will result in an even more significant number of requests. So, the developers found making multiple requests to get the data they needed for a single page problematic. The API responses contained more data than was needed about a specific resource, and multiple requests needed to be made (one for each type of resource). This can be slow and expensive in terms of money and infrastructure bandwidth.
- **The app was still coupled to the API** - Although the app wasn't as tightly coupled when HTML was being returned, the app was still coupled to the API. It meant that the app was still dependent on the API, and any changes to the API would likely require changes to be made to the app. Because there can be many versions of an app out in the wild being used, this can make maintenance problematic. Changing the API might mean the app needs to be updated, but not all users will do that. This also meant multiple versions of the API documentation needed to be maintained, which can be a lot of work.

To tackle these issues, some of the developers proposed a new approach to building APIs: GraphQL.

The aims of GraphQL were to:

- Allow API developers to strictly define the fields and the types of data that can be queried using a schema. This would allow the API to be more predictable and allow the API to be more self-documenting.
- Allow API consumers to query multiple resources in a single request. This would reduce the number of requests to be made to the API.
- Allow API consumers to define the exact fields to be returned. This means the API consumers can get exactly what they need and nothing more.
- Allow API consumers to evolve their queries over time. This would allow the API consumers to add new fields to their queries as needed and deprecate old fields. This reduces the need for versioning the API the way you would with a RESTful API and, instead, allows for a single evolving version of the API.

In 2015, Facebook decided to open source GraphQL, and it's since been adopted by many other companies such as GitHub, Meta, and PayPal.

Example API Schema

Let's look at the main components of a GraphQL API and some examples of HTTP requests and responses. Imagine we have an API for a blogging web application. Within this application, we have two different models: `Author` and `Post`.

An `Author` has the following properties:

- `id` - The unique identifier for the author.
- `name` - The name of the author.
- `email` - The email address of the author.
- `verified` - Whether the author's email address has been verified.
- `profilePicture` - The URL to the author's profile picture. This is optional.

A `Post` has the following properties:

- `id` - The unique identifier for the post.

- `title` - The title of the post.
- `content` - The content of the post.
- `author` - The author of the post. Under the hood, this is a foreign key to the `Author` model (presumably `author_id` in the database).

The API has the functionality to do the following:

- Fetch all the authors in the system.
- Fetch a single author by their ID.
- Fetch a single post by its ID.
- Create a new author.
- Create a new post.

Let's take these requirements and build a GraphQL schema to define the API. The schema can be used to specify things such as:

- The API's data types, such as `string`, `boolean`, or even custom fields such as `Author` and `Post`.
- Whether a field is mandatory or optional.
- The relationships between different types of data.
- The queries (read operations) that can be performed on the API.
- The mutations (write operations) that can be performed on the API.

The schema for this simple API may look something like this:

```
type Author {
  id: ID!
  name: String!
  email: String!
  verified: Boolean!
  profilePicture: String
  posts: [Post!]!
```

```
}

type Post {
  id: ID!
  title: String!
  content: String!
  author: Author!
}

type Query {
  author(id: ID!): Author
  authors: [Author!]!
  post(id: ID!): Post
}

type Mutation {
  createAuthor(
    name: String!, email: String!, verified: Boolean!
  ): Author

  createPost(title: String!, content: String!, authorId: ID!): Post
}
```

Let's break down some of the key points from this schema.

We are defining two data types called `Author` and `Post` in our schema using the `type` keyword. Within each of these fields, we then define which properties each type can have.

You may have noticed that the `name` field in the `Author` type has a data type of `String!`, whereas the `profilePicture` field has a data type of `String`. The `!` symbol after the `String` data type means the field is mandatory, whereas the lack of the `!` symbol means the field is optional.

The `Author` type also includes a `posts` field with a type of `[Post!]!`. This means the `posts` field is an array of `Post` objects. The `!` symbol after the `Post` data type means that the array cannot be null, and the `!` symbol after the array means that an array will always be returned (even if it's empty). By adding this definition, it means that we can include the posts for an author in the API response when making queries to fetch authors.

Similarly, the `Post` type also includes an `author` field with a type of `Author!`. This means we can include the author for a post in the API response when making queries to fetch posts.

The `Query` type defines the queries that can be made to the API. In this case, we have defined three queries:

- `author(id: ID!): Author` - Fetch a single author by their ID. The `id` field is mandatory, and the query will return an `Author` object.
- `authors: [Author!]!` - Fetch all the authors in the system. The query will return an array of `Author` objects.
- `post(id: ID!): Post` - Fetch a single post by its ID. The `id` field is mandatory, and the query will return a `Post` object.

The `Mutation` type defines the mutations (creating, updating, and deleting of resources) that can be made via the API. In this case, we have defined two mutations:

- `createAuthor(name: String!, email: String!, verified: Boolean!): Author` - Create a new author. The `name`, `email`, and `verified` fields are mandatory, and the mutation will return an `Author` object.
- `createPost(title: String!, content: String!, authorId: ID!): Post` - Create a new post. The `title`, `content`, and `authorId` fields are mandatory, and the mutation will return a `Post` object.

Example API Requests

Now that we have defined the schema for our API, let's look at how we can make requests to the API. GraphQL APIs are typically accessed via a single endpoint, so we'll assume that our example API's endpoint is `https://www.example.com/graphql`. Although GraphQL APIs can be accessed via the `GET` or `POST` HTTP methods, it's common practice to use the `POST` method.

Please note that the `query` field may be presented on multiple lines in the request examples. This is just for readability purposes, and the `query` field would typically be on a single line when making requests to the API.

First, let's take a look at a request we could make to fetch the IDs and names of all the authors in the system:

```
POST /graphql HTTP/3
Host: www.example.com
Content-Type: application/json

{
  "operationName": "FetchAuthorNames",
  "query": "query FetchAuthorNames {
                authors {
                    id
                    name
                }
            }"
}
```

As we can see, we've passed the query in the `query` field of the request body. We've also passed the name of the query in the `operationName` field. This is optional, but it's good practice to include it, as it can be helpful for debugging.

The response from the API would look something like this:

```
HTTP/3 200 OK
Content-Type: application/json

{
  "data": {
    "authors": [
      {
        "id": "1",
        "name": "John Doe"
      },
      {
        "id": "2",
        "name": "Jane Doe"
      }
    ]
  }
}
```

As we can see, the response contains only the `id` and `name` fields of the authors.

We could take this further and include the post titles for each author in the response. To do this, we can update the query in the request to look like so:

```
POST /graphql HTTP/3
Host: www.example.com
Content-Type: application/json

{
  "operationName": "FetchAuthorsAndPostTitles",
  "query": "query FetchAuthorsAndPostTitles {
              authors {
                  id
                  name
                  posts {
                      title
                  }
              }
          }"
}
```

As we can see, we've added a nested `posts` field to the query. The response from the API would look something like this:

```
HTTP/3 200 OK
Content-Type: application/json

{
  "data": {
    "authors": [
      {
        "id": "1",
        "name": "John Doe",
        "posts": [
          {
            "title": "Post 1"
          },
          {
            "title": "Post 2"
          }
        ]
      },
      {
        "id": "2",
        "name": "Jane Doe",
        "posts": []
      }
    ]
  }
}
```

The response shows that the first user has some posts, which are included in their `posts` field. However, the second user has no posts, so their `posts` field is an empty array.

If we wanted to fetch a single user in the system, we could make use of the `author(id: ID!): Author` query. For example, if we wanted to fetch the ID and name of the author with an ID of `1`, we could make a request like so:

```
POST /graphql HTTP/3
Host: www.example.com
Content-Type: application/json

{
  "operationName": "FetchSingleAuthorName",
  "query": "query FetchSingleAuthorName($id: ID!) {
                author(id: $id) {
                    id
                    name
                }
            }",
  "variables": {
    "id": "1"
  }
}
```

This request includes a `variables` field in the request body where we can pass parameters to the query. In this case, we pass the `id` variable to the query with a value of `1`. The response from the API would look something like this:

```
HTTP/3 200 OK
Content-Type: application/json

{
  "data": {
    "author": {
      "id": "1",
      "name": "John Doe"
    }
  }
}
```

As we can see, the response contains the `id` and `name` fields of the author with an ID of `1`.

All our requests so far have been `query` requests. Let's look at how we can make a `mutation` request. For example, if we wanted to create a new post, we could make a request like so:

```
POST /graphql HTTP/3
Host: www.example.com
Content-Type: application/json

{
  "query": "mutation CreatePost(
                $title: String!,
                $content: String!,
                $authorId: ID!
            ) {
                createPost(
                    title: $title,
                    content: $content,
                    authorId: $authorId
                ) {
                    id
                    title
                    author {
                        name
                    }
                }
            }",
  "variables": {
    "title": "New Post",
    "content": "This is a new post.",
    "authorId": "1"
  }
}
```

As we can see, instead of using the `query` keyword at the beginning of the `query` field, we've used the `mutation` keyword. This tells the API we want to request a `mutation` request. We've also passed the three variables to the mutation needed to create the new blog post for the author with an ID of `1`. The response from the API would look something like this:

```
HTTP/3 200 OK
Content-Type: application/json
Content-Length: length

{
  "data": {
    "createPost": {
      "id": "p3",
      "title": "New Post",
      "author": {
        "name": "John Doe"
      }
    }
  }
}
```

Since we defined that we only wanted the post's ID, title, and author's name to be returned in the response, that's all that's returned.

Advantages of GraphQL APIs

GraphQL provides a number of advantages to both the API developers and the API consumers. Here are some of the main advantages:

Product-centric Approach to APIs

Typically, the responses in a RESTful API are driven by the server, meaning that the API developers will determine what data an API endpoint should return. The data structure is usually determined to be as reusable as possible to cover as many use cases as possible. However, as we've covered, this can lead to under-fetching and over-fetching, which can be problematic if the API receives many requests at once.

Using GraphQL, responses can be more product-specific. API consumers can define exactly what fields they need to get their applications working. This can benefit the API developer as their infrastructure will be less strained. It can also benefit the API consumer as they can get exactly what they need in a single request, which should, theoretically, be faster than making multiple requests.

Strongly Typed Schema

As we've seen above, GraphQL uses a strongly typed schema. This schema can define not only the structure of the data the API will return but also the types of the data. This is useful for API consumers because it makes the responses predictable.

The schema can also generate code and documentation for the API. This can help API consumers understand how to use the API and start using it more quickly.

Single Evolving Version of the API

GraphQL APIs don't typically use the concept of versioning you might see in a REST API. As we've covered, a REST API might use a version number in the URL to indicate the API version the consumer wants to use. For example, `https://example.com/api/v1/users` to fetch all the users using version 1 of the API, or `https://example.com/api/v2/users` to use version 2.

While this can be useful for creating a clear distinction between the APIs, this can also cause a lot of maintenance overhead.

If the consumer wants to use the latest version of the API, they'd need to update their code and potentially spend a lot of time rewriting some features to work with any breaking changes that are introduced. It also means the API developers need to maintain multiple versions of the documentation.

However, with GraphQL, there is typically only a single version of the API. API developers can deprecate fields in the schema and introduce new fields so API consumers can evolve their queries over time and use the new fields as needed.

A benefit of doing this is that the API developers don't need to maintain multiple versions of documentation and can just update the existing one. It also means the API consumers don't need to update their code to use the latest API version; they can simply update their queries to use the new fields when needed.

Continuing with our `Author` type, imagine the API developers want to deprecate the `verified` field. Instead of using a boolean to represent the verification of a user, they decide the verification status of a user may be one of three values: `VERIFIED`, `UNVERIFIED` or `PENDING`. They could deprecate the `verified` field and introduce a new `verificationStatus` field. So the schema may now look something like this:

```graphql
enum VerificationStatus {
  UNVERIFIED
  PENDING
  VERIFIED
}

type Author {
  id: ID!
  name: String!
  email: String
  verified: Boolean! @deprecated(
    reason: "Use 'verificationStatus' instead."
  )
  verificationStatus: VerificationStatus!
  profilePicture: String
  posts: [Post!]!
}
```

As we can see in the example schema, the `verified` field has now been deprecated using the `@deprecated` directive, along with a reason that explains why the field has been deprecated. The API consumer can now update their queries to use the new `verificationStatus` field instead of the deprecated `verified` field.

We have also introduced a new `VerificationStatus` enum using the `enum` keyword to show the possible values the `verificationStatus` field can have.

Data Returned from Multiple Sources

Another aim of GraphQL is to hide the complexity of the data sources from the API consumer. The GraphQL endpoint is the point of entry for the API consumer, but behind the scenes, the data could be coming from multiple sources. For example, parts of the response could be coming from a database, other parts could be coming from a cache, and other parts could even be coming from another API. The API consumer doesn't need to know where the data is coming from; they only need to know how to query it.

Disadvantages of GraphQL APIs

Although GraphQL provides many advantages, it also has some disadvantages. Here are some of the main disadvantages:

Learning Curve

One of the disadvantages of using GraphQL is that it has a relatively steep learning curve, not only for the API developer but also for the API consumer.

The API developer needs to learn how to define the schema and write resolvers — the functions used to fetch the data to build the responses. The API consumer must also learn how to read and understand these schemas to write queries to fetch the necessary data. They'll also need to learn how to write mutations to update the data and how to make the requests to the GraphQL endpoint.

Having a steep learning curve isn't necessarily a bad thing, and that isn't specific to GraphQL either. But if a developer is coming from a RESTful API background, they'll need to learn a lot of new concepts, which might take some time. If the API is better suited as a REST API, the extra complexity of GraphQL might not be worth it, as it might make it harder to maintain and adopt.

Increases Caching Complexity

In REST APIs, the endpoints are typically resourced-based, meaning that if you make an API call to get a resource (e.g. `/api/v1/users/1`), you'll only get that resource's data. This makes it easy to cache the response so that the next time we attempt to fetch that specific resource from the API, we can retrieve it from our cache instead. This is particularly useful if this resource is used in multiple places around the application because we'll likely already have the data we need in our cache.

However, caching responses from GraphQL APIs isn't as straightforward. First, the GraphQL endpoint is typically a single endpoint, so we can't cache responses based on the URL.

Second, the responses are bespoke to the query that was made, so we can't cache the response from one query and use it in another place. For example, let's imagine that we have three separate places where we want to handle or display a user's data that we've fetched from the API:

1. A user profile page - We need the user's profile picture, email, and name.
2. A list of the user's blog posts - We need some of the user's data and a list of their blog posts.
3. A list of the user's friends - We need some of the user's data and a list of their friends.

Since one of the aims of GraphQL APIs is to prevent under-fetching and over-fetching, we could query precisely the data we need in each of these scenarios. As a result, the responses would be bespoke to each situation and make it difficult to reuse in other places. Although we could still cache these responses for reuse in their specific use cases, it reduces the chances of us being able to use the cached responses in other places. Whereas with a REST API, we could likely cache the response from `/api/v1/users/1` and use it in all three places (assuming we also made extra API calls to fetch the blog posts and friends).

Depending on the application, this might not be a problem. You may also be able to find a way to fetch the data in a way that allows you to reuse the response in multiple places. But it's typically more straightforward with a REST API.

Probably Not Needed for Simple APIs

One of the main benefits of GraphQL is that it allows you to fetch exactly the data you need. This can result in the consumer making fewer API calls and being more performant, making it well-suited for APIs that might be used by mobile apps where data usage is important or for APIs constantly receiving many requests (such as Facebook's) that need to be quick.

However, if you're not building something as complex that isn't going to receive a massive amount of requests, it might not be worth the extra complexity of GraphQL. Its benefits shine for complex APIs used by a lot of people, but for simple APIs, it might be overkill. Remember that GraphQL is just a tool and is not always the right tool for the job. Often a traditional REST API would be better suited for your needs.

RPC APIs

Another type of API you may encounter is Remote Procedure Call (RPC). RPC APIs are typically used for server-to-server communication where performance is key. Thus, they're often used to communicate between microservices and distributed systems or to build APIs for mobile applications and IoT devices.

The concept of running procedures in a remote process was first used in the 1970s but is typically credited as being formalized in 1981 by Bruce Jay Nelson. He proposed the concept of RPC in his dissertation while at the University of California. Then, in 1998, Dave Winer created a new protocol based on RPC called "XML-RPC", which focused on using XML as the data format for the messages. JSON-RPC followed this in 2005, which used JSON as the data format. Following this, Google released gRPC (General remote procedure call) in 2015, which is based on HTTP/2 and uses Protocol Buffers (sometimes referred to as "Protobuf") as the data format.

This section will focus on gRPC, which RPC APIs typically use. gRPC powers the APIs of huge companies such as Netflix, IBM, Cisco, Dropbox, and Google.

Whereas REST APIs revolve around resources, RPC APIs revolve around actions. RPC APIs are thus better suited for exposing actions rather than CRUD-like operations on resources like REST. For example, if you were to build an API for sending a message in a REST API, you might send a `POST` request to a `/messages` endpoint. But in an RPC API, only a single API endpoint is available, and the request contains the action you'd like to carry out (as defined by a schema, which we cover next). You would send a request to the single API endpoint with the name of the action to carry out (such as `SendMessage`) along with the necessary data.

gRPC generally has four types of RPC methods:

- **Unary** - Similar to a typical HTTP request where the client sends a request to the server and waits for a response.
- **Server streaming** - The client makes a single request but expects multiple responses from the server. This is used when the client needs a lot of data from the server, such as a large file or video stream.
- **Client streaming** - The client makes many requests to the server, expecting a single response. This is useful when the client needs to send a large amount of data to the server, such as a large file or video upload.
- **Bidirectional streaming** - Both the client and server send data streams to each other. This is useful when the client and server need to send lots of data to each other, such as a chat application.

gRPC APIs use a similar concept to GraphQL and SOAP APIs in that they have a schema definition that can be used to describe the API interface. This allows defining important information about the API, such as the existing endpoints, what data the endpoints accept, the data types, and the data that will be returned. These schemas are typically defined inside `.proto` files by the API developer.

Let's look at examples of what goes into a gRPC schema definition. Imagine we're building a simple gRPC API for a bookstore. We need functionality to add a new book, get a book, and list all books.

```
syntax = "proto3";

package bookstore;

// The book message structure.
message Book {
  string isbn = 1;
  string title = 2;
  string author = 3;
  int32 pages = 4;
  double price = 5;
}

// The request structure to add a new book.
message AddBookRequest {
  Book book = 1;
}

// The response structure after adding a book.
message AddBookResponse {
  string message = 1;
}

// The request structure to get a book.
message GetBookRequest {
  string isbn = 1;
}
```

```
// The request structure to list all books.
message ListBooksRequest {}

// The response structure for listing all books.
message ListBooksResponse {
  repeated Book books = 1;
}

// The BookStore service definition.
service BookStore {
  // Adds a new book to the store.
  rpc AddBook(AddBookRequest) returns (AddBookResponse) {}

  // Retrieves a book's information by its ISBN.
  rpc GetBook(GetBookRequest) returns (Book) {}

  // Lists all books in the store.
  rpc ListBooks(ListBooksRequest) returns (ListBooksResponse) {}
}
```

Let's break down what's going on here. First, we define the syntax version that we're using. Then, we define the package name, which will be used to group the messages and services and will also be used by code generation tools when generating the code.

We then define the different message types that are available in the API:

- `Book` - Defines the structure of a book. It has fields that define a book's properties, such as the ISBN, title, author, number of pages, and price.
- `AddBookRequest` - Defines the request structure to be sent when adding a new book. It has a single field called `book`, of type `Book`. This means when adding a new book, the

client will send a request that contains a `Book` message.
- `AddBookResponse` - Defines the response structure sent after adding a new book. It has a single field called `message` of type `string`. This means when adding a new book, the server will send a response that contains a `string` message.
- `GetBookRequest` - Defines the request structure sent when getting a book. It has a single field called `isbn` of type `string`. This means when getting a book, the client will send a request containing a `string` ISBN.
- `ListBooksRequest` - This defines the request structure sent when listing all books. It has no fields. This means when listing all books, the client will send a request containing no data.
- `ListBooksResponse` - This defines the response structure sent after listing all books. It has a single field called `books` of type `repeated Book`. This means when listing all books, the server will send a response that contains a list of `Book` messages.

You may have noticed that each of the message type's parameters are numbered. This is because gRPC uses Protocol Buffers as the data format for sending the request and response messages. The numbers are used to identify the fields in the serialized data. For example, when serializing a `Book` message, the `isbn` field will be identified by the number `1`, the `title` field will be identified by the number `2`, and so on.

Finally, we define the `BookStore` service. This defines the actions that are available in the API. Each action is defined by an RPC method using the `rpc` keyword. In this case, we have three RPC methods: `AddBook`, `GetBook`, and `ListBooks`. Each RPC method defines the request and response types. For example, the `AddBook` RPC method takes an `AddBookRequest` and returns an `AddBookResponse`.

While gRPC uses HTTP/2 for transport, it's unlike a typical HTTP API such as a REST or GraphQL API, where you can easily make calls using standard HTTP clients or tools like curl or Postman. Instead, gRPC clients and servers must use the gRPC libraries to correctly serialize and deserialize the messages and interact with the HTTP/2 protocol. For this reason, we can't delve into the details of how to make gRPC calls in this guide. However, if you are interested in learning more about consuming a gRPC API using PHP, you can check out the gRPC documentation at https://grpc.io/docs/languages/php.

Advantages of RPC APIs

Here are some advantages RPC APIs provide over other API types, such as REST APIs.

Highly Performant

A key benefit of using gRPC is efficiency and high performance. One reason is that it's built on HTTP/2 and can use features such as multiplexing, which allows multiple requests to be sent over a single TCP connection. This significantly improves performance because a new TCP connection doesn't need to be established for each request.

Efficient

As mentioned, gRPC uses a data format called Protocol Buffers, a binary format designed to be highly efficient. Converting data into a binary format makes it much smaller than it would be if sent in a text-based format such as JSON or XML. This can result in a significant performance improvement and is also perfect for mobile and IoT applications where bandwidth may be limited and energy efficiency is important.

Of course, it is possible to use something like "gzip" (or other compression algorithms) to compress JSON data that may be sent, but this adds an extra layer of complexity and requires that the client and server both support it. As well as this, data sent in protocol buffers is generally still smaller than data that's been compressed using gzip.

Automatic Code and Documentation Generation

As mentioned, gRPC APIs use a schema defined in `.proto` files. This schema allows you to define the messages sent and received by the API.

These schemas allow tools to generate "stubs" for the API in several languages. "Stubs" refers to the code used to convert the data between a format that can be transmitted over the network and the format used in the application. For example, the stubs are used to convert the data from the format used in your application to binary data that can be sent over the network. Then, when the server receives the data, the stubs are used to convert the binary data back into the format used in your application.

By passing in the schema definition, you can use tools to generate the stubs. This is perfect if you want to create any packages or libraries that other developers can use to consume your API.

Similarly, the schema definitions can be used to generate documentation for the API so that it can be shared with other developers.

Disadvantages of RPC APIs

Although RPC APIs provide many advantages, they also have some disadvantages. Here are some of the main disadvantages:

Not Natively Supported by Web Browsers

A significant disadvantage of gRPC APIs is that a web browser can't natively consume them, as browsers don't allow access to the low-level HTTP features required to consume gRPC APIs. Thus, you can't natively use JavaScript to consume a gRPC API in a web browser.

You can use gRPC APIs in a web browser with a JavaScript client library called gRPC-Web. It works with a proxy server, Envoy, which converts between browser-friendly HTTP requests and gRPC requests. Envoy handles sending and receiving data, making it work seamlessly in the browser.

As you can imagine, this can add extra complexity to the architecture of an application and also removes some benefits of using gRPC (such as client streaming and bidirectional streaming capabilities) since the connection is being made to a proxy server rather than directly to the gRPC API.

Not a Lot of Standardization

Compared to other types of APIs, such as REST, there is limited standardization of gRPC APIs, and there isn't much consistency between them. For example, if you wanted to create a new user in a REST API, you would typically send a `POST` request to a `/users` endpoint. However, in a gRPC API, there isn't a standard way of doing this. Some gRPC APIs may use a `createUser` or a `storeUser` action. Although the action names may be self-descriptive and understandable once found, they might be difficult to discover since you need to learn the conventions of each API.

SOAP APIs

Simple Object Access Protocol (SOAP) APIs are a web service that uses the SOAP standard for sending and receiving messages. SOAP APIs are typically used in enterprise applications, so you may encounter them when working on a large-scale application.

It was created in 1998 by Microsoft as a web communication protocol to exchange data between machines. By design, it's language-independent and platform-independent because it follows a standard XML format that enforces a strict structure. This was important when it was first created as it made it easier for different systems to communicate with each other. However, SOAP is typically only used today to provide APIs for enterprise applications.

While REST and GraphQL APIs use HTTP for sending and receiving messages, SOAP APIs can use a variety of protocols, such as HTTP, SMTP (Simple Mail Transfer Protocol), and FTP (File Transfer Protocol). Unlike REST APIs, which can support JSON or XML, SOAP only supports XML for the message structure. In fact, one of the key characteristics of SOAP APIs is that the SOAP standard strictly defines the message structure. A SOAP message contains the following parts:

- **Envelope** - Encapsulates the entire message.
    - **Header** - An optional field containing information about the message, such as authentication details.
    - **Body** - Contains the payload of the message being sent.
        - **Message Block** - Contains the actual data in the payload.
        - **Fault** - An optional field containing information about any errors.

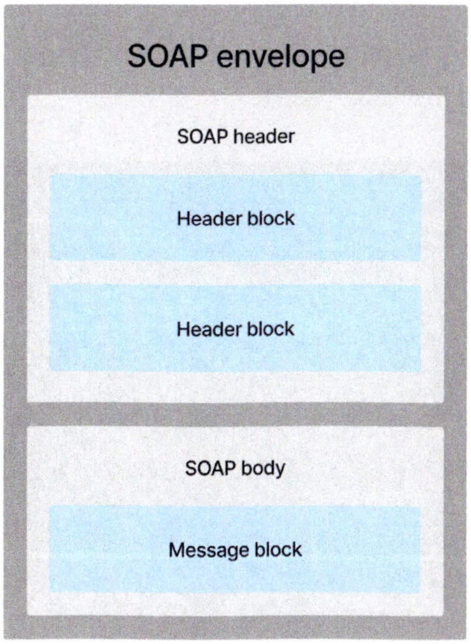

Although you might not come across SOAP APIs as much as REST APIs, SOAP APIs are still very much in use today. SOAP focuses on security rather than performance, so it's ideal for use in enterprise applications where security is a top priority, such as financial transactions, telecommunications, and payment gateways. It's also a stateful protocol, meaning it can chain messages together so they are aware of previous requests. This is useful for things like financial transactions where you might need to make multiple requests to complete a money transfer between bank accounts. This contrasts with REST APIs, which are stateless and know nothing about previous requests. SOAP also used to be a popular choice for building APIs, so you may come across SOAP APIs if you're consuming an older API or working on a legacy application.

SOAP APIs typically use an XML document called a "Web Services Description Language" (WSDL) to describe the API. This is a standardized way to describe the functionality of a SOAP API and what operations it supports. WSDL documents are optional, so they might not always be available — but knowing how to call a SOAP API without a WSDL document can be difficult.

To better understand what interactions with a SOAP API may look like, let's look at an example WSDL, a request, and a response. Imagine a SOAP API available at `https://example.com` that allows you to fetch the name, email, and verification status for a single user. The WSDL document for this API may look something like this:

```
<?xml version="1.0" encoding="UTF-8"?>
<definitions name="UserService"
             targetNamespace="https://www.example.com/user"
             xmlns:tns="https://www.example.com/user"
             xmlns:xsd1="https://www.example.com/user/xsd"
             xmlns:soap12="https://schemas.xmlsoap.org/wsdl/soap12"
             xmlns="https://schemas.xmlsoap.org/wsdl">

  <types>
    <xsd:schema targetNamespace="https://www.example.com/user/xsd"
                xmlns:xsd="https://www.w3.org/2001/XMLSchema">
      <xsd:complexType name="User">
        <xsd:sequence>
          <xsd:element name="name" type="xsd:string" />
```

```
        <xsd:element name="email" type="xsd:string" />
        <xsd:element name="verified" type="xsd:boolean" />
      </xsd:sequence>
    </xsd:complexType>

    <xsd:element name="User" type="xsd1:User"/>
  </xsd:schema>
</types>

<message name="GetUserRequest">
  <part name="userId" type="xsd:string"/>
</message>

<message name="GetUserResponse">
  <part name="User" type="xsd1:User"/>
</message>

<portType name="UserPortType">
  <operation name="GetUser">
    <input message="tns:GetUserRequest"/>
    <output message="tns:GetUserResponse"/>
  </operation>
</portType>

<binding name="UserBinding" type="tns:UserPortType">
  <soap12:binding style="rpc"
      transport="https://schemas.xmlsoap.org/soap/http"/>
  <operation name="GetUser">
    <soap12:operation soapAction="urn:GetUser"/>
    <input>
      <soap12:body use="literal"/>
```

```
      </input>
      <output>
        <soap12:body use="literal"/>
      </output>
    </operation>
  </binding>

  <service name="UserService">
    <documentation>Get User by ID</documentation>
    <port name="UserPort" binding="tns:UserBinding">
      <soap12:address location="https://www.example.com/user"/>
    </port>
  </service>

</definitions>
```

This may look a little overwhelming at first glance, so let's break down what each part of this WSDL is for:

- **`definitions`** - The root element of the WSDL document. It contains all the other elements.
  - **`types`** - Contains the data types used in the WSDL document. We're defining a single data type called `User` with two string fields called `name` and `email` and a boolean field called `verified`.
  - **`message`** (first occurrence) - Defines a message that can be sent or received by the SOAP API. The first occurrence of the `message` in this document defines the request message for the `GetUser` operation. It specifies that a `userId` field should be sent in the request.
  - **`message`** (second occurrence) - Defines a message that can be sent or received by the SOAP API. The second occurrence of the `message` in this document defines the response message for the `GetUser` operation. It specifies that a `User` field should be

sent in the response.

        - `part` - Defines a part of the message.
    - `portType` - Defines the operations the SOAP API supports. We're defining that the SOAP API supports a single operation called `GetUser` that accepts a `GetUserRequest` message and returns a `GetUserResponse` message.
    - `binding` - Defines the concrete protocol and data format specification for the SOAP API. We're defining that the `GetUser` operation should be sent over HTTP using the SOAP protocol.
    - `service` - Defines the service for the SOAP API. It defines the endpoints the SOAP API is available at. This example specifies that the `UserService` service is available at `https://www.example.com/user`.

If we were to send a request to this SOAP API to fetch a user with the ID `123`, it may look something like this:

```
POST /user HTTP/3
Host: www.example.com
Content-Type: application/soap+xml; charset=utf-8

<?xml version="1.0" encoding="UTF-8"?>
<soap12:Envelope
    xmlns:soap12="https://www.w3.org/2003/05/soap-envelope"
    xmlns:usr="https://www.example.com/user"
>
    <soap12:Header/>
    <soap12:Body>
        <usr:GetUserRequest>
            <usr:userId>123</usr:userId>
        </usr:GetUserRequest>
    </soap12:Body>
</soap12:Envelope>
```

The response to this request may look something like this:

```
HTTP/3 200 OK
Content-Type: application/soap+xml; charset=utf-8

<?xml version="1.0" encoding="UTF-8"?>
<soap12:Envelope
    xmlns:soap12="https://www.w3.org/2003/05/soap-envelope"
    xmlns:usr="https://www.example.com/user/xsd"
>
    <soap12:Body>
        <usr:GetUserResponse>
            <usr:User>
                <usr:name>John Doe</usr:name>
                <usr:email>johndoe@example.com</usr:email>
                <usr:verified>true</usr:verified>
            </usr:User>
        </usr:GetUserResponse>
    </soap12:Body>
</soap12:Envelope>
```

Advantages of SOAP APIs

SOAP APIs have a number of advantages over other API types, such as REST and GraphQL. These include:

Standardized Message Structure

The SOAP standard strictly defines the message structure, thereby standardizing it to promote language and platform independence.

Security is a First-Class Citizen

SOAP APIs can use the Web Services Security (WS-Security) protocol built on top of SOAP to secure messages. This standardized way to encrypt and sign SOAP messages is ideal for enterprise applications where security is a top priority. WS-Security focuses on three key areas of security:

- **Confidentiality** - Ensures confidentiality of the message by encrypting it; only the intended recipient can read it (using a decryption key).
- **Integrity** - Ensures the message hasn't been tampered with during transmission. It does this by signing the message using a digital signature and then verifying the signature at the other end to make sure it hasn't been tampered with.
- **Authentication** - Ensures the message's sender is who they say they are by including tokens or certificates.

With other types of APIs, such as REST APIs, security is typically something the API developers must implement themselves. This means it's easy to make mistakes, and each API you deal with may use a different approach to security. However, with SOAP APIs, by making security a first-class citizen built into the standard, it's much easier to secure SOAP messages and know that each SOAP API you deal with will use the same approach to security.

Placing a significant focus on security rather than performance means that SOAP APIs can be ideal for financial transactions, telecommunications, and payment gateways.

ACID-Compliant

By default, SOAP APIs are stateless, meaning requests have no knowledge of previous or future requests. However, SOAP APIs can be stateful, allowing messages to be chained together. This means that SOAP APIs can be used to create complex workflows and messages that are also ACID-compliant through protocols such as WS-AtomicTransaction. WS-AtomicTransaction belongs to the same family of protocols as WS-Security and is used to ensure that a set of operations either all succeed or all fail as a group. This is important when trying to preserve data consistency across multiple operations and distributed systems.

ACID (Atomicity, Consistency, Isolation, and Durability) is a set of properties that guarantee database transactions are processed reliably. The properties are as follows:

- **Atomicity** - Ensures that either all operations in a transaction are processed or none of them are processed. It treats all smaller operations (such as writing data to multiple tables in a database) as a single unit of work.
- **Consistency** - Ensures the data is always in a valid state and never left in a partially-completed state.
- **Isolation** - Ensures the data is isolated from other transactions until the transaction is complete.
- **Durability** - Ensures that once a transaction is complete, the data is permanently stored and won't be lost in the event of power loss, crashes, errors, etc.

These properties are important for things like financial transactions where you need to be sure the transaction is processed correctly and reliably. Although SOAP itself isn't ACID-compliant (because SOAP is a protocol and not a database), the messages can form part of an ACID-compliant transaction. For example, you may have a SOAP API to transfer money between two bank accounts. The API could be used to create a transaction that is ACID-compliant so that if the transfer fails for any reason, the transaction is rolled back, and the money is returned to the original account.

Disadvantages of SOAP APIs

SOAP APIs have some disadvantages. These include:

Complexity

SOAP APIs can have a steep learning curve. The API developer needs to learn the SOAP standard, how to implement it, and how to create a WSDL document to describe the API and create the messages sent to and from the API. The consumer needs to learn how to call the API and interpret the messages returned from the API.

Slower Performance

SOAP API messages contain a lot of verbose XML wrapped inside the envelope, meaning they can be quite large. This can hurt performance because the messages take longer to transmit over the network and parse at the other end.

The performance can also take another hit if the API uses WS-Security to secure the messages, as messages must be encrypted or signed when sent and then decrypted or verified at the other end. This adds overhead on both ends of the API.

As covered, SOAP APIs aren't typically used for things where performance is a top priority. So, depending on the use case, this may not be a problem.

Caching Complexity

When SOAP APIs are consumed using HTTP, the requests are all sent via the `POST` method. Thus, the requests can't be cached by the client or any intermediate proxies at the HTTP level because the `POST` method is non-idempotent — the same request can't be sent multiple times and have the same effect. This means if you're consuming a SOAP API and want to implement caching, you'll likely want to implement it in your application instead of relying on HTTP-level caching. Depending on the use case, this could become complex and involve parsing the SOAP messages and determining which parts you want to cache yourself.

The Benefits of APIs

APIs provide many advantages for your web application and your business. Here are some of the main benefits:

Promotes Automation

Access to APIs allows you to automate tasks that may have been manual before, such as syncing data between systems. Imagine your business has a website and uses a CRM (customer relationship management) system. When a user submits a contact form on your website, you must manually input the details into your CRM. This manual process could be automated. By integrating with your CRM's API, you could automatically create a new contact in your CRM every time a user submits a contact form on your website.

Providing automation like this can speed up business processes and allow you to spend more time on other tasks. An added benefit is that it can reduce the risk of human error, saving time and money.

Improved Services

Allowing users to integrate with other systems and services can increase sales of your application. By providing a way for users to integrate your system into their existing workflows, you can encourage them to want to use your application more.

For example, imagine a new business owner looking for an e-commerce system to sell their products. They might already have a workflow set up with Mailchimp and want to continue using it for their email marketing. They'd like it if every time a new customer bought something from their shop, the customer would be automatically added to their Mailchimp list so they receive newsletters. By integrating with Mailchimp's API, you can allow them to do this.

It would allow them to continue using their existing workflow without significantly changing their business. By reducing the friction a user has in using your application, you can encourage them to use it more.

Improved Security and Mitigation of Risk

Security is a crucial aspect of any web application. Using APIs, you can improve the security of your web application and mitigate the risk of compromising sensitive information by sending it to a third party.

Imagine your web application needs to take payments. You could build your own payment system, but this would require you to be PCI-compliant and do a lot of work. It would also mean you would need to store card details on your own servers, which could incur significant security risks. Instead, you could use a third-party payment system such as Stripe, which would do the hard work of being PCI-compliant and securely storing card details. You can then focus on building the core of your application and let Stripe handle the payment processing.

It's important to note that you should use a third-party payment system you trust. Using third-party systems like Stripe doesn't automatically make your application's payment system secure. You must still ensure you securely handle sensitive information and follow security best practices.

Encourages Innovation and Creativity

From a developer's perspective, APIs can encourage you to build features for your application that you might not have thought of before.

For example, say you want to add SMS messaging to your web application. To add this feature, you'd need to know how telecommunications work and jump through many hoops to get it working correctly. You'd need to ensure that SMSes could be sent and received, get them to work internationally, and you'd want logging so you can check the statuses of the messages — all while adhering to different countries' rules and regulations. As you can imagine, this is a lot of work and would take a lot of time to get right.

Instead, you could use a third-party SMS messaging service like Twilio or Vonage. This would allow you to focus on building the core of your application while relying on the third-party system to handle the complexities of sending and receiving SMS messages.

Drawbacks of APIs

Although APIs provide many benefits, there are drawbacks to be aware of when working with them.

Building the Integration

As with any code you write, you must ensure your API integration code is secure, well-tested, and implemented correctly. If you don't do this, you could end up with a security vulnerability or a bug that causes your application to break.

Depending on the type of API you're integrating with and what you're doing with it, this can mean the integration takes a long time to build — especially when building a complex workflow involving multiple systems. For example, integrating with an API that uses a single API request to send an email would take much less time than building an automated phone call system (involving menus, voice recordings, etc.) using Twilio's API.

Although integrations may remove manual work from your business processes, it doesn't necessarily mean it will be quicker to build the integration. You should decide on a case-by-case basis whether the API integration benefits outweigh the time it takes to build and maintain the integration.

Rate Limiting

Rate limiting constrains the number of requests that can be made to an API in a time period. This helps prevent malicious users or poorly written code from making too many requests to the API and potentially causing it to become unreliable or crash.

This is a handy security feature, but it can cause extra work for developers, particularly on larger projects that send many API requests.

Imagine building a web application to import users from a CSV file. For each imported user, you must send an API request to a CRM system to create them as a new contact. For this example, assume the CRM's API has a rate limit of 1,000 requests a minute.

If the CSV never had more than 1,000 rows, we wouldn't need to worry much about the rate limiting. However, what if the CSV contained 100,000 rows? We'd need to make at least 100,000 API requests to the CRM system. In this case, we'd need to ensure we only make 1,000 requests per minute to the CRM system. This means we'd need to add some kind of rate limiting to our code to ensure we don't exceed the API's rate limit.

Of course, some APIs support batching, meaning you can create multiple users per API call. For instance, if the CRM system supported batching, you could send a single API request to create 1,000 users at once. This means you'd only need to make 100 API requests to the CRM system rather than 100,000, which reduces our rate-limiting concerns. However, it's important to note that not all APIs support batching.

It's important to build out your API integration with rate limiting in mind because it can drastically change how you approach the code for your integration.

Security

When you are working with third parties via an API, you don't know how they are storing and handling your data. You have limited visibility into their security practices and can't be sure they're following security best practices. Thus, you're leaving your data and your users' data in the hands of the third party and trusting they will keep it safe.

Remember — you should only use APIs from third parties that you trust.

Vendor Lock-In

"Vendor Lock-In" refers to becoming overly reliant on a specific vendor's product or service. This is often due to having built your application around the vendor's product or service, making switching to a different vendor extremely difficult.

Imagine you built a web application that uses a third-party API to add a complex feature to your application (such as an automated phone system that includes menus, phone recordings, etc.). If you later decide to switch to a different API vendor, you'd need to rewrite some of your code to use the new API. Depending on the complexity of the integration and code, this could be a lot of work. This can make switching to a different vendor difficult and lead to vendor lock-in.

There are some ways to reduce the risk of vendor lock-in. For example, you could place your code that interacts with the API behind an abstraction layer (using interfaces), allowing you to switch out the implementation of the API code without changing the rest of your application's code.

However, if you're using features that only the vendor's API supports, vendor lock-in may be unavoidable.

Sending Sensitive Information

Depending on the API you're integrating with, you may need to transmit sensitive information, such as when sending credit card details to a payment gateway for payment processing. If sending such information to an API, you must follow security best practices to handle the information securely.

You'll also need to ensure you're informing your users of where their data is being sent for full transparency and privacy reasons. If you don't need to send their personal information, try to avoid doing so.

Authentication

When sending requests to APIs, you must often authenticate to gain access. APIs use several ways of authenticating when making requests. Let's look at some common authentication methods you may encounter.

Bearer Tokens

Bearer tokens are a common authentication method you'll likely encounter when consuming an API. It involves sending a token in your HTTP request that identifies you and grants access to a given resource. A useful way to remember what the term "bearer token" means is to think of the token as a key that gives the "bearer" holding it (your application) access to a resource.

Bearer tokens were initially designed for OAuth 2.0, with the "bearer authentication scheme" being created in RFC (request for change) 6750 of the OAuth 2.0 specification. The idea is that the API consumer would generate an access token in real time using an OAuth service and then pass that token in the subsequent requests. However, it's now common to see bearer tokens used with APIs that don't use OAuth 2.0. This is due to them being a relatively simple authentication method to implement, both for the API developer and the API consumer. We'll go into more depth later in the book about using OAuth and bearer tokens to consume an API.

Typically, the bearer tokens are generated on the API's server and returned to the API consumer. The consumer can then use the bearer token to authenticate themselves when making requests to the API. As briefly mentioned, the tokens may be generated in real time using something like OAuth. But if the service isn't using OAuth, the tokens may be generated in advance, presumably at the point of registering for the API service or when manually creating the token in the API's dashboard. In this case, the tokens may be displayed to the consumer in the API's dashboard.

Generally, the bearer token would be sent using the `Authorization` header in your HTTP request and prefixing the header value with `Bearer `. For example, if we were using the bearer token `abc123`, the `Authorization` header may look something like this:

```
Authorization: Bearer abc123
```

Imagine we want to send a request to an API to list all the users in our account, and we need to authenticate ourselves using a bearer token. We could send a request to the API like so:

```
POST /users HTTP/3
Host: example.com
Content-Type: application/json
Accept: application/json
Authorization: Bearer abc123
```

However, not all APIs use the `Authorization` header, and some may use a different header (such as `X-Auth-Token`, `X-API-Token`, and so on). It's important to check the API's documentation to see how they expect you to send the bearer token.

Depending on the API service, the bearer token may be a cryptographically secure string intended purely for uniquely identifying a user. These tokens wouldn't usually contain personal data and would be stored in the API service's database. However, the token may be a base-64 encoded JSON web token (JWT). We'll be going into more detail about JWTs later in this section, but for now, you just need to know that JWTs are a method of authenticating yourself to an API, are transmitted as a bearer token, and typically aren't stored in a database — rather, user data may be stored in the token itself.

Advantages of Bearer Tokens

Using bearer tokens to authenticate yourself when making requests to an API has a number of advantages.

Firstly, bearer tokens are relatively simple to implement. This is because they don't typically require complex cryptographic algorithms to be used when sending or receiving requests. Of course, a cryptographically secure algorithm must be used to generate the tokens, but after they're generated, they can just be used as a unique identifier for a user in the system. This makes them easy to implement for both the API developer and API consumer because they don't need to worry about using complex algorithms that may add overhead. Instead, a plain-text string can be sent in the request.

If the bearer tokens are stored by the API service (such as in the API service's database) and are used to look up the user to whom the token belongs, they can be easy to revoke. Assuming the API service provides a way to do this, it can be advantageous for the API consumer because they can easily revoke the token. You may want to revoke the token if you suspect that it has been compromised, to prevent the user from accessing the API, or if you are rotating the tokens (changing the token to a new one after a period of time, such as every six months).

Assuming the API service supports this functionality, it can also provide the ability for a bearer token to have limited permissions. For example, rather than creating a single token that identifies yourself and allows you to perform every action in the application, you may want to create a token that identifies yourself and only allows you to read user data. We'll delve into why you might want to do this in the "Granular Permissions" section later on.

Disadvantages of Bearer Tokens

Bearer tokens are simple to use and implement, but they have disadvantages.

Bearer tokens must be stored securely by the consumer and not accidentally leaked. If a bearer token is leaked, it can be used by anyone to make requests on behalf of the token's owner. This also means the bearer token must be sent over a secure channel (such as HTTPS) to prevent it from being intercepted by a malicious user.

JSON Web Tokens (JWT)

JSON web tokens (JWT) are a method of authenticating yourself to an API. They are usually transmitted as a bearer token (as previously discussed) and have an interesting property in that they typically aren't stored in the API service's database. Instead, the token may include information needed for the request, such as user data, permissions, the expiration time of the token, and so on.

JWTs are usually JSON objects that are base-64 encoded so they can be sent in HTTP requests. To get a better understanding of JWTs, let's take a look at an example token that is base-64 encoded:


```
eyJhbGciOiJIUzI1NiIsInR5cCI6IkpXVCJ9.eyJzdWIiOiIxMjM0NTY3ODkwIiwibmFtZSI6IkpvaG4g
RG9lIiwiaWF0IjoxNTE2MjM5MDIyLCJwZXJtaXNzaW9ucyI6WyJ1c2VyLXJlYWQiLCJ1c2VyLXdyaXRlI
l19.reQ3Ksp0usSC6hrDZGiDEqzQf6HIYMSDtXM9TFZdjY0
```


Like bearer tokens, the JWT is sent in the `Authorization` header of the HTTP request like so:

```
Authorization:
eyJhbGciOiJIUzI1NiIsInR5cCI6IkpXVCJ9.eyJzdWIiOiIxMjM0NTY3ODkwIiwibmFtZSI6IkpvaG4g
RG9lIiwiaWF0IjoxNTE2MjM5MDIyLCJwZXJtaXNzaW9ucyI6WyJ1c2VyLXJlYWQiLCJ1c2VyLXdyaXRlI
l19.reQ3Ksp0usSC6hrDZGiDEqzQf6HIYMSDtXM9TFZdjY0
```

Of course, this token doesn't really make much sense, but if you look closely, you'll notice that the token is split into three parts, separated by a `.` character. These three parts are the header, payload, and token signature, using the format: `HEADER.PAYLOAD.SIGNATURE`. If we were to decode the token, we'd get the following three parts:

1. Header

The header of the token is a JSON object containing information about the token itself, such as the algorithm used to sign the token and the token type. For example, the header of our example token is:

```
{
    "alg": "HS256",
    "typ": "JWT"
}
```

The header tells us that the token is a JWT and has been signed using the HMAC-SHA256 algorithm. The API service needs to know what algorithm was used to sign the token to verify that the token is valid and hasn't been tampered with.

2. Payload

The payload contains the data needed for the request. You may sometimes see the payload fields referred to as "claims", as they are claims about who the user is and what they can do with this particular JWT. For example, the payload of our example token is:

```
{
    "sub": "1234567890",
    "name": "John Doe",
    "iat": 1516239022,
    "permissions": ["user-read", "user-write"]
}
```

This payload has four separate claims:

- `sub` - The subject of the token. This is usually a unique identifier for the user that the token belongs to.
- `name` - The name of the user the token belongs to.
- `iat` - The time the token was issued, in Unix time.
- `permissions` - The permissions that the user has.

Claims for JWTs can be split into one of three categories:

- Registered claims - Claims predefined by the JWT specification. They are not required but are recommended, as they provide a set of useful claims so that the token can be used for a variety of purposes.
- Public claims - Claims that are universally accepted and documented online that provide additional information in a token. They are not required.
- Private claims - Claims defined by the developer that are usually specific to the application generating and using the tokens. They are not required but can be used to add additional information to the token.

Examples of the registered claims are:

- `iss` (Issuer) - The issuer of the token. This may be something like the URL of the API service that issued the token.
- `exp` (Expiration time) - The token's expiration time, in Unix time.

- `aud` (Audience) - The audience of the token. This may be something like the URL of the API service that the token is intended for.
- `nbf` (Not before) - The time that the token can first be used, in Unix time.
- `iat` (Issued at) - The time the token was issued, in Unix time.
- `jti` (JWT ID) - The ID of the token. This is a case-sensitive string that can be used to identify the token.
- `sub` (Subject) - The subject of the token. This is usually a unique identifier for the user that the token belongs to.

Examples of some public claims, along with their registered descriptions, are:

- `name` - Full name.
- `given_name` - Given name(s) or first name(s).
- `nickname` - Casual name.
- `profile` - Profile page URL.
- `zoneinfo` - Time zone.
- `address` - Preferred postal address.
- `email` - Preferred email address.

Examples of some private claims you may want to use are:

- `permissions` - The permissions that the user has access to.
- `roles` - The roles that the user has.
- `employee_id` - The ID of the employee that the user is.

The ability to add custom claims to the token makes JWTs very flexible, so they can be tailored to fit an API's needs. As an API consumer, you won't usually need to be aware of the contents of the JWT, as the payload is only used by the API service. However, unless JWTs are encrypted (which typically isn't the case, as they are usually signed), anyone can decode and read the payload. This means that they should never be used to store sensitive information and should only ever contain information needed by the API service.

3. Signature

The final part of the JWT is the signature. The API service generates this string at the time of issuing the token.

In the case of our token, it's the following string:


```
cmVRM0tzcDB1c1NDNmhyRFpHaURFcXpRZjZISVlNU0R0WE05VEZaZGpZMA==
```


This signature is generated by base-64 encoding the header and payload sections of the token and concatenating them together using a `.` as the separator. This is then hashed using the algorithm specified in the header of the token (in our case, the HMAC-SHA256 algorithm), using a secret key that the API service has stored. The resulting hash is then base-64 encoded to produce the signature and is attached to the JWT.

When the API service receives a request using the JWT for authentication and authorization, it will extract the header and payload sections and try to generate a signature using the same algorithm and secret key. If the signature it generates matches the token's signature sent with the JWT, we can be sure it is valid. If the signature doesn't match, it can indicate that the token has been tampered with and is invalid.

Advantages of JSON Web Tokens

As a result of JWTs being stateless and able to contain many claims, it's possible for an API service to authenticate and authorize a user without needing to access the database. For example, suppose an API endpoint contains information about the user and their roles or permissions. In that case, they can be extracted from the JWT and used to determine whether the user is allowed to access the endpoint without checking the database. This can help when scaling an API service, as it can reduce the number of database queries that need to be made.

Since the JWTs can contain all the roles and permissions a user has, tokens can be created with fine-grained control (assuming the API service provides this functionality). It means you can have separate JWTs with different levels of access.

Disadvantages of JSON Web Tokens

Despite the advantages JWTs provide, they have some disadvantages. Since JWTs are usually signed and not encrypted, anyone can read the information in the payload. Thus, you should never store sensitive information in the payload of a JWT and must make a conscious decision when deciding what information to include in the payload when generating it.

Also, since JWTs are stateless, the data contained in them can be outdated. For example, if a user updates their name in an application, the JWT they have will still contain their old name — if the API service uses the name in the JWT to display the user's name, it will be incorrect. This can be solved if the API service checks the database for the latest information, but this almost defeats the purpose of having a JWT that contains the user's name in the first place.

As a result of JWTs not being stored in the database, revoking tokens can be difficult. With a bearer token used to identify and look up a user in a database, the token can be revoked by deleting the token from the database. However, since JWTs are stateless, this is more complex. To revoke a JWT, you could store each token's `jti` (the JWT ID) in the database and then check whether that token exists in the database on each request. Similarly, you could store a list of revoked tokens' `jti` values in the database and then check on each request whether the token's `jti` value is in the list. However, storing the `jti` values in the database or storing a list of revoked tokens in the database can both be seen as defeating the purpose of using a JWT.

Basic Authentication

Another form of authentication you may encounter a bit less often than bearer tokens is basic authentication. This form of authentication relies on a username and password to authenticate a user.

When using basic authentication to authenticate with an API, the username and password are combined into a string in the `username:password` format. This string is then base-64 encoded, prefixed with `Basic` and sent in the `Authorization` header of the request to the API.

Imagine we are attempting to authenticate with an API that has the following credentials:

- Username: `john.doe`
- Password: `password123`

These would be combined into the following string:

```
john.doe:password123
```

This would then be base-64 encoded to produce the following string:

```
am9obi5kb2U6cGFzc3dvcmQxMjM=
```

This would then be prefixed with `Basic` and added to the `Authorization` header of the request to the API, resulting in the following header:

```
Authorization: Basic am9obi5kb2U6cGFzc3dvcmQxMjM=
```

Imagine we wanted to send a request to an API to list all the users in our account, and we needed to authenticate ourselves using basic authentication. We could send a request to the API like so:

```
POST /users HTTP/3
Host: example.com
Content-Type: application/json
Accept: application/json
Authorization: Basic am9obi5kb2U6cGFzc3dvcmQxMjM=
```

Advantages of Basic Authentication

Basic authentication is very simple to implement. Since it only requires combining the username and password into a string and base-64 encoding it, it's easy to add to the API requests you send. Basic authentication is also built into the HTTP protocol, so it's supported by all HTTP clients (such as browsers, HTTP libraries, etc.).

It's also worth noting that basic authentication is used in several of the flows of OAuth 2. Later in the book, we'll delve into OAuth and look at how we can use basic authentication to send requests to an OAuth server.

Disadvantages of Basic Authentication

Basic authentication may have more disadvantages than benefits despite its ease of use. Firstly, in most cases, basic authentication relies on you needing to send the username and password with every request to the API. Since these are likely the username and password you'd also use to sign in to the application in a web browser, it means if someone could intercept the request, they'd have the potential to gain access to your account. It's important to remember that the credentials in the `Authorization` header are base-64 encoded, not encrypted, so anyone who intercepts the request can decode the credentials.

Further, basic authentication generally doesn't support fine-grained permissions. Typically, an API using basic authentication will only have a single username and password that can be used to authenticate with the API. If you need different levels of access to the API, you'll need to create multiple users with different permissions and use the appropriate credentials for the level of access you need. However, this isn't always the case. For example, some GitHub API endpoints use basic authentication and allow you to pass personal access tokens instead of a password. This means that instead of using the `username:password` combination to authenticate with the API, you can use `username:token` instead. This means you can create multiple personal access tokens with different permissions and use the appropriate token for the level of access you need. But this isn't supported by all APIs using basic authentication.

API Integration Security

When building out your API integration, there are things that you should keep in mind to ensure your integration is secure. This section covers some of the most common security issues I see when working with APIs.

Allowing Specific Domains or IP Addresses

Some APIs may provide the ability to restrict domains or IP addresses that can make requests to the API with a given API key. This feature is often provided to help prevent malicious users from making requests to the API if the API key is compromised.

If you're using an API that provides this feature, you should ensure you're only allowing domains or IP addresses that you need to make requests to the API. For example, you may only want to allow requests from your app servers' IP addresses.

Avoiding Hardcoded API Keys

You should always avoid hard-coded API keys in your code, whether in the application's code, as config defaults, or in an `.env.example` file. If you need an API key in your code, you should always use an environment variable.

Suppose your Laravel app interacts with the Mailgun API in one of your classes. To make the requests to the API, you'll need a Mailgun API key. I've seen service classes that look something like this:

```php
class MailgunService
{
    public const MAILGUN_SECRET = 'abc123';

    public function sendBulkEmail(
        string $to,
        string $subject,
        string $body
    ): void {
        // Send email here...
    }
}
```

Hard-coding the key in the code like this has a few problems we should address.

Difficult to Change the Key Immediately

If we ever needed to change that key, we would need to release a new version of our code. This could be problematic if you found that the API key had been compromised and needed to be changed instantly. It could also cause issues if you wanted to use a new API key with different abilities/scopes than the one you already have.

Additionally, you may regularly rotate your API keys, meaning you'll delete your old API key and create a new one. Some services, such as HubSpot, advise that you rotate your keys at least every six months. This is a good security practice, as it means that if your API key is compromised, it will only be valid for a short time. If you have hard-coded API keys in your code, this will mean that you'll need to update your code every time you rotate your API keys, and you could miss occurrences of the key in your code.

Committed to Version Control

Another major downside to including API keys in your code is that it likely means that the keys are committed in your version control. This adds an attack vector that a malicious attacker could use to compromise your system. Rather than needing to get access to your server (and maybe server management system, such as Laravel Forge) to get access to your API keys, they could also try to compromise your version control accounts (like GitHub, GitLab, Bitbucket, etc.).

Say you have five developers on your team with access to the project on GitHub. That's five new potential attack vectors that someone could use to access your keys. Of course, strong passwords and two-factor authentication can reduce the chance of this happening. But how confident are you that all your team members follow these security practices? It's important to remove hard-coded keys from your committed code.

Hard to Use Multiple Keys

You'll likely have multiple environments set up with the external API. You may have a development environment, a staging environment, and a production environment, each with its own API keys. If you are hard-coding API keys in your code, using different keys for each environment can be difficult. For instance, you may be forced to use the production API key in your development environment, which could cause issues if you're testing out new features that have yet to be released.

The Fix

The best way to fix this would be to extract the fields out into config fields using your `.env` file. If you do find any keys that have been hard-coded, you might want to rotate them and create new keys when you extract them to your `.env`. Your old keys will still be present in your project's git history, giving you confidence that you wouldn't still be as vulnerable if the version control were ever compromised.

Let's take our example from above and update it to use environment variables instead of hard-coded values:

```
class MailgunService
{
    private string $mailgunSecret;

    public function __construct()
    {
        $this->mailgunSecret = config('services.mailgun.secret');
    }

    public function sendBulkEmail(
        string $to,
        string $subject,
        string $body
    ): void {
        // Send email here...
    }
}
```

In the example above, we've extracted the API key into the `config/services.php` config file. The config file may look something like this:

```php
return [

    // ...

    'mailgun' => [
        'domain' => env('MAILGUN_DOMAIN'),
        'secret' => env('MAILGUN_SECRET'),
        'endpoint' => env('MAILGUN_ENDPOINT', 'api.mailgun.net'),
        'scheme' => 'https',
    ],

    // ...
];
```

In the `services.php` config file, we can see that we're grabbing the `mailgun.secret` field from the `MAILGUN_SECRET` environment variable. Our `.env` file may contain something like this:

```
MAILGUN_SECRET=abc123
```

Now, changing the API key is much easier if we ever need to.

Granular Permissions

It's important to always follow the "principle of least privilege" if the service allows it. The principle of least privilege states that a subject should be given only those privileges needed to complete its task. In the context of API keys, this means creating API keys with the lowest possible scopes/abilities needed. For example, if you're interacting with an API and only need to read data, create an API key that can only read data. Don't create an API key that has the ability to write data.

This adds extra security and means that if the API key is ever compromised, it will reduce the amount of things an attacker can do with it.

It can be tempting to allow all abilities when creating an API key because it can make future development easier, but make sure not to do it. Remember: less is more secure. If you need extra abilities in the future, you can easily create a new API key and drop it into your `.env` file.

Use HTTPS

This point may seem obvious, and you may not have any other choice, but always use HTTPS where you can. Although a large amount of the popular APIs will only allow you to use HTTPS, some APIs you're interacting with may still support HTTP, so you may accidentally use HTTP instead of HTTPS.

By using HTTPS, you ensure your data is encrypted and secure. If you're using HTTP, your data is sent in plain text and can be intercepted by an attacker. So, it's important to always use HTTPS, especially when dealing with sensitive or personal data.

Avoid Using API Keys in the URL

Some APIs allow you to use an API key in the URL or in request headers. If you're using an API that provides this option, you should always use the request headers instead of the URL. In general, you should avoid putting sensitive information in the URL, whether a password, API key, or anything else.

The reason to avoid doing this is because it increases the chances of the API key being leaked. For example, the URL may be stored in some logs, browser history, or cache, depending on where the API request is initiated. Each of these places adds another attack vector that a malicious actor could use to access the API key.

By including the API keys in the request headers, you can reduce (but not eliminate) the likelihood of these leaks happening.

Conclusion

In this section, we've examined what APIs are and how they work. An examination of different types of APIs has introduced REST, GraphQL, RPC, and SOAP APIs. We've also looked at security concerns you must be aware of when interacting with APIs. Using what you've learned from this section, you should understand the theory behind how to interact with an API.

In the following sections, we'll look at some code techniques you can use to interact with APIs in your Laravel applications before diving into writing code to consume the GitHub API.

Code Techniques

Before we dive into building API integrations, it is essential to understand many of the general techniques used in this book to improve the quality of your code. By understanding these concepts now, you can focus on the API-related subject matter in each chapter without as much concern for understanding the rationale for these patterns at that time.

This chapter covers using strict type-checking, final classes, data transfer objects (DTOs), `readonly` classes and properties, interfaces, the service container, enums, and more. By the end, you should understand how to use these techniques to make your API integration code maintainable, testable, and extensible.

Strict Type-Checking

Strict type-checking is a feature you can enable in PHP applications to improve type safety. Let's examine what this means, the benefits of using strict types, and how to enable it in your applications.

To enable strict type-checking, add `declare(strict_types=1)` to the top of your PHP files. This statement enforces strict typing for your application's function parameters and return types so that if a function expects a particular parameter or return value, PHP will throw an error if the wrong type is used.

Here's a simple example that doesn't use `declare(strict_types=1)`:

```
function add(int $a, int $b): int
{
    return $a + $b;
}
```

Let's call this function with string arguments:

```
echo add('1', '2');

// Output:
// 3
```

PHP happily converts the string parameters to integers and returns the result `3`.

In some cases, you may be satisfied with this behaviour, like when you are intending to capture user input in a string format and don't want to attempt typecasting it first. But this could also have unintended consequences that cause bugs in your application.

Let's add `declare(strict_types=1);` to the top of the example:

```
declare(strict_types=1);

function add(int $a, int $b): int
{
    return $a + $b;
}
```

Now, if we call the `add` function with string parameters, PHP will throw an error:

```
echo add('1', '2');

// Output:
// Fatal error: Uncaught TypeError: Argument 1 passed to add() must
// be of the type int, string given
```

PHP throws an error because the `add` function expected integers to be passed but received strings instead.

If strict type-checking is enabled and we try to return the wrong data type from the method, PHP will also throw an error. For example, say our `add` function now accepts floats instead of integers and that we don't have strict type-checking enabled:

```
function add(float $a, float $b): int
{
    return $a + $b;
}
```

We could call the function like so:

```
echo add(1.25, 2.25);

// Output:
// 3
```

Did you spot the problem in the output?

The answer we should have received is `3.5`. However, because we have defined the return type as `int`, PHP converted the float to an integer and lost precision. As you can imagine, this could cause some issues in other parts of our application where we're using this result and the precision may have been needed.

Now let's fix this issue by using `declare(strict_types=1)`:

```
declare(strict_types=1);

function add(float $a, float $b): int
{
    return $a + $b;
}
```

We could then call the function like so:

```
echo add(1.25, 2.25);

// Output:
// Fatal error: Uncaught TypeError: add(): Return value must be of
// type int, float returned
```

As we can see, enabling strict type-checking shows that the function isn't returning the correct data type. This is useful because it could highlight a possible bug we didn't know about. We could then take the necessary steps to either:

- Update the return types if they are incorrect
- Update the type hints if they are incorrect
- Update the function body to return the correct data type if it's incorrect
- Fix any bugs in the code calling the function that may be passing the incorrect data type to it

Should You Use Strict Types?

I think it's a good idea to use `declare(strict_types=1)` in all your PHP files. It gives you confidence that you're using the correct data types in your code and can help to spot bugs, particularly when adding it to older codebases.

If you're using an integrated development environment (IDE) such as PhpStorm, you can update your templates so that new PHP files created within the IDE automatically include `declare(strict_types=1)` at the top of the file. Then you don't need to remember to add it manually.

In PhpStorm, you can update your template for creating new PHP classes to look something like so:

```php
<?php

declare(strict_types=1);

#parse("PHP File Header.php")

#if (${NAMESPACE})
namespace ${NAMESPACE};

#end
class ${NAME} {

}
```

You can also publish the default Laravel file stubs for creating PHP files when running Artisan commands such as `php artisan make:controller`. Publishing the stubs allows you to edit them and add `declare(strict_types=1)` to the top. This means the files you create using Artisan commands will be created with stricter type safety already enabled.

Of course, if you are going to add stricter type-checking to your existing files, I recommend having a good-quality test suite in place first. Your PHP code may have been allowing incorrect data types to be passed without throwing errors. But, by enabling strict type-checking, your code will become much less forgiving and may start throwing errors. This could cause your application to break in unexpected ways for your users.

You may also need to refactor some of your code to make it compatible with `declare(strict_types=1)`. I wouldn't see this as a bad thing, though. Instead, see it as an opportunity to improve the quality of your code.

To help add `declare(strict_types=1)` to your code, you can use a tool like PHPStan that may pick up on these type mismatches for you.

Composition Over Inheritance

"Composition over inheritance" is a design principle that encourages us to use composition (building a class's functionality using smaller, more-focused classes) instead of inheritance (extending from a parent class) to share code between classes. Inheritance can be useful, but if it's misused, it can lead to code that is difficult to maintain, test, and update.

To better understand composition over inheritance, let's look at an example. Imagine we have a software-as-a-service (SaaS) application that allows users to connect to their GitHub and GitLab accounts to perform actions on their repositories (such as fixing code style issues, running tests, etc.) directly from the application. We'll imagine that users can only perform a given number of requests per month. If they exceed this limit, they must upgrade their plan, so we want to keep track of how many actions each user has performed.

Imagine the application has several service classes:

- `BillingService` - Handles billing-related functionality (taking payments, upgrading plans, etc.).
- `UserService` - Handles user registration, login, etc.
- `GitHubService` - Handles GitHub API requests.
- `GitLabService` - Handles GitLab API requests.

We'll also imagine each service class extends a single `Service` class. The intention of this `Service` class is to contain any shared functionality that the other service classes may need.

Let's say the `GitHubService` and `GitLabService` both require access to a method that records the action so we can track the total number of actions performed in a month. We'll call this method `recordAction` and assume that it accepts an `ActionDetails` object containing the action's details. You may be tempted to add this method to your `Service` class so it can be easily accessed and reduce code duplication. This would result in your `GitHubService`, `GitLabService`, and `Service` classes looking something like so:

```php
class Service
{
    public function recordAction(ActionDetails $actionDetails): array
    {
        // Record the action in the database here...
    }
}
```

```php
class GitHubService extends Service
{
    public function fixRepoStyling(string $repoName): void
    {
        $this->recordAction(
            new ActionDetails(
                service: 'github',
                action: 'fix_repo_styling',
                userId: $this->user->id,
                happenedAt: now(),
            )
        );

        // Run the code style fixer here...
    }

    // ...
}
```

```php
class GitLabService extends Service
{
    public function fixRepoStyling(string $repoName): void
    {
        $this->recordAction(
            new ActionDetails(
                service: 'gitlab',
                action: 'fix_repo_styling',
                userId: $this->user->id,
                happenedAt: now(),
            )
        );

        // Run the code style fixer here...
    }

    // ...
}
```

Although this may seem like a good idea initially, this approach has some issues.

Firstly, the `BillingService` and `UserService` classes are entirely unrelated to the `GitHubService` and `GitLabService`. They have no relation to them and do not need the `recordAction` method because it's only used for recording actions against GitHub and GitLab repositories. So they shouldn't have or need access to it.

As well as this, all our child service classes are tightly coupled to the `Service` class. This means that if we ever need to change the `Service` class, we'll need to be careful not to break the `GitHubService` and `GitLabService` classes. This may not seem like a big issue in smaller projects, but it can lead to unintended behaviour and bugs in larger projects — particularly ones that may not have a good-quality test suite covering this functionality.

We could use composition instead of inheritance to improve the code in this scenario. So instead of sharing the common methods from a single `Service` class, we'll create smaller classes to "compose" (or build) up our service classes. Let's look at how we could do this.

Seeing as the `GitHubService` and `GitLabService` classes both require access to the `recordAction` method, we could create a `UsageService` class that contains this method and is focused solely on recording and accessing the recorded usage for users. We could then inject this class into our `GitHubService` and `GitLabService` classes. This would result in our classes looking something like so:

```
class UsageService
{
    public function recordAction(ActionDetails $actionDetails): array
    {
        // Record the action in the database here...
    }
}

class GitHubService
{
    public function __construct(private UsageService $usageService)
    {

    }

    public function fixRepoStyling(string $repoName): void
    {
        $this->usageService->recordAction(
            new ActionDetails(
```

```
                service: 'github',
                action: 'fix_repo_styling',
                userId: $this->user->id,
                happenedAt: now(),
            )
        );

        // Run the code style fixer here...
    }

    // ...
}
```

As shown in the method above, we can now access the `recordAction` method from the `UsageService` class. This means that we're able to share the functionality between the `GitHubService` and `GitLabService` classes, and none of our service classes need to extend a single `Service` class.

This encourages us to write smaller classes focused on a single responsibility which helps us write cleaner, more maintainable code. For instance, the `BillingService` and `UserService` are no longer aware of the `recordActions` method and can focus solely on their intended purposes. Doing this also makes writing unit tests much easier because the functionality will likely be more focused.

It's important to remember that composition isn't a silver bullet and is not always the best solution. There are cases where inheritance may be a better solution. It's important to understand the differences between the two and when to use each one.

If you keep your classes specific rather than generalized, inheritance can still be useful. For example, you may have noticed that by default in your Laravel applications, your controller classes extend from a single `App\Http\Controllers\Controller` class. This is because they all share common functionality useful to all controller classes. You can also confidently say that your `UserController`, `BookingController`, `PricingController`, etc. are all controllers. So it makes sense for them to extend from a `Controller` class. The `Controller` class is a focused class that is specific to controllers. It's not a generalized class (such as our `Service` class) that contains functionality shared between all service classes in your application.

Final Classes

Final classes are a powerful yet often overlooked feature of PHP. They can be a controversial topic and cause a lot of debate. But when used correctly, they can be a handy tool in your arsenal.

In short, final classes are PHP classes with the `final` keyword in the class definition. For example, we could have a class that looks something like so:

```
final class GitHubService
{
    // ...
}
```

Final classes are designed to prevent inheritance, meaning a final class cannot be extended. Using our example `GitHubService` class above, we wouldn't be able to extend it like so:

```
class ExtendedGitHubService extends GitHubService
{
    // ...
}
```

I hear you asking, "But why would we want to prevent inheritance?". That's a valid question, especially since inheritance is a core feature of object-oriented programming (OOP). But, as with most things in development, there are pros and cons to using final classes. So let's take a look at them.

Advantages of Final Classes

To understand how final classes can help improve our code, let's look at some advantages they provide.

Immutability of Class Implementation

One of the benefits of using final classes is that you can have confidence that the class's functionality cannot be extended and then overwritten. This can be beneficial if you want to be sure that the class is not going to be changed in any way.

Confirmation of No Inheritance

Another advantage of using final classes is that you can have visual confirmation that a class is not being extended. For example, let's imagine we have the following class:

```
class GitHubService
{
    // ...
}
```

At first glance, it's not obvious whether this class is being extended or not. If you needed to update any logic within the service class, you wouldn't know whether this would affect any other classes that may be extending it. Although this may not be as much of a problem in smaller codebases, this can sometimes cause issues in larger codebases. Speaking from experience, this is more of a problem when working with legacy codebases that have been around for a while and have had multiple developers working on them for a long time.

Of course, an IDE such as PhpStorm makes it easier to spot whether a class is being extended, but it's still not always obvious.

By prepending the `final` keyword to the class definition, you'll be able to get a visual confirmation that the class is not being extended. Additionally, PHP will throw an error if you try to extend a final class, so you can get more protection against it accidentally happening.

Promotes Composition Over Inheritance

Another benefit, and potentially the biggest, is that final classes promote "composition over inheritance".

Since final classes can't be extended, they encourage you to use composition to build up your class's functionality. This can improve your code's maintainability and make testing easier by keeping your class's functionality focused.

Disadvantages of Final Classes

Although final classes can benefit your application, they also have some disadvantages. Let's take a look at some of them.

Can't Be Extended

As already mentioned, final classes can't be extended. This can lead to code duplication if you need to use a similar class in your application but change a small piece of the code.

Of course, if the final class is part of your own application's code, you can remove the `final` keyword from the class definition. As a result, you'll then be able to extend the class, assuming it's safe to do so without causing any issues. However, if the final class is part of a third-party package, it will be difficult to extend the class without modifying the package's code (whether through a fork, pull request, or monkey patching).

For these reasons, if you're building your API integration as part of a package that you may be sharing among different projects or distributing publicly, then you'll have to consider whether you want to allow the classes to be extended. This is a controversial topic, and there are arguments for both sides. So it's up to you to decide what's best for your package and anyone using it.

Difficult To Mock

Another disadvantage of using final classes is that they can be difficult to mock. This can sometimes make it difficult to write unit tests for your code.

To explain this further, let's look at an example. We'll imagine we have a simple `RequestBuilder` class responsible for building and sending HTTP requests to the GitHub API. The class may look something like so:

```
declare(strict_types=1);

namespace App\Services\GitHub;

final class RequestBuilder
{
    public function get(string $url): array
    {
        // Make the request to the URL and return the body.
    }

    // ...
}
```

We'll then imagine we have a `GitHubService` class responsible for fetching the user's GitHub repositories. It will use the `RequestBuilder` class to make the request to the GitHub API, parse the results, and then return the repositories. The class may look something like so:

```
declare(strict_types=1);

namespace App\Services\GitHub;

final readonly class GitHubService
{
    public function __construct(
        private string $username,
        private string $token,
    ) {}

    public function getRepos(): array
    {
        $requestBuilder = app(RequestBuilder::class);

        $response = $requestBuilder->get('url-goes-here');

        // Parse the response and return the repos.
    }

    // ...
}
```

If we were writing tests for the `GitHubService`, we may want to write them as unit tests that isolate the service and don't actually run the code inside the `RequestBuilder` class. One way to do this would be to mock the `RequestBuilder` class so that when we try to resolve it from the service container (using `app(RequestBuilder::class)`) it will return a mocked version instead. The test may look something like so:

```
declare(strict_types=1);

namespace Tests\Unit\Services\GitHub;

use App\Services\GitHub\GitHubService;
use App\Services\GitHub\RequestBuilder;
use Tests\TestCase;

class GetReposTest extends TestCase
{
    /** @test */
    public function request_is_sent_to_fetch_repos(): void
    {
        $this->mock(RequestBuilder::class)
            ->shouldReceive('get')
            ->once()
            ->andReturn([
                'dummy-contents-here'
            ]);

        $service = new GitHubService('username', 'token');

        $service->getRepos();
    }
}
```

In the test, we're mocking the `RequestBuilder` class and telling it to expect the `get` method to be called once and to return some dummy content when called. We're then creating a new instance of the `GitHubService` class and calling the `getRepos` method on it. This will then call the `get` method on the mocked `RequestBuilder` class and return the dummy content that we specified. This is all done using the `mock` method provided by Laravel.

However, if we try to run this test, we'll get an error that looks something like so:

```
Mockery\Exception: The class \App\Services\GitHub\RequestBuilder is marked final
and its methods cannot be replaced. Classes marked final can be passed in to
\Mockery::mock() as instantiated objects to create a partial mock, but only if
the mock is not subject to type hinting checks.
```

This is because final classes cannot be mocked by default in our mocking library "Mockery", so we'll need to make some changes to our code to allow us to mock the `RequestBuilder` class.

One solution to solve the issue would be to remove the `final` keyword from the `RequestBuilder` class. However, if that isn't possible, you may want to approach the mocking process differently.

Instead, you may want to create the mock yourself using Mockery rather than using Laravel's `mock` helper method. This will allow you to create the mock like in the updated test below:

```
declare(strict_types=1);

namespace Tests\Feature\Services\GitHub;

use App\Services\GitHub\GitHubService;
use App\Services\GitHub\RequestBuilder;
use Mockery;
```

```php
use Tests\TestCase;

class GetReposTest extends TestCase
{
    /** @test */
    public function request_is_sent_to_fetch_repos(): void
    {
        // Define your mock.
        $mock = Mockery::mock(RequestBuilder::class, new RequestBuilder());

        // Define the mock's expectations.
        $mock->shouldReceive('get')
            ->once()
            ->andReturn([
                'dummy-contents-here'
            ]);

        // Register the mock in the service class.
        $this->app->instance(RequestBuilder::class, $mock);

        $service = new GitHubService('username', 'token');

        $service->getRepos();
    }
}
```

Using the above approach, Mockery will do the mocking via a proxy class that records and forwards the method calls, rather than creating a subclass of the class you're mocking (as it usually would). In some cases, this may be fine. However, it's worth noting that this approach may not work if the class that you're mocking is subject to type hinting checks. Let's look at some examples of code that would no longer work.

Since the mocked class is not a subclass of the original class, we would not be able to use `instanceof`:

```
if ($requestBuilder instanceof RequestBuilder) {
    // We cannot enter here.
}
```

We also wouldn't be able to use the class as a return type:

```
public function getRequestBuilder(): RequestBuilder
{
    return app(RequestBuilder::class);
}
```

As well as this, we also wouldn't be able to use it as a type hint for a method either:

```
public function __construct(RequestBuilder $requestBuilder)
{
    // ...
}
```

The Mockery documentation suggests that to get around this, you can create an interface that the `RequestBuilder` class will implement. The mocked proxy class that Mockery creates will also implement this same interface so that you can use the interface as a type hint instead. This will allow you to use the mocked class in place of the original class. We could update our code examples above to use an interface instead. We'll assume we have created a new `RequestBuilderInterface` that the `RequestBuilder` class implements. We'll also assume that we have updated the `GitHubService` class to use the interface instead of the concrete class.

Our code examples would then look like so:

```
if ($requestBuilder instanceof RequestBuilderInterface) {
    // We cannot enter here.
}
```

```
public function getRequestBuilder(): RequestBuilderInterface
{
    return app(RequestBuilder::class);
}
```

```
public function __construct(RequestBuilderInterface $requestBuilder)
{
    // ...
}
```

Of course, being able to make changes like this to your code isn't always possible, especially if the final classes are part of third-party vendor packages. If this is the case, you may need to choose a different approach for testing your code.

Another approach to writing these tests is to use test doubles. We'll discuss how to use test doubles later in the book in the "Testing API Integrations" section of the "Building an API

Integration Using Saloon" chapter.

Should You Use Final Classes?

Deciding whether to use final classes is a decision you'll need to make for yourself. As we've seen above, either approach has pros and cons.

I like using final classes for all the advantages we've discussed and making all of my classes final by default. They make me second guess whether to use inheritance, as I have to consciously and explicitly remove the `final` keyword. From working on legacy projects that have suffered from "inheritance hell" that are difficult to maintain and update, I feel like using `final` can help to avoid falling into the same traps with newer code that's written.

However, I am fully aware of the limitations that they can cause, so I don't maintain a 100% "this class *HAS* to be final" philosophy. Just like with any other part of development, there are many nuances to consider, and you should always use your best judgement based on the project you're working on and follow your team's existing conventions.

Data Transfer Objects

In PHP, arrays are both a blessing and a curse. They are flexible, and you can put almost anything you want in them, which makes them great for moving data around your application's code.

However, misusing them can make your code more difficult to understand and can make it unclear what data they contain. Additionally, arrays can make it more difficult to fully benefit from features such as PHP's type system.

For these reasons, I like to use classes such as "data transfer objects" (DTOs) instead of arrays where possible. Using these allows you to benefit from PHP's type system, get better autocomplete suggestions from your IDE, and reduce the chance of bugs.

Later in the book, we'll use DTOs to represent the data we're sending (in an HTTP request) and receiving (in an HTTP response) using Saloon. Saloon is a package you can use to interact with external APIs and comes with some convenient features. For this example, you don't need to know the specifics of how Saloon works under the hood — we'll cover how to build your own API integrations using Saloon later in the book in the "Building an API Integration Using Saloon" chapter.

Let's look at a code example to understand the advantages of using DTOs in our code.

Imagine we have an `app/Services/GitHubService` service class that can be used to interact with the GitHub API. The service class may have a `getRepo` method that can be used to fetch data about a single GitHub repository. The outline of the method may look something like so:

```php
public function getRepo(string $owner, string $repo): array
{
    return $this->client()
        ->send(new GetRepo($owner, $repo))
        ->json();
}
```

In the example, assume the `$this->client()` call returns a Saloon client to send the request and that the `GetRepo` class is a Saloon request class used to build the request. You don't need to understand how the request is being sent, but it's important to note that the `json` method converts the API response to an array.

Now we have to ask an important question about this method: "*What data is inside the array that's being returned?*".

Without checking GitHub's API documentation or using something like XDebug, `log()`, `dd()`, or `ray()` to inspect the data, we have no clear indication of what data is available in the array. We also don't know the data types of the values in the array. The API response for fetching a GitHub repository's data is large and contains 95 fields by default (including integers, strings, booleans, and arrays). As a result, it can be difficult to know how to use the data being returned to us.

Another issue that can arise from these types of scenarios is that we may accidentally reference a key that doesn't exist. For example, the API response contains a `private` boolean field which indicates whether the GitHub repository is public or private. In our code, we may correctly reference this field like so:

```php
$repoData = app(GitHubService::class)->getRepo('ash-jc-allen', 'short-url');

$isPrivate = $repoData['private'];
```

However, somewhere else in our code, we may accidentally reference a non-existent `is_private` key instead of the `private` key:

```
$repoData = app(GitHubService::class)->getRepo('ash-jc-allen', 'short-url');

$isPrivate = $repoData['is_private'];
```

As you'd imagine, this would throw a PHP error. Assuming this error was caught during the development process, you would need to either check the API documentation or inspect the API response to find the correct key name. This can be a tedious task and can slow down your development process. In the worst-case scenario, this error might only be spotted in the production environment, which could result in your application crashing for your users.

To reduce the likelihood of these issues occurring, we can use a DTO to represent the data being returned from the API. For example, we could create a `GitHubRepoData` class that looks like so:

```php
declare(strict_types=1);

namespace App\DataTransferObjects;

use Carbon\CarbonInterface;

final readonly class Repo
{
    public function __construct(
        public int $id,
        public string $name,
        public string $fullName,
        public bool $isPrivate,
        public string $description,
        public CarbonInterface $createdAt,
    ) {
        //
    }
}
```

You may have noticed that we only have a subset of the fields (6 out of the 95) returned in the API response. This can help keep your DTOs manageable by only including the fields you need for your application. If you need to add more fields later, you can do so without updating any of the code that uses the DTO. This helps keep your DTOs focused and indicates what data you're currently using in your codebase. However, suppose you're building a package that other developers will use to interact with an API. In that case, you'll likely want to include all the fields returned in the API response because you can't predict what fields other developers may need.

Using constructor property promotion and readonly classes/properties (covered in the next chapter), we can avoid creating "setter" or "getter" methods and don't need to assign the property values inside the constructor. So we can have a simple immutable object that doesn't need to be updated after instantiation.

Now that we have our DTO that represents the data being returned from the API, we can update our `getRepo` method to return an instance of the DTO instead of an array.

```
public function getRepo(string $owner, string $repo): Repo
{
    return $this->client()
        ->send(new GetRepo($owner, $repo))
        ->dtoOrFail(Repo::class);
}
```

You might wonder what the `dtoOrFail` method is and where it originated. We'll cover this in more detail in a later section, but the `dtoOrFail` method is provided by Saloon and converts a JSON response to an instance of a specified class. In our `GetRepo` class, a `createDtoFromResponse` method would need to be specified that handles mapping the API response to fields in a DTO that we can return like so:

```php
/**
 * @param \Saloon\Http\Response $response
 * @return \App\DataTransferObjects\Repo
 */
public function createDtoFromResponse(Response $response): mixed
{
    $responseData = $response->json();

    return new Repo(
        id: $responseData['id'],
        name: $responseData['name'],
        fullName: $responseData['full_name'],
        isPrivate: $responseData['private'],
        description: $responseData['description'] ?? '',
        createdAt: Carbon::parse($responseData['created_at']),
    );
}
```

Now that we've updated our `getRepo` method to return an instance of our DTO, we can update our code to use the DTO instead of an array:

```php
$repoData = app(GitHubService::class)->getRepo('ash-jc-allen', 'short-url');

$isPrivate = $repoData->isPrivate;
```

Making these changes has improved the maintainability of our code because we are decoupling our application's code from the raw API response. For instance, we have been able to convert the `created_at` field to a `Carbon` object rather than leaving it as a string.

It has also allowed us to use PHP's type system to improve the type safety of our application. By defining the data types of each field in the `Repo` DTO, we can have more confidence that we're working with the correct data types in the rest of our codebase.

An additional benefit is that we have also improved the predictability of our code. If you're using an integrated development environment (IDE) such as PhpStorm, you can get autosuggestions for the fields available on the DTO. This reduces the likelihood of referencing a non-existent field and helps speed up your development process by allowing you to write code faster and more confidently without leaving your editor.

Readonly Classes and Properties

A powerful feature introduced in PHP 8.1 is readonly properties. It allows us to prevent properties from being changed after they have been set and can give us confidence we aren't accidentally changing a property we shouldn't.

PHP 8.2 then introduced the ability to make entire classes readonly. This can be particularly useful for DTOs because it allows us to prevent all the properties from being changed after the DTO has been instantiated.

Let's look at an example to understand the benefits of using readonly classes and properties. We'll use our Repo DTO from the previous class (excluding the `readonly` keyword when defining the class):

```
final class Repo
{
    public function __construct(
        public int $id,
        public string $name,
        public string $fullName,
        public bool $isPrivate,
        public string $description,
        public CarbonInterface $createdAt,
    ) {
        //
    }
}
```

At the moment, our DTO is mutable, meaning we can change the values of any of the properties after the DTO has been instantiated. For example, we could do the following:

```
$repo = new Repo(
    id: 123,
    name: 'short-url',
    fullName: 'ash-jc-allen/short-url',
    isPrivate: false,
    description: 'A URL shortener',
    createdAt: Carbon::now(),
);

$repo->name = 'short-url-2';
```

The code in the example would allow us to update the `name` property of the DTO from `"short-url"` to `"short-url-2"`. This is because the `name` property is currently public and can be updated from inside or outside of the class. Depending on how you're using the DTOs, you may not want to allow this. Prior to PHP 8.1, to prevent the property from being changed, we would need to add a private property and a public getter method to retrieve the value of the property:

```
final class Repo
{
    public function __construct(
        private int $id,
        private string $name,
        private string $fullName,
        private bool $isPrivate,
        private string $description,
        private CarbonInterface $createdAt,
    ) {
        //
    }

    public function getName(): string
    {
        return $this->name;
    }

    // Other getter methods here...
}
```

Changing each of the properties to be private would prevent them from being changed after the class is instantiated, whether it be accidental or intentional. However, this approach has several drawbacks:

- It requires us to add a getter method for each property we want to access from outside the class.
- It adds a lot of boilerplate code to the class that adds cognitive load when reading it.

To solve these issues, we could change this DTO to use readonly properties instead:

```php
final class Repo
{
    public function __construct(
        public readonly int $id,
        public readonly string $name,
        public readonly string $fullName,
        public readonly bool $isPrivate,
        public readonly string $description,
        public readonly CarbonInterface $createdAt,
    ) {
        //
    }
}
```

As a result of using the `readonly` keyword, we've been able to remove the getter methods from the class. We've also been able to change the visibility of the properties to `public` because we can be confident that the fields cannot be updated after the class has been instantiated.

If any code was written, whether intentional or accidental, to update the value of any of the properties, PHP would throw an error. For example, if we tried to update the `name` property of the DTO, PHP would throw the following error:

```
Cannot modify readonly property App\DataTransferObjects\Repo::$name
```

To take this further, if you are confident that no property in the DTO should ever be changed after the class has been instantiated, you can make the entire class readonly:

```php
final readonly class Repo
{
    public function __construct(
        public int $id,
        public string $name,
        public string $fullName,
        public bool $isPrivate,
        public string $description,
        public CarbonInterface $createdAt,
    ) {
        //
    }
}
```

As a result of making the class readonly, PHP will throw an error if our code attempts to change any of the properties' values.

By default, I like to make as many of my classes and properties readonly as possible. Although it may sometimes seem overkill and unneeded, I like the visual cue it gives me when reading my code — especially when I'm reading code I wrote several months ago. It clearly indicates that a given class or property isn't updated anywhere in the codebase after it's instantiated. If the code needs to be updated to allow a property to be changed, I can remove the `readonly` keyword.

Using Interfaces and the Service Container

When building your API integrations, it's important to make the most of interfaces and the Laravel service container. Using these features allows you to write testable, maintainable code that is decoupled from the implementation details.

Before we get into the details of how to use interfaces and the service container, let's look at what interfaces and the service container actually are.

In basic terms, interfaces describe what a class should do. They can be used to ensure any class implementing the interface includes each public method defined inside it.

Interfaces can be:

- Used to define public methods for a class.
- Used to define constants for a class.

Interfaces cannot be:

- Instantiated on their own.
- Used to define private or protected methods for a class.
- Used to define properties for a class.

Interfaces define the public methods a class should include. It's important to remember that only the method signatures are defined and don't include the method body (like in a method in a class). This is because the interfaces only define communication between objects rather than defining the communication and behaviour like in a class. They let you know what you can do with a class and what it will return, but not how it will do it.

For example, imagine we want to create an API integration with GitHub. We could create an interface that defines the methods we want to communicate with the GitHub API:

```php
interface GitHubServiceInterface
{
    public function getRepo(string $owner, string $repo): array;

    public function getRepos(string $owner): array;
}
```

We've created an interface that specifies that any class implementing it must include two methods: `getRepo` and `getRepos`.

We could then create a class (that we'll imagine is using Saloon to make the API requests) that implements this interface like so:

```php
class GitHubService implements GitHubServiceInterface
{
    public function getRepo(string $owner, string $repo): array
    {
        // Make API request to GitHub API and return the response.
    }

    public function getRepos(string $owner): array
    {
        // Make API request to GitHub API and return the response.
    }
}
```

As we can see, the `GitHubService` class implements the `GitHubServiceInterface` interface and includes the two methods defined in the interface. If we were to remove one of the methods from the `GitHubService` class or change their signature (so they no longer match the signatures in the interface), PHP would throw an error because the class would no longer implement the interface correctly.

As a result of creating the interface, we know that any class implementing it will include the methods needed to communicate with the GitHub API. This is where we can now use Laravel's service container to write some really powerful code!

According to the Laravel documentation, the service container is a core feature of Laravel "for managing class dependencies and performing dependency injection". We can use it when instantiating classes to automatically inject any dependencies that the class requires.

Let's look at an example of what this looks like in practice. Traditionally, we might instantiate a class like so:

```
use App\Services\GitHubService;

$gitHubService = new GitHubService();
```

However, if we wanted to use the service container, we could instead do the following:

```
use App\Services\GitHubService;

$gitHubService = app(GitHubService::class);
```

Using the `app` helper method, we are resolving the `GitHubService` class from the service container.

Depending on which parts of your project you're working on, you may have already used the service container without realizing it. For example, if we wanted to resolve the `GitHubService` in a controller method, we could do the following:

```
use App\Services\GitHubService;

final class GitHubController extends Controller
{
    public function index(GitHubService $gitHubService)
    {
        // Use the GitHubService here.
    }
}
```

As you can see in the code example, we've only needed to define the service class as an argument for the controller method. If an argument is defined in a controller method signature, Laravel will automatically attempt to resolve the class from the service container and inject it into the method.

Although we have managed to resolve the `GitHubService`, our code is still tightly coupled to our Saloon implementation that we're using to make the API requests. This means if we want to create a different class for interacting with the GitHub API (such as a `GitHubGuzzleService` that directly uses the Guzzle package to make requests), we would have to go through our codebase and update every place where we're using the `GitHubService` class.

To decouple our code from this implementation detail, we could instead resolve an instance of the `GitHubServiceInterface` from the service container. We could do this like so:

```php
use App\Interfaces\GitHubServiceInterface;

$gitHubService = app(GitHubServiceInterface::class);
```

If we were to run this code, a PHP error would be thrown because interfaces cannot be instantiated on their own. However, we can tell Laravel how to resolve the interface by binding it to a concrete class in the service container. We can do this by adding the following code to the `register` method of the `AppServiceProvider` class:

```php
use App\Interfaces\GitHubServiceInterface;
use App\Services\GitHubService;
use Illuminate\Support\ServiceProvider;

class AppServiceProvider extends ServiceProvider
{
    public function register()
    {
        $this->app->bind(
            abstract: GitHubServiceInterface::class,
            concrete: GitHubService::class
        );
    }

    public function boot()
    {
        //
    }
}
```

By doing this, whenever we try to resolve the `GitHubServiceInterface` from the service container, an instance of the `GitHubService` class will be returned instead. This also means that if we wanted to change the implementation in the future, we could change this mapping in the `AppServiceProvider` class and not have to change any of the code that uses the `GitHubServiceInterface`.

As a result, we can ensure that none of our code (outside the service class and Saloon classes) is aware of Saloon or how we're making the API requests.

To take this concept further, we can also bind these interfaces to a specific instance of a concrete class. For instance, let's say that our `GitHubService` class has the following constructor:

```
class GitHubService implements GitHubServiceInterface
{
    public function __construct(
        private string $username,
        private string $token,
    ) {
        //
    }
```

The constructor specifies that a `username` and `token` must be passed to the class when it is instantiated. Both of these fields will be used as part of the authentication when making the API requests. Assume both fields are accessible via the `services.github.username` and `services.github.token` config fields.

We could update our binding in the `AppServiceProvider` like so:

```php
$this->app->bind(
    abstract: GitHubServiceInterface::class,
    concrete: fn () => new GitHubService(
        username: config('services.github.username'),
        token: config('services.github.token'),
    )
);
```

In the code example, we're creating a specific instance of the `GitHubService` class that has the necessary arguments passed to it.

Later in the book, we'll take interfaces and service container concepts further and explore how to use them to make your API integration more testable by using "test doubles" in the "Building an API Integration Using Saloon" chapter.

Redacting Sensitive Parameters

When working with external APIs in your application, you'll likely need to pass sensitive data (such as passwords and API keys) to your service classes as method parameters. In these scenarios, you may wish to prevent those parameters from being logged in your application's logs and stack traces.

To provide some context, let's look at an example of where we might want to redact sensitive parameters.

Imagine we are building an API integration that requires us to pass a username and password to an identity API endpoint that will return a token we can use to interact with the rest of the API. The code to do this might look something like this:

```
class IdentityApiService
{
    public function authenticate(
        string $username,
        string $password
    ): string {
        // Authenticate the user and return the token.
    }
}
```

If, for any reason, an exception is thrown within this method, the exception may be logged in your application's logs. This means that the username and password will be logged in plain text, which we want to avoid. For instance, imagine we called this method using the following code:

```
$identityApiService->authenticate('ash-jc-allen', 'PASSWORD HERE');
```

If an exception were thrown, the following lines would be found in the stack trace logged in your application's logs:

```
Something went wrong! {"exception":"[object] (Exception(code: 0): Something went
wrong! at /Users/ash/www/api-project/app/Services/IdentityApiService.php:13)
Stack trace:
#0 /Users/ash/www/api-project/app/Services/ApiService.php(48):
App\\Services\\IdentityApiService->authenticate('ash-jc-allen', 'PASSWORD HERE')
```

As we can see in the stack trace, the password is logged in plain text. To prevent this from happening, we could update the `authenticate` method to redact the password from the stack trace by using the `#[\SensitiveParameter]` attribute:

```
class IdentityApiService
{
    public function authenticate(
        string $username,
        #[\SensitiveParameter] string $password
    ): string {
        // Authenticate the user and return the token.
    }
}
```

As a result of doing this, if the `authenticate` method threw an exception, the password would be redacted from the stack trace:

```
Something went wrong! {"exception":"[object] (Exception(code: 0): Something went
wrong! at /Users/ash/www/api-project/app/Services/IdentityApiService.php:13)
Stack trace:
#0 /Users/ash/www/api-project/app/Services/ApiService.php(48):
App\\Services\\IdentityApiService->authenticate('ash-jc-allen',
Object(SensitiveParameterValue))
```

As we can see in the stack trace, the password has been redacted and replaced with an instance of the `SensitiveParameterValue` class. This means the password will no longer be logged in plain text.

Redacting sensitive parameters in your projects can be beneficial because it can prevent them from being transmitted to an external logging or bug-reporting system (such as Honeybadger, Flare, or Bugsnag). Sending this data to an external service introduces a new attack vector to your application. For example, if the external system was to be compromised (such as someone gaining access to your account or the service accidentally leaking data), this could allow malicious hackers to see any sensitive data that was logged. As a result, they may be able to gain access to the API you're using and cause damage. For instance, if you use a third-party API to send SMS messages, and the API key is logged in plain text, a malicious hacker could use this to send SMS messages to premium rate numbers, which could cost a lot of money.

However, there may be times when you must log your parameters in plain text. This may be for debugging reasons or because you're using a third-party package that prevents you from being able to redact the parameters. In these scenarios, you'll need to decide on a case-by-case basis whether you're happy taking the risk with the sensitive data being logged in plain text.

It's worth noting that most third-party error monitoring services allow you to define a list of parameters or fields that you'd like to redact and prevent transmitting to them. Make sure to check the documentation for the service you're using to see if this is something that they support.

Enums

Enums (or "enumerations") are a powerful feature introduced in PHP 8.1 that we can use to write cleaner, safer, and more expressive code.

They provide a type-safe way of representing a set of distinct values and can be used for representing things like states, options, or flags in your code. Later in the book (in the "Webhooks" chapter), we'll cover how we can use enums to represent the delivery status of an email when handling webhooks.

Benefits of Using Enums

By using enums in our code, we can:

- **Improve readability** - Enums can make your code more expressive and easier to understand by giving meaningful names to distinct values.
- **Reduce errors** - Enums can remove the need for passing raw string values around your code, which can lead to confusion, typos, and needing boilerplate code to validate the values.
- **Improve encapsulation** - Enums allow you to group related values, which can help you organize your code and reduce the risk of name conflicts with other constants or variables.
- **Improve autocompletion and error detection** - If you're using an IDE (such as PhpStorm), your editor can provide autocomplete suggestions and highlight errors when passing the incorrect enum types to methods.

Reducing Errors Using Enums

Let's look at how we can use enums to improve our code. We'll imagine we're building an integration to consume the GitHub API that allows us to fetch a user's repositories and filter them by one of the given types:

- All
- Owner
- Public
- Private
- Member

Before PHP 8.1, if we wanted to represent these values in PHP, we could use class constants. Here's an example of how we could do this:

```
class RepoType
{
    public const ALL = 'all';
    public const OWNER = 'owner';
    public const PUBLIC = 'public';
    public const PRIVATE = 'private';
    public const MEMBER = 'member';
}
```

If we were to imagine we had a `getReposByType` method in a `GitHubService` class that accepted a repository type as a parameter, the method might look something like this:

```php
class GitHubService
{
    public function getReposByType(string $type): array
    {
        if (! in_array($status, $this->validTypes(), true) {
            throw new InvalidArgumentException('Invalid type.');
        }

        // Get and return the repos here.
    }

    public function validTypes(): array
    {
        return [
            RepoType::ALL,
            RepoType::OWNER,
            RepoType::PUBLIC,
            RepoType::PRIVATE,
            RepoType::MEMBER,
        ];
    }
}
```

As we can see in the code example, we're checking whether the repository type is valid by using the `validTypes` method to get a list of valid types. If the repository type is not valid, we throw an `InvalidArgumentException`. But, as you can imagine, this isn't a very elegant solution. It now means that we must maintain a separate list of valid type values in our code, which is prone to errors and can easily become out of sync if we add any new constants. It also means we have to add additional validation logic to our code, which adds extra cognitive overhead when you're reading it.

We could call the `getReposByType` method like so:

```
app(GitHubService::class)->getReposByType(RepoType::PUBLIC);
```

However, because we're using a string to represent the language, we could also call the `getReposByType` method by passing a raw string:

```
app(GitHubService::class)->getReposByType('is_public');
```

Can you spot the error in that line of code?

We're passing `"is_public"` as the language, but that's not a valid type; instead, we should be passing `"public"`. If this error is caught during the development process, this could be easily solved by passing the correct raw string value or using one of the `RepoType` constants. But if this code made it to production, it could cause a bug in our code that would crash the application.

This is where enums come in and can help us. Let's look at how we could use enums to represent the repository types. We could start by defining our enum like so:

```php
enum RepoType: string
{
    case All = 'all';
    case Owner = 'owner';
    case Public = 'public';
    case Private = 'private';
    case Member = 'member';
}
```

It's worth noting that this `RepoType` enum is referred to as a "backed enum". This is because each of the enum cases has a value associated with them (in this case, they are strings). For example, calling `RepoType::All->value` would give you the value `"all"`, and calling `RepoType::Owner->value` would give you the value `"owner"`. Backed enums are incredibly useful in Laravel applications because they can be used as route parameters (for route binding, which we'll cover in the "Webhooks" section of the book) and can be used to represent columns in your database when they're defined as casts in your Eloquent models. You may not always need a value associated with the enum cases, so you can also create enums without a backing value. However, this guide will continue to use backed enums for the rest of the examples.

We can now update our `GitHubService` class to use the enum instead of a string:

```php
class GitHubService
{
    public function getReposByType(RepoType $repoType): array
    {
        // Get and return the repos here.
    }
}
```

Now the `getReposByType` method can only be called by passing a `RepoType` enum to the method. Passing any other type of value would result in a PHP type error being thrown. As a result, we could remove our checks from the beginning of the method and keep our code lean and focused. We can now call the `getReposByType` method like so:

```
app(GitHubService::class)->getReposByType(RepoType::All);
```

You may have noticed that the code doesn't look any different from the previous example. This is because we access enum cases using the same syntax as we'd access constants in a class. However, the key difference is that we're passing a `RepoType` instance to the method rather than a string in this example.

Adding Methods to Enums

Sometimes you want to take your enums a step further and add methods to them. Doing this can be extremely helpful when you want to encapsulate logic specific to the enum. As a basic example to show how this could be done, let's imagine we want to add a `toFriendly` method to our enum that returns a friendly name for the enum case. This friendly name might be displayed in the UI of our application. We could do this by adding the following method to our `RepoType` enum:

```php
enum RepoType: string
{
    case All = 'all';
    case Owner = 'owner';
    case Public = 'public';
    case Private = 'private';
    case Member = 'member';

    public function toFriendly(): string
    {
        return match ($this) {
            self::All => 'All',
            self::Owner => 'User is an Owner',
            self::Public => 'Public Repository',
            self::Private => 'Private Repository',
            self::Member => 'User is a Member',
        };
    }
}
```

By doing this, we can then do the following:

```php
RepoType::All->toFriendly(); // Returns "All"
RepoType::Owner->toFriendly(); // Returns "User is an Owner"
RepoType::Public->toFriendly(); // Returns "Public Repository"
RepoType::Private->toFriendly(); // Returns "Private Repository"
RepoType::Member->toFriendly(); // Returns "User is a Member"
```

Instantiating Enums from Values

When parsing an API request's response, you may want to create an enum from a raw value. For example, if you're parsing the response of a GitHub API request, you may want to create a `RepoType` enum from the value of the `type` key in the response. You can do this using the enum's `from` or `tryFrom` method.

Let's continue with our `Repo` example from earlier in this section and imagine that our DTO now has a `repoType` property that must be a `RepoType` enum. In our `createDtoFromResponse` method of our Saloon request class (where we map the API response data to the values of our new DTO), we could do the following:

```
/**
 * @param \Saloon\Http\Response $response
 * @return \App\DataTransferObjects\Repo
 */
public function createDtoFromResponse(Response $response): mixed
{
    $responseData = $response->json();

    return new Repo(
        id: $responseData['id'],
        // ...
        repoType: RepoType::from($responseData['type']),
    );
}
```

The `from` method allows us to take a raw value that represents one of the cases in the enum (in this case, "all", "owner", "public", "private", or "member") and instantiates the matching enum.

For instance, calling `RepoType::from('public')` would return the `RepoType::Public` enum case.

If no enum case exists with the given value, a `ValueError` will be thrown. For example, if we called `RepoType::from('INVALID')`, a `ValueError` would be thrown with the following error message:

```
"INVALID" is not a valid backing value for enum App\Enums\RepoType
```

However, there may be times when you don't want an exception to be thrown if the enum cannot be found. In these scenarios, you can use the `tryFrom` method instead. The `tryFrom` method will return `null` if the enum cannot be found. For example, if we called `RepoType::tryFrom('INVALID')`, `null` would be returned.

Conclusion

In this chapter, we've reviewed what strict-type checking is, its benefits, and how to use it to reduce bugs in your code. We also learned about composition over inheritance and how it can help to keep your code lean and focused. We also learned how to use final classes, data transfer objects, and readonly classes to help us achieve this. Additionally, we learned how we can use interfaces and Laravel's service container to help decouple code to make it more maintainable and testable. As well as this, we learned about how we can redact sensitive parameters from our stack traces to help reduce the chance of sensitive data being leaked. Finally, we showed how enums can help reduce bugs by ensuring only valid values are passed to methods.

Using the techniques we've learned in this chapter, you should feel confident enough to use them in your Laravel applications.

In the next chapter, we look at how to use these techniques alongside Saloon to build a robust and maintainable API client to consume the GitHub API.

Building an API Integration Using Saloon

Now that we've covered the basics of what APIs are and some code techniques we can use when building our integrations, let's look at how we can actually consume an API in our Laravel applications.

To do this, we'll use a package called Saloon, created by Sam Carré. We'll start by looking at what Saloon is, its benefits, and alternative approaches you may want to use. We'll then step through how you can install and use Saloon in your Laravel applications. We'll look at aspects of building an API integration, such as authentication, making requests, handling errors, caching responses, and testing our integrations.

In this section, we'll write code that can consume the GitHub API. By the end of this chapter, you should feel confident enough to use Saloon in your applications to consume APIs.

In the next chapter, we'll look at how to use Saloon to consume an OAuth API.

What is Saloon?

Saloon is a PHP library created and maintained by Sam Carré that allows you to easily consume APIs in your PHP applications.

It uses an elegant, expressive, object-oriented approach that makes it easy to build API integrations without worrying about the underlying implementation. Saloon has many features that make it easy to build API integrations, such as authentication handling, concurrent requests, pagination, error handling, and caching.

It ships with handy default settings that make it easy for you to get started. But it also allows you to customize these settings to suit your needs.

A key benefit of Saloon is that it comes with powerful tools you can use for writing tests for your API integrations. This makes it simpler to write tests that are easy to read and maintainable.

Saloon is also an excellent choice for consuming APIs in your Laravel applications as it encourages you to abstract your code into classes, such as "connectors" and "requests", which we'll cover later in this chapter. By logically separating the code, it makes it much easier for you to maintain and extend your integrations in the future.

This chapter will focus on using Saloon v3. Specifically, we'll be using Saloon's Laravel driver, which allows us to easily integrate Saloon into our Laravel application by providing features such as:

- Artisan commands for creating new connectors and request classes
- Facade for mocking and recording requests for testing
- Access to Laravel's `HTTP` sender rather than the default `Guzzle` sender

Alternatives to Saloon

If you're building an API integration for your Laravel application, you can take several approaches to making HTTP requests. Let's take a quick look at some of the alternatives to Saloon:

Guzzle

Guzzle is a popular PHP HTTP client that you can use to make HTTP requests. It's a great choice for making API requests, especially as it ships in the default installation of Laravel, so it doesn't require you to install any additional dependencies.

It is relatively straightforward to use and also has tools that you can use for mocking responses in your tests.

The core Saloon package actually uses Guzzle under the hood to make HTTP requests.

An example request using Guzzle may look something like this:

```php
$client = new GuzzleHttp\Client();

$response = $client->get('https://api.github.com/user', [
    'headers' => [
        'Authorization' => 'Bearer '.config('services.github.token'),
    ]
]);

$statusCode = $response->getStatusCode();
// $statusCode is: 200

$contentType = $response->getHeader('content-type')[0];
// $contentType is: "application/json; charset=utf-8"

$contents = json_decode(
    json: $response->getBody()->getContents(),
    associative: false,
    depth: 512,
    flags: JSON_THROW_ON_ERROR
);
// $contents is: {"login": "ash-jc-allen", ...}
```

Http Facade

The `Http` facade is a class that ships with Laravel that you can use to make HTTP requests. It's a wrapper around Guzzle that simplifies some of Guzzle's functionality and makes it easier to use.

In my opinion, the `Http` facade provides two main benefits over using Guzzle directly:

- The `Http` facade includes many methods you can use for testing. It allows you to mock the responses for individual calls and inspect HTTP requests to ensure your application sends them with the correct data.
- All the requests made via the `Http` facade can be logged in Laravel Telescope (a package that provides a dashboard for debugging and inspecting your Laravel application). This makes it easy to visually inspect your requests and responses and debug any issues you may have.

As a side note, if you'd like to log your HTTP requests made by Saloon, you can install the `saloonphp/laravel-http-sender` package and configure Saloon to use the `Http` facade as the sender rather than Guzzle. We'll cover how to do this in more depth later in this chapter.

Continuing with our GitHub example from earlier, an example request using the `Http` facade may look something like this:

```
$response = Http::withToken(config('services.github.token'))
    ->get('https://api.github.com/user');

$statusCode = $response->status();
// $statusCode is 200

$contentType = $response->header('content-type');
// $contentType is: "application/json; charset=utf-8"

$contents = $response->json();
// $contents is: {"login": "ash-jc-allen", ...}
```

As we can see, the `Http` facade hides away some of Guzzle's functionality for us to keep the code understandable and easy to read. For example, instead of needing to call `getBody()->getContents()` to get the response body and then using `json_decode`, we can simply call `json()` to get the response body as an array.

cURL

Another option that you can use to make HTTP requests is "Client for URL" (cURL). PHP supports `libcurl`, a library you can use to make different types of requests, such as HTTP requests.

In fact, Guzzle uses cURL under the hood to make HTTP requests by default because it's a powerful and flexible library that's been around for a long time and is typically available on servers. This means that when using Saloon, you're indirectly using cURL under the hood.

However, although cURL is a powerful tool, it is a lot of work to use and can be verbose. For example, take our example GitHub request and write it using cURL:

```php
$ch = curl_init();

curl_setopt($ch, CURLOPT_URL, 'https://api.github.com/user');
curl_setopt($ch, CURLOPT_HTTPHEADER, [
    'Authorization: Bearer '.config('services.github.token'),
    'User-Agent: My-Laravel-App'
]);
curl_setopt($ch, CURLOPT_RETURNTRANSFER, true);

$output = curl_exec($ch);

if(curl_errno($ch)){
    echo 'Curl error: ' . curl_error($ch);
} else {
    $statusCode = curl_getinfo($ch, CURLINFO_HTTP_CODE);
    // $statusCode is 200

    $contentType = curl_getinfo($ch, CURLINFO_CONTENT_TYPE);
    // $contentType is: "application/json; charset=utf-8"

    $contents = json_decode($output, false, 512, JSON_THROW_ON_ERROR);
    // $contents is: {"login": "ash-jc-allen", ...}
}

curl_close($ch);
```

We can see that it's a lot more verbose than the Guzzle and `Http` facade examples. This makes it harder to read, understand, and maintain. A general rule I like to follow when writing code is to make it read like an English sentence as much as possible. The more plain English is used, the easier it will be for new developers to understand the code, and the easier it will be for me to understand it in the future. I don't feel cURL helps achieve this goal.

You're unlikely to encounter cURL requests in your Laravel applications, but if you're working on an older application with some legacy code, you may encounter it.

API SDK

Sometimes, you must build an API integration for your Laravel application and find that the third-party service has a software development kit (SDK) available. In the context of PHP applications, an SDK is typically a Composer package you can download and install into your application that provides a wrapper around the API you're integrating.

For instance, imagine you want to interact with the Stripe API to take payments from your web application's customers. To do this, you may want to install Stripe's official PHP SDK (`stripe/stripe-php`). As a basic example, you could write the following code to create a new customer using the Stripe package:

```
use Stripe\StripeClient;

$stripe = new StripeClient(config('services.stripe.secret'));

$customer = $stripe->customers->create([
    'description' => 'John Doe',
    'email' => 'john@example.com',
    'payment_method' => 'pm_card_visa',
]);
```

As you can see, the SDK provides a convenient wrapper around the API, making it easy to interact with and removing the need to worry about the underlying HTTP requests and responses. This way, you can focus on the business logic of your application.

Generally, SDKs are built and maintained by the third-party service companies themselves. They act as a way to encourage developers to integrate with their API and make it as easy as possible to do so — they're essentially a marketing tool. For this reason, they're typically well-maintained and kept up to date with the latest API changes. Thus, you don't need to worry about keeping up to date with the API changes yourself, as the SDK will do this for you. You'll have the added benefit of the SDK including tests to ensure it works as expected. So, you can write your own tests to ensure that the SDK's methods are being called correctly without needing to test the underlying HTTP requests.

However, I strongly recommend inspecting an SDK before you start using it. As mentioned, these packages and libraries are a marketing tool for third-party services. As with any other aspect of business, building and maintaining them costs money. If the package isn't especially popular, it may not be well-maintained. If this is the case, you may find that the SDK is outdated and doesn't support the latest API changes. This could cause issues for your application and may mean that you must write your own wrapper around the API.

To help decide whether you should use an SDK, here are several questions to ask when inspecting it:

- **How many downloads does the package have?** - This isn't a perfect metric, but it can give you a good idea of a package's popularity. It's likely to be well-maintained and updated if it has many downloads. It can also indicate that more people have been using it, meaning there's an increased chance bugs have been spotted and fixed. It's likely not very popular and may not be maintained very much if it has very few downloads.
- **How many open issues does the package have?** - Check out the issues for the package and see what types of problems you're seeing. Many issues may be feature requests, which aren't necessarily alarming. The issues you want to look out for are things like "this package doesn't work with the latest version of the API" or "this package doesn't work with the latest version of PHP". These issues can indicate that the package isn't well-

maintained.

- **How many open pull requests does the package have?** - If there are open pull requests to fix bugs or add new features, this indicates community interest. Note the frequency of recent merges and whether minor fixes have been ignored for long periods to gauge maintainer activity.

Should I Use Saloon?

When planning your API integration, you might ask, "Should I use Saloon, Guzzle, the `Http` facade, cURL, or the API SDK?". That's a valid question you'll need to answer based on your project's needs.

Let's start by saying it's doubtful that you'll want to use cURL directly. Although it's a very powerful library, and you'll be interacting with it regardless of the other options you choose, it's not very easy to use and can be quite verbose. It's also not very easy to test compared to the other approaches, making it difficult to write tests for your application. It's important to remember that we must ensure that tests are easy to write. The easier they are to write, the more motivation you'll feel to write them. If tests are difficult to write, you'll be less likely to write them, which means you'll have less confidence in your application.

You may want to use Guzzle or the `Http` facade to build your integration. These are both perfectly valid approaches and ones I've used many times. They both have testing utilities and come packed with many convenient methods to simplify sending requests and reading responses. Of these two approaches, I would lean more towards the `Http` facade as it makes the code look cleaner and more readable — and readability is very important. If you're only going to send a single API request in your application, you may want to use one of these rather than installing Saloon. Sam Carré, the creator of Saloon, has stated in the past that it may be easier to use one of these approaches rather than installing a new dependency (Saloon) and keeping it up to date in your application.

If the third-party service you're using offers an SDK for interacting with their API, you may want to opt for that. This is, of course, assuming that it's well-maintained and that you're happy with the quality of the code. Using their package, you can take advantage of the code they've written. This will also reduce the burden of updating your code with the latest API changes.

If there isn't a well-maintained SDK available, you can use the Saloon package. Saloon allows you to use an object-oriented approach to building your integration code with small, focused classes that are highly testable. You'll also have access to Saloon features such as caching responses, error handling, OAuth handling, plugins, and more. You can take advantage of all these features to build very extensive integrations.

Another benefit of Saloon is its popularity and the fact that it's well maintained. As mentioned, it's important to ask questions before installing a new dependency in your application. You want to make sure that it's still actively being maintained and that it will be around for a long time. At the time of writing, Saloon boasts over 460k downloads (averaging at around 60k downloads per month), 1.6k stars on GitHub, and has had over 80 releases. The package also has a good-quality test suite with a high level of code coverage. These are all good indicators that the package is well maintained and is safe to use in your application.

As a side note, you can also use Saloon to build your own API SDK. You may want to do this if you're building an API service and want other developers to start using it.

No matter which of these approaches you take, I recommend writing a thin abstraction layer over your code. You can do this using interfaces and dependency injection, as we've already covered in the "Code Techniques" section. Doing this can make it easier to switch out your implementation in the future. For example, imagine you have written your API integration using an SDK that is now abandoned and won't receive any more updates. You may want to use Saloon to rewrite the API calls and logic in this situation. If the code is abstracted away behind interfaces, you'll be able to swap out the implementation without needing to change any of the code that uses the API integration. This is a very powerful technique and one that I recommend using.

Connectors, Requests, and Senders

Before we start using Saloon, there are three concepts we must understand: connectors, requests, and senders.

Connectors and requests are two types of classes Saloon uses to build your API integration. They have different responsibilities and are used in different ways. They form an integral part of Saloon and are what you'll mainly interact with when using the package.

After installing and configuring Saloon, you won't likely need to worry about senders. But they are an important part of Saloon, and it's important to understand what they are and how they fit into your integration.

Let's understand these three concepts before writing any code.

Connectors

According to the Saloon documentation, connectors are "classes that hold the basic requirements of an API integration. Connectors communicate with the HTTP client (sender)". They are the classes you use to define things like the base URL for an API, common headers that should be sent (such as an API key), and any other configuration you want to use across all of your API requests to a particular service. A core purpose of Saloon is to standardize your integrations, and connectors are a key part of this. They help you reduce repeated code and make integrations a lot tidier.

Typically, you create a connector for each third-party service you're integrating. For example, if you're integrating with GitHub, you would create a `GitHubConnector` class. Likewise, if you were interacting with `Xero`, you may want a `XeroConnector`. You can then send requests to the API using the connector you've created. So you can think of a connector in a literal sense that they define how you want to connect to a particular service and send requests to it.

Connectors created using the Saloon's Artisan commands (covered later) are stored in the `app/Http/Integrations` directory by default. For example, a `GitHubConnector` class for a `GitHub` integration would be stored in `app/Http/Integrations/GitHub/GitHubConnector.php`.

A basic example of a connector looks like this:

```php
namespace App\Http\Integrations\GitHub;

use Saloon\Http\Connector;
use Saloon\Traits\Plugins\AlwaysThrowOnErrors;

final class GitHubConnector extends Connector
{
    use AlwaysThrowOnErrors;

    public function resolveBaseUrl(): string
    {
        return 'https://api.github.com/';
    }

    public function defaultHeaders(): array
    {
        return [
            'Accept' => 'application/vnd.github+json',
        ];
    }
}
```

The above connector has three main parts:

- `use AlwaysThrowOnErrors` - The connector uses one of Saloon's built-in plugins that throws an exception if the API returns an error response. Since this is applied to the connector, it will work with all the requests sent through it, so we don't need to apply it to each request class. We'll delve into plugins and error handling later.
- `resolveBaseUrl` - This method is used to define the base URL for the API. This means that in our request classes, we can just define the path for the request rather than the whole, absolute URL.
- `defaultHeaders` - This method is used to define any default headers that are sent with each request. In this case, we're defining a default `Accept` header that GitHub advises should be sent with each request.

Requests

Saloon requests are classes that define the logic and information for a single API request. They are the classes you'll use to define things such as the URL to which requests should be sent, the HTTP method to use, building the request body data, and mapping the response body data to a data transfer object (DTO).

Typically, a Saloon request would represent a single request. So, for example, if you wanted to send three types of requests to GitHub (fetch all GitHub repositories for a user, fetch a single GitHub repository, create a new repository), you may have three separate request classes: `GetAllRepos`, `GetRepo`, `StoreRepo`. These request classes would then be sent using the connector class for the integration, such as a `GitHubConnector`.

Saloon requests are typically stored in the `app/Http/Integrations/{IntegrationName}/Requests` directory. For example, a `CreateRepo` request class for a `GitHub` integration would be stored in `app/Http/Integrations/GitHub/Requests/CreateRepo.php`.

Let's look at a basic request class:

```php
namespace App\Http\Integrations\GitHub\Requests;

use App\DataTransferObjects\GitHub\NewRepoData;
use Saloon\Contracts\Body\HasBody;
use Saloon\Enums\Method;
use Saloon\Http\Request;
use Saloon\Traits\Body\HasJsonBody;

final class CreateRepo extends Request implements HasBody
{
    use HasJsonBody;

    protected Method $method = Method::POST;

    public function __construct(
        private readonly NewRepoData $newRepoData,
    ) {}

    public function resolveEndpoint(): string
    {
        return '/user/repos';
    }

    protected function defaultBody(): array
    {
        return [
            'name' => $this->newRepoData->name,
            'description' => $this->newRepoData->description,
            'private' => $this->newRepoData->isPrivate,
        ];
```

```
    }
}
```

The above request class has five main parts:

- `use HasJsonBody` - This trait defines the request body data. In this case, we're using the `HasJsonBody` trait, which means the `Content-Type: application/json` header will be added to the request.
- `protected Method $method = Method::POST` - This property defines the HTTP method that should be used for the request. In this case, we're using the `POST` method.
- `__construct` - This is the constructor for the request class. We're using the constructor to pass a data transfer object (DTO) to the request class containing the data we want to send in the request body.
- `resolveEndpoint` - This method defines the endpoint to which the request should be sent. In this case, we're sending the request to the `/user/repos` endpoint.
- `defaultBody` - This method defines the default request body data. In this case, we're using the data from the DTO that we passed to the request class in the constructor.

As we can see, Saloon provides a readable and obvious structure for defining requests. This makes it easy to understand what a request is doing and what data it's sending. We can further extend the functionality of our requests by using additional methods, plugins, and middleware. This chapter will delve into these features and examine how to write powerful and flexible requests.

Although you'll typically send your requests through a connector, Saloon provides a handy feature called "Solo Requests". These are request classes that can be sent on their own without using a connector. We'll delve into these later in this chapter.

Senders

In Saloon, a sender is the underlying HTTP client responsible for sending your HTTP request and handling the response.

As mentioned, Saloon uses Guzzle by default to send HTTP requests and this uses the `GuzzleSender` class. However, you may want to use Laravel's `Http` facade to send your requests, which allows you to take advantage of Laravel features, such as logging your requests in Telescope for debugging purposes. To use the `HttpSender` class, you'll need to install the `saloonphp/laravel-http-sender` Composer package. We'll look at how to do this in the "Installing Saloon" section of this chapter.

In most cases, you won't need to change the sender that Saloon uses, and it's likely not something you'll think about after installing Saloon. However, depending on your application, you can create your own sender class or use a different one for a specific integration.

Under the hood, Saloon makes use of PSR-7, PSR-17, and PSR-18 standards. PSR-7 defines how the HTTP request messages are built before sending. PSR-17 defines HTTP factories and is used for creating things like the URI, streams, and the request. PSR-18 defines HTTP client interfaces and is used for sending the request. Following these standards makes Saloon robust and able to switch to different senders in the future without affecting your code.

Installation and Configuration

With an understanding of what Saloon is, let's write code to make requests to the GitHub API.

Installing Saloon

We can start by installing Saloon using Composer by running the following command in our project's root:

```
composer require saloonphp/saloon "^3.0" saloonphp/laravel-plugin "^3.0"
```

It's worth noting that we are installing the core Saloon package (`saloonphp/saloon`) along with the Laravel plugin package (`saloonphp/laravel-plugin`). This is because we are using Laravel and want to take advantage of the Laravel-specific features that Saloon provides (such as Artisan commands for generating our connector and request classes). However, if you use Saloon in a non-Laravel project, you can just install the `saloonphp/saloon` package instead.

Configuration

At the time of writing this book, the only configuration option available is to change the default sender class that Saloon uses. As mentioned, you likely won't need to change this, so you won't need to publish the configuration file. However, if this is something you think you may want to change, you can publish the configuration file by running the following command:

```
php artisan vendor:publish --tag=saloon-config
```

After running this command, you should have a `config/saloon.php` file in your project.

Using the Laravel HTTP Sender

As mentioned, Saloon provides the functionality to define the sender used to send your HTTP requests. By default, Saloon uses Guzzle to send your requests, but if you'd like to use Laravel `Http` sender instead, you can install the `saloonphp/laravel-http-sender` Composer package by running the following command:

```
composer require saloonphp/laravel-http-sender
```

After installing the package, you'll need to update the `sender` configuration option in your `config/saloon.php` file to use the `HttpSender` class like so:

```
use Saloon\HttpSender\HttpSender;

return [
    'default_sender' => HttpSender::class,
];
```

Saloon will now be configured to use Laravel's HTTP client for sending requests rather than the default Guzzle client.

Available Artisan Commands

Since we are using the Laravel plugin for Saloon (the `saloonphp/laravel-plugin` package), we have Artisan commands to help us generate the classes needed for our integration. You're not required to use these commands, but they can speed up the creation of files for your project.

The following commands are available:

saloon:connector

This command generates a connector class for the specified integration.

The command structure is:

```
saloon:connector {Integration Name} {Connector Name}
```

For example, if we wanted to create a new connector class for GitHub, we could run the following command:

```
php artisan saloon:connector GitHub GitHubConnector
```

This would create a new `app/Http/Integrations/GitHub/GitHubConnector.php` file.

saloon:request

This command generates a request class for the specified integration.

The command structure is:

```
saloon:request {Integration Name} {Request Name}
```

For example, if we wanted to create a new request class for our GitHub integration, we could run the following command:

```
php artisan saloon:request GitHub GetAllRepos
```

This would create a new `app/Http/Integrations/GitHub/Requests/GetAllRepos.php` file.

saloon:response

This command generates a response class for the specified integration. You can use custom response classes to add logic or override Saloon's default response class. This can be helpful if you're repeating the same logic for multiple requests and want to abstract it into a single class.

The command structure is:

```
saloon:response {Integration Name} {Response Name}
```

For example, if we wanted to create a new response class for our GitHub integration, we could run the following command:

```
php artisan saloon:response GitHub GitHubResponse
```

This would create a new `app/Http/Integrations/GitHub/Responses/GitHubResponse.php` file.

saloon:plugin

This command generates a plugin class for the specified integration. A plugin allows you to add functionality to your integrations' connectors and requests. Later, this chapter covers plugins in more depth.

The command structure is:

```
saloon:plugin {Integration Name} {Plugin Name}
```

For example, if we wanted to create a new plugin class for our GitHub integration, we could run the following command:

```
php artisan saloon:plugin GitHub GitHubPlugin
```

This would create a new `app/Http/Integrations/GitHub/Plugins/GitHubPlugin.php` file.

saloon:auth

This command generates a custom authenticator class for the specified integration. This allows adding authentication logic to your connectors and requests, such as adding headers to requests containing API keys. We'll see later how to create custom authentication classes.

The command structure is:

```
saloon:auth {Integration Name} {Authenticator Name}
```

If we want to create a new authenticator class for our GitHub integration, we could run the following command:

```
php artisan saloon:auth GitHub GitHubAuthenticator
```

This would create a new `[app/Http/Integrations/GitHub/Auth/GitHubAuthenticator.php` file.

Preparing the API Integration

Before building our integration, we need to prepare. We'll build a simple integration with GitHub to highlight some of Saloon's key features. To make requests to GitHub, we need an API key (or personal access token) to be sent in all our requests to identify ourselves.

For this chapter, we will be storing our API key in our `.env` file and accessing it using Laravel's `config` helper function. Depending on the type of application you're building, you may want to do this differently. For example, you may want your users to be able to add their API keys to your application. You might allow this by entering API keys into a form (such as on a "settings" page), or you might use something like OAuth to allow users to authenticate with GitHub and then store their access token in your database. We'll be covering how you can use OAuth for this purpose in the next chapter.

Imagine we have generated a new API key for our GitHub account. We'll store it in our `.env` file like so:

```
GITHUB_TOKEN=github-token-goes-here
```

We can now add an entry to `config/services.php` so we can access the API key in our application:

```
return [
    // ...

    'github' => [
        'token' => env('GITHUB_TOKEN'),
    ],

    // ...
];
```

If we were to run `config('services.github.token')` in our application, we would get the value of the `GITHUB_TOKEN` environment variable. This makes our API key accessible in our codebase.

Building the Interface and Classes

Let's plan what we want to build and how we want to build it. Imagine building a simple API client to do the following:

- Fetch all GitHub repositories that belong to the authenticated user.
- Fetch a single GitHub repository.
- Fetch the languages a GitHub repository uses (e.g., PHP, JavaScript, etc.)
- Create a new GitHub repository.
- Update an existing GitHub repository.
- Delete a GitHub repository.

We must plan what we want to build before writing any code, which helps us identify potential issues early on and leads to cleaner, more maintainable code.

One process we'll focus on in this chapter is abstracting Saloon from the rest of our application. We want to ensure our application code has no knowledge of Saloon. This way, if we ever decide to change the underlying implementation of our integration, we can do so without needing to change any code outside our integration classes.

In principle, you should be able to swap out Saloon for another API client library, and your application code should still work. This is why we will use interfaces to define our integration service class. We'll then use Laravel's service container to bind our interfaces to their concrete implementations.

Building the Interface

Let's build our interface first. We'll create a new `GitHub` interface in an `app/Interfaces` directory. This interface will define the methods that we want our integration service class to have.

It will look something like this:

```
namespace App\Interfaces;

use App\Collections\GitHub\RepoCollection;
use App\DataTransferObjects\GitHub\NewRepoData;
use App\DataTransferObjects\GitHub\Repo;
use App\DataTransferObjects\GitHub\UpdateRepoData;

interface GitHub
{
    public function getRepos(): RepoCollection;

    public function getRepo(string $owner, string $repoName): Repo;

    public function getRepoLanguages(string $owner, string $repoName): array;

    public function createRepo(NewRepoData $repoData): Repo;

    public function updateRepo(
        string $owner,
        string $repoName,
        UpdateRepoData $repoData
    ): Repo;

    public function deleteRepo(string $owner, string $repoName): void;
}
```

We have defined six methods to implement in our integration service class. You may have noticed we reference classes that don't exist yet: `RepoCollection`, `Repo`, `NewRepoData`, and `UpdateRepoData`. We'll create these classes in the following few sections.

The `Repo` class is a data transfer object (DTO) to hold the data for a single GitHub repository. The `RepoCollection` class is a Collection of `Repo` objects. The `NewRepoData` and `UpdateRepoData` classes are DTOs to hold data for creating and updating a GitHub repository.

Building the DTOs

As mentioned in this book, DTOs are simple classes that hold data. They allow us to pass data around our application in a structured way and use PHP's type system to ensure we pass the correct data to our methods.

Thanks to some of Saloon's features, it's simple to use DTOs to represent the data we want to send to and receive from the API.

Building the Repo DTO

We'll create a `Repo` DTO representing a single GitHub repository. GitHub returns 95 fields in the API responses containing repository information by default. However, we will only use a few of these fields for our example:

- ID of the repository
- Owner of the repository
- Name of the repository
- Full name of the repository (e.g., `owner/repo-name`)
- Whether the repository is private or not
- Description of the repository
- Date the repository was created

If you're building the integration for your own application, you may want to follow this same approach. It helps to keep your DTO focused and ensures that you only use the data you need. However, if you're building your integration as part of a library or package other developers might use, you don't know what data other developers might need. Thus, you'll likely want to include all the data GitHub returns.

Let's create our new `Repo` DTO and place it in the `app/DataTransferObjects/GitHub` directory:

```
namespace App\DataTransferObjects\GitHub;

use Carbon\CarbonInterface;

final readonly class Repo
{
    public function __construct(
        public int $id,
        public string $owner,
        public string $name,
        public string $fullName,
        public bool $private,
        public string $description,
        public CarbonInterface $createdAt,
    ) {}
}
```

As we can see in the code example, we've made the DTO a final, readonly class. As a result, it can't be extended by another class or mutated after it has been instantiated.

Building the NewRepoData and UpdateRepoData DTOs

We'll create two more DTOs to be passed to our integration's request classes when making API calls to create or update a repository. For this reason, they will be very similar to each other. In fact, in this particular example, they will be identical. However, I prefer to split them into two separate classes as it can help maintainability. For instance, if we want to pass a new field in the request to create a repository, we can add it to the `NewRepoData` DTO without worrying about it affecting the `UpdateRepoData` DTO. If we didn't use two separate DTOs, we would have to be careful about adding new fields to the DTO as it could break the update functionality, so we may have to create a new DTO anyway. Consequently, I like to create two separate DTOs from the start to avoid this problem.

When creating or updating a repository in GitHub, we'll need to pass the following data:

- Name of the repository
- Whether the repository is private or not
- Description of the repository

Let's create our `NewRepoData` DTO and place it in the `app/DataTransferObjects/GitHub` directory:

```php
namespace App\DataTransferObjects\GitHub;

final readonly class NewRepoData
{
    public function __construct(
        public string $name,
        public string $description,
        public bool $isPrivate,
    ) {}
}
```

We'll also create our `UpdateRepoData` DTO and place it in the same directory:

```php
namespace App\DataTransferObjects\GitHub;

final readonly class UpdateRepoData
{
    public function __construct(
        public string $name,
        public string $description,
        public bool $isPrivate,
    ) {}
}
```

Building the Collections

Laravel Collections are an extremely powerful tool that allows us to work with arrays of data very expressively. They contain useful methods and are a great way to work with data we receive from an API.

For this reason, we'll use a Collection to hold the `Repo` objects we receive from the GitHub API. Rather than just using an `Illuminate\Support\Collection` instance, we'll create our own `RepoCollection` class that extends that class. This is a perfect example of where inheritance can be used to our advantage.

Let's create our `RepoCollection` class and place it in the `app/Collections/GitHub` directory:

```
namespace App\Collections\GitHub;

use App\DataTransferObjects\GitHub\Repo;
use Illuminate\Support\Collection;

/** @extends Collection<int,Repo> */
final class RepoCollection extends Collection
{

}
```

As we can see in the code example, we've extended the `Illuminate\Support\Collection` class and specified that the items in the collection will be instances of our `Repo` DTO. This means we can use the `RepoCollection` class like any other `Collection`, but we get the added benefit of static analysis tooling being able to detect if we're not passing `Repos` to the Collection. As well as this, we can also benefit from our integrated development environment (IDE), such as

PhpStorm, being able to detect that our `RepoCollection` contains `Repo` objects and providing us with code completion and other useful features.

Although we won't add any methods to our `RepoCollection`, you may add methods such as `addRepo(Repo $repo)`. This is a great way to add some extra type-safety to your code and ensure you only add `Repo` objects to the collection.

However, in this case, we will keep our `RepoCollection` as a simple extension of the `Illuminate\Support\Collection` class. In our code examples, we'll be able to use the `ensure` method to ensure that all the items in the `RepoCollection` are `Repo` objects. For example, we can run it like this:

```
$repos = new RepoCollection([
    new Repo(...),
    new Repo(...),
]);

$repos->ensure(Repo::class);
```

If all the `RepoCollection` items are instances of `Repo` classes, the code will continue running as expected. Otherwise, an `UnexpectedValueException` will be thrown.

Creating the Integration Service Class

Now that we have our interface, DTOs, and Collection prepared, we can create the actual class used to interact with the GitHub API.

For this book, we won't add any code to our class's methods just yet. Instead, we'll add the code to each method as we go through this chapter. This allows us to see how each method works, and we'll be able to highlight different aspects of the code as we go.

Let's create a new `GitHubService` class and place it in the `app/Services/GitHub` directory. The class may look something like this:

```
use App\Collections\GitHub\RepoCollection;
use App\DataTransferObjects\GitHub\NewRepoData;
use App\DataTransferObjects\GitHub\Repo;
use App\DataTransferObjects\GitHub\UpdateRepoData;
use App\Interfaces\GitHub;

final readonly class GitHubService implements GitHub
{
    public function __construct(
        private string $token,
    ) {}

    public function getRepos(): RepoCollection
    {
        // ...
    }

    public function getRepo(string $owner, string $repoName): Repo
    {
        // ...
    }

    public function getRepoLanguages(string $owner, string $repoName): array
    {
        // ...
    }
```

```php
    public function createRepo(NewRepoData $repoData): Repo
    {
        // ...
    }

    public function updateRepo(
        string $owner,
        string $repoName,
        UpdateRepoData $repoData
    ): Repo {
        // ...
    }

    public function deleteRepo(string $owner, string $repoName): void
    {
        // ...
    }
}
```

You may have noticed that we added a constructor that accepts a `$token` parameter. This is our GitHub personal access token we added to our `.env` file earlier. I like to pass all required data to my integration code's constructor so I can run any of the public methods on the class with the confidence that I have all the needed to make the request.

However, you may want to take a different approach. For example, you may want to add a `setToken` method on the class that allows you to set the token after the class has been instantiated. This is a perfectly valid approach, and it's up to you which approach to take.

Binding the Interface to the Concrete Implementation

As mentioned earlier, we'll use interfaces in our code so we can easily swap out the concrete implementation of the integration code. This means we'll never directly access the `GitHubService` class in our code. Instead, we'll use the `GitHub` interface.

To make this work, we must bind the interface to the concrete implementation. We can do this with a service provider. You may want to create your own service provider that's responsible for all these bindings. However, for the sake of simplicity, we'll add the binding to the `AppServiceProvider` class that's already included in a new Laravel application.

We'll update our `app/Providers/AppServiceProvider` class like so:

```php
namespace App\Providers;

use App\Interfaces\GitHub;
use App\Services\GitHub\GitHubService;
use Illuminate\Support\ServiceProvider;

class AppServiceProvider extends ServiceProvider
{
    public function register(): void
    {
        $this->app->bind(
            abstract: GitHub::class,
            concrete: fn (): GitHub => new GitHubService(
                token: config('services.github.token'),
            )
        );
    }

    // ...
}
```

As we can see here in the code example, we've bound the `GitHub` interface to the `GitHubService` class. We've also ensured that the `GitHubService` class is instantiated with the token we've added to our `config/services.php` file.

This now means that to get an instance of our `GitHubService` class, we can resolve the `GitHub` interface from the service container like so:

```
$gitHub = app(GitHub::class);

// $github is an instance of App\Services\GitHub\GitHubService
```

Preparing the Connector

We're nearly ready to start making requests to the GitHub API. However, before we do that, we need to create a connector class responsible for making the HTTP requests.

Creating the Connector Class

We'll use Saloon's Artisan command to create our connector. We'll run the following Artisan command in our terminal:

```
php artisan saloon:connector GitHub GitHubConnector
```

This command creates a new `GitHubConnector` class in the `app/Http/Integrations/GitHub` directory. The class may look something like this:

```php
namespace App\Http\Integrations\GitHub;

use Saloon\Http\Connector;
use Saloon\Traits\Plugins\AcceptsJson;

class GitHubConnector extends Connector
{
    use AcceptsJson;

    public function resolveBaseUrl(): string
    {
        return '';
    }

    protected function defaultHeaders(): array
    {
        return [];
    }

    protected function defaultConfig(): array
    {
        return [];
    }
}
```

The connector class contains several methods we can use to configure the connector. Earlier in this chapter, we looked at the `resolveBaseUrl` and `defaultHeaders` methods. But we haven't come across the `defaultConfig` method yet. This method can be used to add any default configuration to the connector that the HTTP client (in most cases, Guzzle) should use. For example, we can add a default timeout to the connector. However, for this book, we won't add any default configuration to the connector. So, to keep our class clean and focused, we can remove the `defaultConfig` method.

All the URLs of our requests to the GitHub API will begin with `https://api.github.com/`. Therefore, we can add this URL to the `resolveBaseUrl` method like so:

```
public function resolveBaseUrl(): string
{
    return 'https://api.github.com/';
}
```

GitHub recommends that every request to their API should include an `Accept` header with the value of `application/vnd.github+json`. We can update our `defaultHeaders` method to include this header like so:

```
public function defaultHeaders(): array
{
    return [
        'Accept' => 'application/vnd.github+json',
    ];
}
```

Adding the Connector to the Service Class

Now that we've created our connector class, we'll add it to our `GitHubService` class. I like to add a `connector` method to my service classes that returns an instance of the connector. This means that if we need to change the connector (such as calling a method on it to add a new header), we can do so in one place, and it will be applied to all the methods in the service class.

Let's add a new `connector` method to our `GitHubService` class like so:

```
namespace App\Services\GitHub;

use App\Http\Integrations\GitHub\GitHubConnector;
use App\Interfaces\GitHub;

final readonly class GitHubService implements GitHub
{
    public function __construct(
        private string $token,
    ) {}

    // ...

    private function connector(): GitHubConnector
    {
        return app(GitHubConnector::class)->withTokenAuth(
            token: $this->token,
        );
    }
}
```

As we can see in our code example, we're creating and returning an instance of the `GitHubConnector` class. We're also using the `withTokenAuth` method to add the token authentication to the connector, so every request we make with the connector will include the token in the `Authorization` header. In the next section, we'll go into more detail about the available authentication methods.

As a result, instead of repeating the `withTokenAuth` method in every method in our service class, we can simply call the `connector` method, and it will return an instance of the connector with the token authentication already applied.

Authentication

Most APIs require you to authenticate requests. Thankfully, Saloon provides handy helper methods to make this process simple.

Let's examine the authentication methods available and where you might use them in your integration's code.

Where to Use Authentication

Saloon provides the functionality to apply authentication to either the connector or the request itself.

Connector Authentication

For our GitHub code examples, we'll apply the authentication in the connector by using the `withTokenAuth` method on the `GitHubConnector` class. This includes the token in the `Authorization` header in every request we make with the connector.

In previous examples, we've called the `withTokenAuth` method on the connector class. However, you may want to call the method inside the connector class. For example, you can pass the token to the connector class in the constructor and then apply the authentication like so:

```php
namespace App\Http\Integrations\GitHub;

use Saloon\Http\Connector;

class GitHubConnector extends Connector
{
    public function __construct(string $token) {
        $this->withTokenAuth($token);
    }

    // ...
}
```

As a result of doing this, you could then instantiate the connector class like so:

```php
$connector = new GitHubConnector($token);
```

Default Connector Authentication

Depending on the integration you're building, you may want to apply the authentication to the connector by default, rather than passing in the token to the connector class.

This is ideal if you have a single token that you'll be using for all requests to the API. To do this, you can use the `defaultAuth` method on the connector. For example, to use this method in our `GitHubConnector` class, we can do so like this:

```php
namespace App\Http\Integrations\GitHub;

use Saloon\Contracts\Authenticator;
use Saloon\Http\Connector;
use Saloon\Http\Auth\TokenAuthenticator;

class GitHubConnector extends Connector
{
    // ...

    protected function defaultAuth(): ?Authenticator
    {
        return new TokenAuthenticator(config('services.github.token'));
    }
}
```

This approach means we don't need to call the `withTokenAuth` method on the connector class. Instead, the token authentication is applied to the connector by default.

Although this approach is handy for building small integrations, I prefer to pass the token to the connector class. This way, the connector can stay as flexible as possible. For example, say the initial version of our GitHub integration is built to use our application's API key. However, in the future, we may want to allow our users to provide their own API keys (whether manually or through OAuth). If we used the `defaultAuth` method, this may become difficult to implement, and we'll need to use a different approach (such as the `withTokenAuth` method). It's important to consider how you may want to use your integration in the future. If you never intend to use other API keys, then using the `defaultAuth` method may be the most suitable approach.

Request Authentication

Sometimes, you might want to avoid specifying the authentication on the connector. Instead, you could apply the authentication to the request when sending it. To apply the token authentication to a `GetRepo` request, we can do so like this:

```
$request = new GetRepo('ash-jc-allen', 'short-url');
$request->withTokenAuth($this->token);
```

This means the token authentication would only be applied to this request and not any other requests made with the connector.

Types of Authentication

As we've seen, Saloon provides the `withTokenAuth` method to apply token authentication to requests and connectors. However, you may need to use other types of authentication when consuming an API. Let's take a quick look at the different authentication types available.

Token Authentication

Saloon allows you to add an `Authorization` header to your requests using the `withTokenAuth` method like so:

```
$connector = new GitHubConnector();
$connector->withTokenAuth($token);
```

This adds an `Authorization` header prefixed with `Bearer` to your requests. For example, calling `withTokenAuth('api-key-here')` would apply an `Authorization: Bearer api-key-here` header to your requests.

Sometimes, you may need a different prefix for token authentication. For example, some APIs may require you to use `Idaas` instead of `Bearer`. You can pass the prefix as the second argument to the `withTokenAuth` method to do this. For example:

```
$connector = new GitHubConnector();
$connector->withTokenAuth($token, 'Idaas');
```

This will add an `Authorization: Idaas api-key-here` header to your requests.

Basic Authentication

Saloon allows you to use HTTP basic authentication with your requests. To apply this authentication, call the `withBasicAuth` method on the connector. For example:

```
$connector = new GitHubConnector();
$connector->withBasicAuth($username, $password);
```

Digest Authentication

Saloon also allows you to use HTTP digest authentication with your requests. To apply this authentication, you can call the `withDigestAuth` method on the connector. For example:

```php
$connector = new GitHubConnector();
$connector->withDigestAuth($username, $password);
```

Query Authentication

Saloon also provides a `withQueryAuth` method that allows you to add authentication to the query string of your requests. For example:

```php
$connector = new GitHubConnector();
$connector->withQueryAuth('api-key', $password);
```

For example, running this code would add `?api-key=password` to your request URL. However, remember that it's highly discouraged to pass sensitive data (such as API keys) in the query string of your requests.

Custom Authentication Classes

Sometimes, you may work with an API that doesn't use conventional authentication. For example, the API may require an `X-Api-Key` header rather than an `Authorization` header.

I've worked with APIs that use bespoke headers for authentication. For example, imagine the application is called `BookStore`. They may require you to pass an `X-BookStore-Key` header to authenticate your requests.

In these scenarios, you must create a custom authenticator class that applies this authentication to your requests. Let's see how to do this. Imagine we need to pass our API key in an `X-BookStore-Key` header.

We'll create the custom authenticator by running the following command:

```
php artisan saloon:auth BookStore BookStoreAuthenticator
```

This creates an `app/Http/Integrations/BookStore/Auth/BookStoreAuthenticator.php` file containing an empty constructor and `set` method. Let's update this class and then see what it looks like:

```php
namespace App\Http\Integrations\BookStore\Auth;

use Saloon\Contracts\Authenticator;
use Saloon\Http\PendingRequest;

class BookStoreAuthenticator implements Authenticator
{
    public function __construct(private string $token)
    {
        //
    }

    public function set(PendingRequest $pendingRequest): void
    {
        $pendingRequest->headers()->add('X-BookStore-Key', $this->token);
    }
}
```

As we can see in the code example, we've specified in the `set` method that an `X-BookStore-`

`Key` header should be added to the request. We can then use this authenticator like so:

```
$connector = new BookStoreConnector();
$connector->authenticate(new BookStoreAuthenticator($token));
```

The connector will now be ready to send requests to the API, and each request will contain the necessary authentication.

Although this particular example is quite simple, and you could achieve a similar result by using the `defaultHeaders` on a connector or request, it should highlight the steps you can take if needed. This approach is useful when working with APIs that use more complex authentication systems. For example, an API may require you to authenticate and generate a single-use token before each request you make to the API service. In this scenario, using a custom authenticator class would be ideal as it allows you to generate the token and add it to each request before it's sent.

Sending Requests

Now that we've built our boilerplate service class and created a connector that is authenticated and ready to send requests, we can start making requests to the API.

Fetching a Single Resource

Let's start by making the easiest type of request: fetching a single resource. In this case, we'll fetch a single repository from GitHub.

To make this request, we'll first need to create a new `GetRepo` request class. We can do this by running the following command:

```
php artisan saloon:request GitHub GetRepo
```

Running this command should create an empty `app/Http/Integrations/GitHub/Requests/GetRepo.php` file. Let's update this file and then take a look at what it would look like:

```php
namespace App\Http\Integrations\GitHub\Requests;

use Saloon\Enums\Method;
use Saloon\Http\Request;
use Saloon\Http\Response;

final class GetRepo extends Request
{
    protected Method $method = Method::GET;

    public function __construct(
        private readonly string $owner,
        private readonly string $repo
    ) {}

    /**
     * Define the endpoint for the request
     *
     * @return string
     */
    public function resolveEndpoint(): string
    {
        return '/repos/'.$this->owner.'/'.$this->repo;
    }
}
```

There are three parts of this class that we should take notice of:

- The `$method` property is set to `Method::GET`. This tells Saloon that this request should be

sent using the `GET` HTTP method.
- The constructor accepts two arguments: `$owner` and `$repo`. These are the arguments we'll pass when we instantiate the request.
- The `resolveEndpoint` method defines the relative URL for the request. In this case, we're using the `$owner` and `$repo` arguments to build the endpoint.

We can send our request using our `GitHubConnector` class like so:

```
$connector = new GitHubConnector();
$response = $connector->send(new GetRepo('laravel', 'laravel'));
```

Saloon provides many methods we can call on the response to get the information from it. Here are common methods you're most likely to use, along with what they return:

- `body` - response body as a string
- `json` - JSON response body as an array
- `collect` - JSON response body as a Collection
- `dto` - JSON response body as a DTO
- `dtoOrFail` - JSON response body as a DTO or throws an exception if the request was unsuccessful
- `stream` - response body as a stream
- `headers` - all the headers from the response
- `header` - a specific header from the response
- `status` - HTTP status code from the response

In this list, there are many ways to access the response body, as Saloon doesn't make assumptions about how you want to consume the response. Instead, it provides you with different methods so you can choose the method that best suits your needs.

For this book, we'll use the `dtoOrFail` method. This powerful method allows us to map the response body to a DTO. In our case, we'll want the request to return an instance of the `Repo`

DTO we created earlier.

To do this, we define a `createDtoFromResponse` method on the `GetRepo` class. We can add the method to the request class like so:

```
namespace App\Http\Integrations\GitHub\Requests;

use App\DataTransferObjects\GitHub\Repo;
use Carbon\Carbon;
use Saloon\Http\Response;

final class GetRepo extends Request
{
    // ...

    public function createDtoFromResponse(Response $response): mixed
    {
        $responseData = $response->json();

        return new Repo(
            id: $responseData['id'],
            owner: $responseData['owner']['login'],
            name: $responseData['name'],
            fullName: $responseData['full_name'],
            private: $responseData['private'],
            description: $responseData['description'] ?? '',
            createdAt: Carbon::parse($responseData['created_at']),
        );
    }
}
```

In the code example, we're using the `json` method on the response to get the response body as an array. We're then using this array to create a new instance of the `Repo` DTO.

You may find that many of the API responses contain the same structure. In our case, the repository structure is the same in the responses for fetching a single repository, fetching a list of repositories, creating a repository, and updating a repository. Consider adding a `fromResponse` method to the DTO in this scenario. This method would create a new instance of the DTO from the response body, allowing you to reuse the logic across multiple requests. For example, you could update your `createDtoFromResponse` method to look like this:

```
public function createDtoFromResponse(Response $response): mixed
{
    return Repo::fromResponse($response->json());
}
```

The `fromResponse` method would then look like this:

```
public static function fromResponse(array $response): static
{
    return new static(
        id: $response['id'],
        owner: $response['owner']['login'],
        name: $response['name'],
        fullName: $response['full_name'],
        private: $response['private'],
        description: $response['description'] ?? '',
        createdAt: Carbon::parse($response['created_at']),
    );
}
```

This can be useful for cleaning up your request classes and DTOs. However, it's important to note that this approach can lead to coupling between your DTOs and the API responses. Adding logic to your DTOs can become messy and defeat the purpose of a DTO. As with most things, finding a balance that works for you and your team is important. A general rule I follow with DTOs is "If I have to write tests for the logic, then that logic should be moved out of the DTO." I like to keep them as simple as possible. If different requests have a slightly different structure, keeping the logic in the request class also makes sense. This avoids needing a `fromResponse` method on the DTO that handles different structures or many methods such as `fromCreateResponse`, `fromUpdateResponse`, etc.

No matter which approach you take to adding the `createDtoFromResponse` method to your request class, we can now use the `dtoOrFail` method to get an instance of the `Repo` DTO. We can do this like so:

```
$connector = new GitHubConnector();
$repo = $connector->send(new GetRepo('laravel', 'laravel'))->dtoOrFail();

// $repo is an instance of App\DataTransferObjects\GitHub\Repo
```

We can now bring all this together and update the `getRepo` method on the `GitHubService` class like so:

```php
namespace App\Services\GitHub;

use App\DataTransferObjects\GitHub\Repo;
use App\Http\Integrations\GitHub\Requests\GetRepo;
use App\Interfaces\GitHub;

final readonly class GitHubService implements GitHub
{
    // ...

    public function getRepo(string $owner, string $repoName): Repo
    {
        return $this->connector()
            ->send(new GetRepo($owner, $repoName))
            ->dtoOrFail();
    }

    // ...
}
```

We can now use the `getRepo` method to fetch the data for a given repository. For example, to fetch the data for the `laravel/framework` repository, we can do the following:

```php
use App\Interfaces\GitHub;

$repo = app(GitHub::class)->getRepo('laravel', 'framework');
```

The `$repo` variable will now contain an instance of the `Repo` DTO with details all about the `laravel/framework` repository.

Let's look at an example controller to give more context about how this may fit inside a Laravel application. Imagine the controller is responsible for fetching details of a given repository and displaying them in a view. The controller may look like this:

```php
namespace App\Http\Controllers;

use App\Interfaces\GitHub;
use Illuminate\Contracts\View\View;

final class GitHubController extends Controller
{
    public function show(string $owner, string $name, GitHub $gitHub): View {
        $repo = $gitHub->getRepo(
            owner: $owner,
            repoName: $name,
        );

        return view('repos.show')->with([
            'repo' => $repo,
        ]);
    }
}
```

In the code example, we're using dependency injection to instantiate the `GitHub` interface and then using the `getRepo` method to fetch the details of the repository. We then pass the `Repo` DTO to the view to display it to the user.

Fetching a List of Resources

Now that we've seen how to fetch a single resource, let's see how we can make a request that returns a list of resources.

In this case, we want to fetch a list of languages (e.g., PHP, JavaScript, etc.) used in a given repository. We'll use this example as it's a simple request that does not use pagination. This allows us to focus on the basics of making a request that returns a list of resources. We'll look at making requests that use pagination in the next chapter.

We'll create a `GetRepoLanguages` request class by running the following command:

```
php artisan saloon:request GitHub GetRepoLanguages
```

Running this command will create a new request class at `app/Http/Integrations/GitHub/Requests/GetRepoLanguages.php`. Let's make some changes to the class so that it looks like the following:

```php
namespace App\Http\Integrations\GitHub\Requests;

use Saloon\Enums\Method;
use Saloon\Http\Request;

final class GetRepoLanguages extends Request
{
    protected Method $method = Method::GET;

    public function __construct(
        private readonly string $owner,
        private readonly string $repo,
    ) {}

    public function resolveEndpoint(): string
    {
        return '/repos/'.$this->owner.'/'.$this->repo.'/languages';
    }
}
```

We've updated the request class by adding two properties: `$owner` and `$repo`. We've also updated the `resolveEndpoint` method to return the correct endpoint for the request.

If we were to run this request, we'd get a response similar to this:

```json
{
  "PHP": 50,
  "JavaScript": 50,
  "CSS": 25
}
```

We can use the `GetRepoLanguages` request class in our `GitHubService` to fetch the languages for a given repository. We can do this like so:

```php
use App\Http\Integrations\GitHub\GitHubConnector;
use App\Http\Integrations\GitHub\Requests\GetRepoLanguages;
use App\Interfaces\GitHub;

final readonly class GitHubService implements GitHub
{
    // ...

    public function getRepoLanguages(string $owner, string $repoName): array
    {
        return $this->connector()
            ->send(new GetRepoLanguages($owner, $repoName))
            ->collect()
            ->keys()
            ->all();
    }
}
```

In the code example, we send the request to the GitHub API and then use the `collect` method on the response. This converts the response body into an `Illuminate\Support\Collection` instance. We then use the `keys` method on the collection to get the keys of the collection (in this case, `PHP`, `JavaScript`, and `CSS`). Finally, we use the `all` method to convert the collection into a standard PHP array and return it.

This is a simple example of how to use Saloon to fetch a list of resources from an API. In this example, I've opted against using a DTO to represent the result of the API request since the response body is just an array of strings and doesn't justify creating a DTO. However, if you wanted to, you could create a DTO to represent the response body and then use the `dto` method on the response to convert the response body into an instance of the DTO.

We can run the following code to fetch the languages for the `laravel/framework` repository:

```
use App\Interfaces\GitHub;

$languages = app(GitHub::class)->getRepoLanguages('laravel', 'framework');

// $languages would be an array of strings
```

Creating a New Resource

So far, we've looked at making simple `GET` requests. Let's now look at how to make `POST` requests containing a request body. We'll create a request that allows us to create a new repository on GitHub.

Let's create a new `CreateRepo` request class by running the following command:

```
php artisan saloon:request GitHub CreateRepo
```

Running this command will create a new request class at `app/Http/Integrations/GitHub/Requests/CreateRepo.php`. Let's make some changes to the class so that it looks like the following:

```
namespace App\Http\Integrations\GitHub\Requests;

use App\DataTransferObjects\GitHub\NewRepoData;
use App\DataTransferObjects\GitHub\Repo;
use Saloon\Contracts\Body\HasBody;
use Saloon\Enums\Method;
use Saloon\Http\Request;
use Saloon\Http\Response;
use Saloon\Traits\Body\HasJsonBody;

final class CreateRepo extends Request implements HasBody
{
    use HasJsonBody;

    protected Method $method = Method::POST;

    public function __construct(
        private readonly NewRepoData $newRepoData,
    ) {}

    public function resolveEndpoint(): string
    {
        return '/user/repos';
    }

    protected function defaultBody(): array
```

```php
    {
        return [
            'name' => $this->newRepoData->name,
            'description' => $this->newRepoData->description,
            'private' => $this->newRepoData->isPrivate,
        ];
    }

    public function createDtoFromResponse(Response $response): mixed
    {
        return Repo::fromResponse($response->json());
    }
}
```

As we can see, this request class has more going on than the previous request classes we've created. But it should still be simple to understand. Let's dig into what we've done.

The request class implements the `Saloon\Contracts\Body\HasBody` interface. Without this interface, Saloon won't send a request body with the request, so it's important that we add this.

The request class is also using the `Saloon\Traits\Body\HasJsonBody` trait. This trait automatically adds the `Content-Type: application/json` header to the request and converts the request body to JSON. It also defines a new `body` method on the request class that we can use to set the request body on the fly. For example, we could do the following to add a new key to the request body:

```php
$request = new CreateRepo($newRepoData);
$request->body()->add('name', 'my-repo-name-here');
```

Or we could add multiple keys to the body like so:

```
$request = new CreateRepo($newRepoData);
$request->body()->merge([
    'name' => 'my-repo-name-here',
    'description' => 'my-repo-description-here',
]);
```

In fact, there are multiple methods available via the `body` method:

- `add(string $key, mixed $value)` - Add items to the JSON body
- `remove(string $key)` - Remove items from the JSON body
- `merge(...$items)` - Merge items into the JSON body
- `set(array $items)` - Overwrite the JSON body
- `all(): array` - Get all items from the JSON body
- `isEmpty(): bool` - Check if the JSON body is empty
- `isNotEmpty(): bool` - Check if the JSON body is not empty

Although these methods are handy, we won't use them in our example. Instead, we'll use the `defaultBody` method to define the request body. As we can see in the example, we've defined that an instance of `App\DataTransferObjects\GitHub\NewRepoData` should be passed to the request class. This DTO contains all the information we need to create a new repository in GitHub. So we can map the DTO fields to the request body fields in the `defaultBody` method.

We've also defined a `createDtoFromResponse` method to get a `Repo` DTO from the response body. To keep the example focused, we used a `fromResponse` method on the `Repo` DTO to create an instance of the DTO. However, as mentioned, you can also manually build the DTO directly in the response class.

This means we can then send the request from our `GitHubService` like so:

```php
namespace App\Services\GitHub;

use App\DataTransferObjects\GitHub\NewRepoData;
use App\DataTransferObjects\GitHub\Repo;
use App\Http\Integrations\GitHub\Requests\CreateRepo;
use App\Interfaces\GitHub;

final readonly class GitHubService implements GitHub
{
    // ...

    public function createRepo(NewRepoData $repoData): Repo
    {
        return $this->connector()
            ->send(new CreateRepo($repoData))
            ->dtoOrFail();
    }
}
```

In the example, we can see that we're sending the request through the connector and then converting the response to a Repo DTO that we return. Let's look at how we might call this method:

```php
use App\DataTransferObjects\GitHub\NewRepoData;
use App\Interfaces\GitHub;

$repo = app(GitHub::class)->createRepo(
    new RepoData(
        name: 'my-repo-name-here',
        description: 'My repo description here',
        isPrivate: true,
    )
)

// $repo is an instance of App\DataTransferObjects\GitHub\Repo
```

Updating an Existing Resource

Another common request is to update an existing resource. Let's see how we can update an existing repository in GitHub.

This example will be very similar to creating a new repository. The only differences are that we'll use the `PATCH` method rather than `POST` and an `UpdateRepoData` DTO rather than a `NewRepoData` DTO.

Let's create our `UpdateRepo` request class with the following command:

```
php artisan saloon:request GitHub UpdateRepo
```

This creates an `UpdateRepo` request class in the

`app/Http/Integrations/GitHub/Requests` directory. Let's make some updates to the request class and then look at what we've done:

```
namespace App\Http\Integrations\GitHub\Requests;

use App\DataTransferObjects\GitHub\Repo;
use App\DataTransferObjects\GitHub\UpdateRepoData;
use Saloon\Contracts\Body\HasBody;
use Saloon\Enums\Method;
use Saloon\Http\Request;
use Saloon\Traits\Body\HasJsonBody;

final class UpdateRepo extends Request implements HasBody
{
    use HasJsonBody;

    protected Method $method = Method::PATCH;

    public function __construct(
        private readonly string $owner,
        private readonly string $repoName,
        private readonly UpdateRepoData $updateRepoData,
    ) {}

    public function resolveEndpoint(): string
    {
        return '/repos/'.$this->owner.'/'.$this->repoName;
    }

    protected function defaultBody(): array
```

```
    {
        return [
            'name' => $this->updateRepoData->name,
            'description' => $this->updateRepoData->description,
            'private' => $this->updateRepoData->isPrivate,
        ];
    }

    public function createDtoFromResponse(Response $response): mixed
    {
        return Repo::fromResponse($response->json());
    }
}
```

As we can see, the request class is very similar to the `CreateRepo` request class. The main differences are:

- The endpoint for creating a new repository was `/user/repos`, whereas the endpoint for updating an existing repository is `/repos/{owner}/{repo}`.
- The method for creating a new repository was `POST`, whereas the method for updating an existing repository is `PATCH`.
- We have passed multiple arguments to the constructor. We've passed the owner of the repository, the name of the repository, and an instance of `UpdateRepoData`. This is because we need to know which repository we're updating and what data we're updating it with.

This request can then be sent like so:

```php
namespace App\Services\GitHub;

use App\DataTransferObjects\GitHub\Repo;
use App\DataTransferObjects\GitHub\UpdateRepoData;
use App\Http\Integrations\GitHub\Requests\UpdateRepo;
use App\Interfaces\GitHub;

final readonly class GitHubService implements GitHub
{
    // ...

    public function updateRepo(
        string $owner,
        string $repoName,
        UpdateRepoData $repoData
    ): Repo {
        return $this->connector()
            ->send(new UpdateRepo($owner, $repoName, $repoData))
            ->dtoOrFail();
    }
}
```

We can then call this method like so:

```php
use App\DataTransferObjects\GitHub\UpdateRepoData;
use App\Interfaces\GitHub;

$repo = app(GitHub::class)->updateRepo(
    owner: 'owner-name-here',
    repoName: 'repo-name-here',
    repoData: new UpdateRepoData(
        name: 'my-new-repo-name-here',
        description: 'My new repo description here',
        isPrivate: false,
    )
)

// $repo is an instance of App\DataTransferObjects\GitHub\Repo
```

As you can see, by using techniques such as DTOs, the service container, interfaces, and named arguments, we can write code that is very easy to read and understand. The code's intentions are clear, and it's easy to see what will be returned from the method.

Deleting a Resource

Another common request to make is to delete a resource. Let's look at how we can delete an existing repository in GitHub.

Generally, when we delete a resource, the request doesn't contain a request body, and the response doesn't always contain a response body. If it does, it's likely just a confirmation message or boolean field to indicate whether the resource was deleted. Therefore, these types of requests are usually straightforward to make.

Let's create our `DeleteRepo` request class by running the following command:

```
php artisan saloon:request GitHub DeleteRepo
```

This creates a new `DeleteRepo` request class in the `app/Http/Integrations/GitHub/Requests` directory. Let's update the request class and then look at what we've done:

```
namespace App\Http\Integrations\GitHub\Requests;

use Saloon\Enums\Method;
use Saloon\Http\Request;

final class DeleteRepo extends Request
{
    protected Method $method = Method::DELETE;

    public function __construct(
        private readonly string $owner,
        private readonly string $repo
    ) {}

    public function resolveEndpoint(): string
    {
        return '/repos/'.$this->owner.'/'.$this->repo;
    }
}
```

As we can see, the request class is very simple. We've specified that the `DELETE` HTTP method should be used, and we passed the repository's owner and name to the constructor. We then resolved the endpoint using the owner and repository name.

This request can then be sent like so from our `GitHubService`:

```
namespace App\Services\GitHub;

use App\Http\Integrations\GitHub\Requests\DeleteRepo;
use App\Interfaces\GitHub;

final readonly class GitHubService implements GitHub
{
    // ...

    public function deleteRepo(string $owner, string $repoName): void
    {
        $this->connector()
            ->send(new DeleteRepo($owner, $repoName));
    }
}
```

As we can see in the example, we aren't returning anything from the method. We assume that the repository will be deleted if the request is successful. Otherwise, if the request fails, an exception will be thrown. (We'll go into more depth about errors and exceptions later in this chapter.) Either way, we don't need to return anything from the method.

We can then call this method like so:

```php
use App\Interfaces\GitHub;

app(GitHub::class)->deleteRepo(
    owner: 'owner-name-here',
    repoName: 'repo-name-here',
);
```

Pagination

Pagination is a common feature of many APIs and something you may have even implemented yourself in your own APIs or applications. You'll likely encounter paginated data when working with API endpoints that can contain a large amount of data. For example, GitHub's API endpoint for getting a list of repositories belonging to a user uses pagination. A user may have hundreds or even thousands of repositories, so returning all their repositories in a single response is not feasible. Instead, the API will return a subset of the repositories and provide pagination data in the response, allowing you to get the next page of results.

Interacting with paginated API endpoints can be tricky and may require additional logic to handle the pagination data. However, Saloon makes it very easy to interact with paginated API endpoints.

By default, Saloon supports three types of pagination:

- Paged pagination (e.g., `?page=1&per_page=10`)
- Limit/offset pagination (e.g., `?limit=10&offset=0`)
- Cursor-based pagination (e.g., `?cursor=abc123`)

Understanding Paginated Responses

The concepts for working with each pagination type are similar, with a few minor differences. To demonstrate how pagination works in Saloon, we'll look at how to interact with a paginated API endpoint that uses paged pagination.

Before we start, let's look at an example JSON response we may receive that contains paginated data:

```json
{
  "total": 50,
  "per_page": 15,
  "current_page": 1,
  "last_page": 4,
  "first_page_url": "https://example.com/users?page=1",
  "last_page_url": "https://example.com/users?page=4",
  "next_page_url": "https://example.com/users?page=2",
  "prev_page_url": null,
  "path": "https://laravel.app/users",
  "from": 1,
  "to": 15,
  "data": [
    {
      "id": 1,
      "name": "Record 1"
    },
    {
      "id": 2,
      "name": "Record 2"
    }
  ]
}
```

You might have noticed this is the same format Laravel uses for its pagination data. Let's break down what each of these fields are for:

- `total` - The total number of available records.
- `per_page` - The number of records returned per page.
- `current_page` - The current page of results being returned. For example, this would be `2`

on the next page.

- `last_page` - The last page of results available. For example, if there are four pages of results, this would be `4`.
- `first_page_url` - The URL for the first page of results.
- `last_page_url` - The URL for the last page of results.
- `next_page_url` - The URL for the next page of results.
- `prev_page_url` - The URL for the previous page of results. In this case, this is `null` because we're on the first page. If we were on the second page, this would be `https://example.com/users?page=1`.
- `path` - The base URL for the endpoint without any query parameters.
- `from` - The index of the first record in the current page of results. For example, if we're on the first page, this would be `1`. If we're on the second page, this would be `16`.
- `to` - The index of the last record in the current page of results. For example, if we're on the first page, this would be `15`. If we're on the second page, this would be `30`.
- `data` - The actual data we want to retrieve.

In this example, we have been provided a lot of data about the paginated results. This can make it very easy to parse the response and use the information about the pages in your code. However, there may be times when the API doesn't provide this information in the response. For example, you may have a response that looks like this:

```json
{
  "first_page_url": "https://example.com/users?page=1",
  "last_page_url": "https://example.com/users?page=4",
  "next_page_url": "https://example.com/users?page=2",
  "prev_page_url": null,
  "data": [
    {
      "id": 1,
      "name": "Record 1"
    },
    {
      "id": 2,
      "name": "Record 2"
    }
  ]
}
```

In this example, we're only provided information about the URLs for the first, last, next, and previous pages. We're not provided with the current page, the total number of pages, or the total number of records. This means we need to do additional work to calculate this information ourselves if we need any of it.

You may also find the pagination information nested inside a field, such as `meta`, `pages`, or `pagination`, like so:

```json
{
  "meta": {
    "first_page_url": "https://example.com/users?page=1",
    "last_page_url": "https://example.com/users?page=4",
    "next_page_url": "https://example.com/users?page=2",
    "prev_page_url": null
  },
  "data": [
    {
      "id": 1,
      "name": "Record 1"
    },
    {
      "id": 2,
      "name": "Record 2"
    }
  ]
}
```

There may also be times when the pagination data is provided via a `Link` header in an API response. GitHub uses this approach for its API when returning paginated data. The `Link` header in the response may look something like this:

```
Link: <https://api.github.com/user/repos?per_page=10&page=1>; rel="prev",
      <https://api.github.com/user/repos?per_page=10&page=3>; rel="next",
      <https://api.github.com/user/repos?per_page=10&page=10>; rel="last",
      <https://api.github.com/user/repos?per_page=10&page=1>; rel="first",
```

For readability, I've split this into multiple lines. But, in practice, the contents of this header would all be on a single line.

In the `Link` header returned from the `https://api.github.com/user/repos` endpoint, we can see that four links are returned, each separated by a `,`. Each link has a `rel` attribute that describes what the link is for. In this case, we have links for the previous page, the next page, the last page, and the first page.

Sending Requests to Paginated Endpoints in Saloon

With a better understanding of how page-based paginated responses work and what type of information can be available, let's look at how to send paginated requests in Saloon.

To illustrate paginated requests, we'll use the GitHub API again. Specifically, we'll query the `https://api.github.com/users/user/repos` endpoint to fetch a user's repository list, which comes back as a paginated response.

Installing the Pagination Plugin

We'll first need to install the pagination plugin for Saloon to get started. We can do this by running the following Composer command:

```
composer require saloonphp/pagination-plugin
```

This command should install the plugin so we can use it in our application.

Configuring the Connector

We can then update our connector class to implement the `Saloon\PaginationPlugin\Contracts\HasPagination` interface. This interface requires that our connector class implement a `paginate` method. We can update our `App\Http\Integrations\GitHub\GitHubConnector` class to look like so:

```
namespace App\Http\Integrations\GitHub;

use Saloon\Http\Connector;
use Saloon\Http\Request;
use Saloon\PaginationPlugin\Contracts\HasPagination;
use Saloon\PaginationPlugin\Paginator;

final class GitHubConnector extends Connector implements HasPagination
{
    // ...

    public function paginate(Request $request): Paginator
    {
        // ...
    }
}
```

As we can see in the code example, we've added a `paginate` method to our connector and implemented the `Saloon\PaginationPlugin\Contracts\HasPagination` interface. This means that once we've specified in the `paginate` method how we should handle paginated responses, we'll be able to call it using `(new GitHubConnector())->paginate($request)`.

Let's implement the `paginate` method now and then explain what's happening in the code:

```php
use GuzzleHttp\Psr7\Header;
use Saloon\Http\Connector;
use Saloon\Http\Request;
use Saloon\Http\Response;
use Saloon\PaginationPlugin\Contracts\HasPagination;
use Saloon\PaginationPlugin\PagedPaginator;

final class GitHubConnector extends Connector implements HasPagination
{
    // ...

    public function paginate(Request $request): PagedPaginator
    {
        return new class(
            connector: $this, request: $request
        ) extends PagedPaginator {
            protected function isLastPage(Response $response): bool
            {
                $linkHeader = Header::parse($response->header('Link'));

                return collect($linkHeader)
                    ->where(fn(array $link): bool => $link['rel'] === 'next')
                    ->isEmpty();
            }

            protected function getPageItems(
                Response $response,
                Request $request
```

```
            ): array {
                return $response->dtoOrFail()->toArray();
            }
        }
    }
}
```

In the code example, we're returning an anonymous class that extends the `Saloon\PaginationPlugin\PagedPaginator` class. The pagination plugin provides this class, which offers useful methods for handling paginated responses. It requires that our anonymous class implements two methods: `isLastPage` and `getPageItems`.

The `isLastPage` method contains the logic that we can use to determine whether the response we've received is the last page. If it's the last page, we should return `true`, and no more requests will be made for more pages. Otherwise, we should return `false`. Since the GitHub API returns the pagination information in the `Link` header, we need to use a `GuzzleHttp\Psr7\Header::parse()` method. This will parse the header for us and return an array like so:

```
[
    [
        0 => "<https://api.github.com/user/repos?per_page=30&page=2>",
        "rel" => "next"
    ],
    [
        0 => "<https://api.github.com/user/repos?per_page=30&page=4>",
        "rel" => "last"
    ],
]
```

We then use the `collect` helper to convert this array into a Laravel collection and check whether a URL exists in the array with a `rel` of `next`. If it does, we know there is another page of results, and we should return `false`. If no `next` link exists, we know we're on the last page and should return `true`.

If the API endpoint returned the pagination information in the response body, we wouldn't need to parse these headers. For example, let's assume the response returned a `next_page_url` nested inside a `meta` field in the body. In this case, the `isLastPage` method would look like so:

```
protected function isLastPage(Response $response): bool
{
    return empty($response->json('meta.next_page_url'));
}
```

In our paginator, we've also implemented the `getPageItems` method. This method tells the paginator how to get the items from the response. In our case, we're calling the `dtoOrFail` method on the response, which will return a `Collection` of `Repo` DTOs representing the response. We'll be defining the logic to create this `Collection` later when we create our request class. We then call the `toArray` method on the DTO to get the items from the response.

You may have also noticed that we've updated the `paginate` method on our connector class to return an instance of `Saloon\PaginationPlugin\PagedPaginator` instead of `Saloon\PaginationPlugin\Paginator`. This isn't something you have to do, but I like adding the type hint so it's clear that we're returning a paginator designed to handle page-based pagination.

Sometimes, you want to explicitly define the number of items that should be returned per page rather than using the API's default page size. For example, the GitHub API returns 30 items per page by default. But you may want to return 100 items per page. To do this, you can set a `perPageLimit` property on your paginator class like so:

```php
namespace App\Http\Integrations\GitHub;

use Saloon\Http\Connector;
use Saloon\Http\Request;
use Saloon\PaginationPlugin\Contracts\HasPagination;
use Saloon\PaginationPlugin\PagedPaginator;

final class GitHubConnector extends Connector implements HasPagination
{
    // ...

    public function paginate(Request $request): PagedPaginator
    {
        return new class(
            connector: $this, request: $request
        ) extends PagedPaginator {
            protected ?int $perPageLimit = 100;

            // ...
        }
    }
}
```

This means all paginated requests sent through this connector will attempt to return 100 items per page. However, Saloon provides the ability for you to override this on the fly if needed. For example, imagine you want to return 50 items per page for the `GetAuthUserRepos` request. You could override the page size by calling the `setPerPageLimit` method on the paginator like so:

```
use App\Http\Integrations\GitHub\GitHubConnector;
use App\Http\Integrations\GitHub\Requests\GetAuthUserRepos;

$connector = new GitHubConnector();

$paginator = $connector->paginate(new GetAuthUserRepos());

$paginator->setPerPageLimit(50);

$results = $paginator->collect();
```

In the code example, we're calling `setPerPageLimit` on the paginator and specifying that we only want 50 items per page. We can then call the `collect` method on the paginator to get all the items from all the pages of results.

By default, Saloon will pass `page` and `per_page` parameters to determine which page of results should be fetched. But the API you're consuming might not support these query parameters, so you may want to override them. To do this, override the `applyPagination` method on the `Saloon\PaginationPlugin\PagedPaginator` instance you're returning from the `paginate` method. You might want to do this on a connector level (for all your requests) or a request level (for a specific request). For example, assume we want to use a `current_page` query parameter instead of `page` and `page_size` rather than `per_page`. We could define these fields in the `applyPagination` method like so:

```
namespace App\Http\Integrations\GitHub;

use Saloon\Http\Connector;
use Saloon\Http\Request;
use Saloon\PaginationPlugin\Contracts\HasPagination;
```

```php
use Saloon\PaginationPlugin\PagedPaginator;

final class GitHubConnector extends Connector implements HasPagination
{
    // ...

    public function paginate(Request $request): PagedPaginator
    {
        return new class(
            connector: $this, request: $request
        ) extends PagedPaginator {
            // ...

            protected function applyPagination(Request $request): Request
            {
                $request->query()->add('current_page', $this->page);

                if (isset($this->perPageLimit)) {
                    $request->query()->add('page_size', $this->perPage);
                }

                return $request;
            }
        }
    }
}
```

In this example, we add the `current_page` query parameter as expected in the `applyPagination` method. We then check whether a `perPageLimit` property exists on the paginator class (which we assume we have added). If it exists, this will then add the `page_size` query parameter to the request. If it doesn't exist, the `page_size` query parameter won't be added to the request.

Sending the Requests to the API

Now that we have configured our connector class, we can send requests to the API.

Let's start by creating a new `GetAuthUserRepos` request class that can be used to get all the authenticated user's repositories. We'll do this by running the following Artisan command:

```
php artisan saloon:request GitHub GetAuthUserRepos
```

After we've configured the endpoint, the request class may look something like so:

```php
namespace App\Http\Integrations\GitHub\Requests;

use App\DataTransferObjects\GitHub\Repo;
use Illuminate\Support\Collection;
use Saloon\Enums\Method;
use Saloon\Http\Request;
use Saloon\Http\Response;
use Saloon\PaginationPlugin\Contracts\Paginatable;

final class GetAuthUserRepos extends Request implements Paginatable
{
    protected Method $method = Method::GET;

    public function resolveEndpoint(): string
    {
        return '/user/repos';
    }

    /**
     * @param Response $response
     * @return Collection<Repo>
     */
    public function createDtoFromResponse(Response $response): mixed
    {
        return $response->collect()
            ->map(fn (array $repo): Repo => Repo::fromResponse($repo));
    }
}
```

In the code example, we're also defining a `createDtoFromResponse` method so we can call `dtoOrFail` on the response. This method makes a Collection of `App\DataTransferObjects\GitHub\Repo` objects from the response and then returns it. This is the method that will be called by the paginator's `getPageItems` method when we're iterating through the pages of results.

It's also important to note that we've implemented the `Saloon\PaginationPlugin\Contracts\Paginatable` interface. This interface doesn't require us to add any methods to our class. Instead, it's used internally by Saloon and is required for any requests that should be paginated.

Let's now take a look at how we can use the request in the `getRepos` method of our `App\Services\GitHub\GitHubService` class:

```php
namespace App\Services\GitHub;

use App\Collections\GitHub\RepoCollection;
use App\DataTransferObjects\GitHub\Repo;
use App\Http\Integrations\GitHub\GitHubConnector;
use App\Http\Integrations\GitHub\Requests\GetAuthUserRepos;
use App\Interfaces\GitHub;
use Illuminate\Support\Collection;
use Saloon\Http\Response;

final class GitHubService implements GitHub
{
    // ...

    public function getRepos(): RepoCollection
    {
        $repos = $this->connector()
            ->paginate(new GetAuthUserRepos())
            ->collect()
            ->ensure(Repo::class);

        return RepoCollection::make($repos);
    }

    // ...
}
```

In our code example, we first call the `paginate` method on our connector class and pass an instance of our `GetAuthUserRepos` request class. We then call the `collect()` method, which will return an `Illuminate\Support\LazyCollection` containing the `Repo` DTOs representing each of the repositories in the response. Note that the `paginate` method returns an iterator, so we can also use a `foreach` loop to iterate over the pages. For instance, you may want to use something like:

```
foreach ($this->connector()->paginate(new GetAuthUserRepos()) as $page) {
    // ...
}
```

However, for this example, we'll stick to using the `collect` method to make the most of Laravel's Collection methods.

Finally, we call the `ensure` method to ensure all the items in the collection are instances of `App\DataTransferObjects\GitHub\Repo`.

Once we're sure we only have `App\DataTransferObjects\GitHub\Repo` objects, we create a new `App\Collections\GitHub\RepoCollection` containing them and return it.

This means that we can now use the `getRepos` method in our controller like so:

```php
namespace App\Http\Controllers;

use App\Interfaces\GitHub;
use Illuminate\Contracts\View\View;

final class GitHubController extends Controller
{
    public function index(GitHub $gitHub): View
    {
        return view('repos.index')->with([
            'repos' => $gitHub->getRepos(),
        ]);
    }

    // ...
}
```

In the code example, we inject the `App\Interfaces\GitHub` interface into the controller's `index` method, giving us an instance of our `App\Services\GitHub\GitHubService` class. We then call the `getRepos` method on the service so we can pass the `App\Collections\GitHub\RepoCollection` to the view.

Solo Requests in Saloon

Sometimes, you only need to send a single type of request to an API. In this case, you may not need a full integration that uses connectors.

Saloon provides a handy feature called "solo requests" that allows you to do this. You can send a single request without needing a separate connector class.

To demonstrate how solo requests work, let's look at how we can convert our `GetRepo` request into a solo request.

We'll start by updating our `GetRepo` class so it extends the `Saloon\Http\SoloRequest` class like so:

```
namespace App\Http\Integrations\GitHub\Requests;

use Saloon\Enums\Method;
use Saloon\Http\SoloRequest;

final class GetRepo extends SoloRequest
{
    protected Method $method = Method::GET;

    public function __construct(
        private readonly string $owner,
        private readonly string $repo
    ) {}

    public function resolveEndpoint(): string
    {
```

```
        return 'https://api.github.com/repos/'.$this->owner.'/'.$this->repo;
    }

    public function defaultHeaders(): array
    {
        return [
            'Accept' => 'application/vnd.github+json',
        ];
    }

    // ...
}
```

As we can see in the code example, the request looks very similar to a typical Saloon request class. The main difference is that we define the full, absolute endpoint URL in the `resolveEndpoint` method rather than just a relative path. We also define the default headers in the `defaultHeaders` method.

This is all that's needed for us to be able to send this request.

By extending the `Saloon\Http\SoloRequest` class, we can now send this request using the `send` method available on the request class. Let's take a look at how we can send this request:

```php
namespace App\Services\GitHub;

use App\DataTransferObjects\GitHub\Repo;
use App\Http\Integrations\GitHub\Requests\GetRepo;
use App\Interfaces\GitHub;

final readonly class GitHubService implements GitHub
{
    // ...

    public function getRepo(string $owner, string $repoName): Repo
    {
        return (new GetRepo($owner, $repoName))
            ->send()
            ->dtoOrFail();
    }
}
```

We see it can be sent very similarly to how we send requests using a connector. The only difference is that we don't need to pass the request to a connector's `send` method. Instead, we can just call the `send` method directly on the request class.

Although solo requests are a handy tool, I recommend taking a moment to think about the future of your integration. For example, solo requests are a great option if you only intend to make a single request to the API. However, if you ever intend to make multiple requests to the API, I'd recommend building a connector instead. This allows you to build a more robust integration that can be extended in the future. Otherwise, you may end up writing duplicated logic across many solo requests and will need to refactor your code in the future.

Sending Concurrent Requests

When consuming an API, you may need to make multiple requests at once. For example, you might want to make five requests to GitHub, each for a different Git repository. Depending on the feature you're building, sending the requests sequentially (using approaches we've looked at so far) may be fine. However, if you're looking to make a large number of requests or if you're looking to make several requests that are independent of each other, there may be better approaches than sending sequential requests.

In this case, you might want to use Saloon's concurrency and pooling features.

Saloon's concurrency feature uses Guzzle's concurrency implementation, so it's a powerful feature that can lead to substantial performance gains. It allows you to send multiple requests to the API service using the same cURL connection without waiting for the previous request to finish. This can make many applications much faster due to not needing to establish a new connection or wait for each request.

Sequential vs. Concurrent Requests

A typical flow for sending three sequential requests may look like this:

1. Send the first request
2. Wait for the response
3. Send the second request
4. Wait for the response
5. Send the third request
6. Wait for the response

We must wait for each request to finish before sending the next request. This can waste a lot of time, especially if the API service is slow to respond. The total time to send these three requests sequentially would be the sum of the time to send each request. For instance, if each request took 500 milliseconds, the total time to send all three would be 1.5 seconds.

However, if we were to send the same three requests concurrently, the flow would look something like this:

1. Send the first request.
2. Send the second request.
3. Send the third request.
4. Wait for the responses.

This approach is slightly different as we're not waiting for the response of each request before sending the next one. Instead, we're sending all three requests at the same time. This means the total time to send all three requests would be the time to send the slowest request. So, if the slowest request took 500 ms to send, the total time to send all three requests would be 500 ms.

A benefit of using concurrency and request pools is that it allows us to take a more asynchronous approach to handling responses. For example, if we receive the response for a request, we can handle it immediately (such as storing information in the database) while the other requests are still being sent. This makes it perfect for things like making requests to a paginated endpoint. If we did this sequentially, we'd likely need to wait for all the requests to finish, or handle the responses before sending the next request.

Comparing Times

Let's look at an example to provide more context about the difference in time to send requests sequentially or concurrently.

We'll use the GitHub API to send six requests to retrieve information about six different Git repositories. We'll send the requests sequentially and concurrently, then compare the times taken to send the requests each way. We won't act on the responses, so we can focus on the time taken to send the requests and receive the responses using Saloon.

We could send six requests sequentially like so:

```
use App\Http\Integrations\GitHub\GitHubConnector;
use App\Http\Integrations\GitHub\Requests\GetRepo;

$requests = [
    new GetRepo('laravel', 'framework'),
    new GetRepo('laravel', 'laravel'),
    new GetRepo('laravel', 'telescope'),
    new GetRepo('ash-jc-allen', 'short-url'),
    new GetRepo('saloonphp', 'saloon'),
    new GetRepo('saloonphp', 'laravel-plugin'),
];

$connector = new GitHubConnector();

foreach ($requests as $request) {
    $connector->send($request);
}
```

According to the results of my local benchmark, it took an average of 1650 ms to send all six requests and receive responses for them.

Let's now send these same requests concurrently. We have yet to look at any concurrent code in Saloon, so don't worry much about the code — we cover this in more detail later. We could send the requests concurrently like so:

```php
use App\Http\Integrations\GitHub\GitHubConnector;
use App\Http\Integrations\GitHub\Requests\GetRepo;

$requests = [
    new GetRepo('laravel', 'framework'),
    new GetRepo('laravel', 'laravel'),
    new GetRepo('laravel', 'telescope'),
    new GetRepo('ash-jc-allen', 'short-url'),
    new GetRepo('saloonphp', 'saloon'),
    new GetRepo('saloonphp', 'laravel-plugin'),
];

(new GitHubConnector())
    ->pool($requests)
    ->setConcurrency(10)
    ->send()
    ->wait();
```

According to the results of my local benchmark, it took an average of 305 ms to send all six requests and receive responses for them.

This highlights the huge difference between sending requests sequentially and concurrently, with a 1345 ms difference in this example, making the concurrent request example 5.4 times faster than the sequential request example.

It's important to note that these results aren't scientifically accurate. The tests were carried out on a local machine, and the times will vary depending on many factors (such as the machine you're using and your network connection). However, they should give you a good idea of the difference in times between sending requests sequentially and concurrently.

Sending Concurrent Requests

Now that we understand what concurrent requests are and how they can be beneficial, let's look at how we can send concurrent requests using Saloon.

To get started, you'll need to create a request pool to which your requests can be added. You can do this by calling the `pool` method on your connector instance like so:

```
use App\Http\Integrations\GitHub\GitHubConnector;
use App\Http\Integrations\GitHub\Requests\GetRepo;

$requests = [
    new GetRepo('laravel', 'framework'),
    // ...
];

$pool = (new GitHubConnector())
    ->pool($requests);
```

By default, Saloon will have set a concurrency of `5`. This means that Saloon will send a maximum of five requests concurrently at a time on the same connection. However, you can change this limit to optimize it for your situation. To do this, use the `setConcurrency` method on your request pool like so:

```php
use App\Http\Integrations\GitHub\GitHubConnector;
use App\Http\Integrations\GitHub\Requests\GetRepo;

$requests = [
    new GetRepo('laravel', 'framework'),
    // ...
];

$pool = (new GitHubConnector())
    ->pool($requests)
    ->setConcurrency(10);
```

In the code example, we've defined that ten requests can be sent concurrently.

We can then send the requests in the pool by calling the `send` method on the request pool like so:

```php
use App\Http\Integrations\GitHub\GitHubConnector;
use App\Http\Integrations\GitHub\Requests\GetRepo;

$requests = [
    new GetRepo('laravel', 'framework'),
    // ...
];

$pool = (new GitHubConnector())
    ->pool($requests)
    ->setConcurrency(10)
    ->send();
```

In the code example, this would trigger all the requests to be sent. However, any code run after the `send` method would be executed immediately, even if the requests haven't finished sending yet. In some cases, this might not be an issue for you. But, if you'd like to wait for all the requests to be fulfilled before continuing, you can call the `wait` method on the request pool like so:

```
use App\Http\Integrations\GitHub\GitHubConnector;
use App\Http\Integrations\GitHub\Requests\GetRepo;

$requests = [
    new GetRepo('laravel', 'framework'),
    // ...
];

$pool = (new GitHubConnector())
    ->pool($requests)
    ->setConcurrency(10)
    ->send()
    ->wait();
```

Now, any code run after the `wait` method will only execute once all the requests have been fulfilled.

In most cases, you'll want to run some logic based on the responses of the requests. For example, you may want to store some response data in your application's database. To do this, you can use the `withResponseHandler` and `withExceptionHandler` methods on the request pool. Both methods accept a closure where you can define additional logic that should be run. The `withResponseHandler` method is called when a successful response is returned, whereas the `withExceptionHandler` method is called when the response is unsuccessful (i.e., the response has a `4xx` or `5xx` status code).

Let's expand on our current example so we can show how you may want to act on the responses to the requests. We'll assume we have created a `storeInDatabase` method to store the repository in our database. We'll also assume we have created a `logException` method to log any exceptions thrown when sending the requests. We can then use these methods in our request pool like so:

```
use App\Http\Integrations\GitHub\GitHubConnector;
use App\Http\Integrations\GitHub\Requests\GetRepo;
use Saloon\Exceptions\Request\FatalRequestException;
use Saloon\Exceptions\Request\RequestException;
use Saloon\Http\Response;

$requests = [
    new GetRepo('laravel', 'framework'),
    // ...
];

$pool = (new GitHubConnector())
    ->pool($requests)
    ->setConcurrency(10)
    ->withResponseHandler(function (Response $response): void {
        $this->storeInDatabase($response);
    })
    ->withExceptionHandler(function (FatalRequestException|RequestException $e) {
        $this->logException($e);
    })
    ->send()
    ->wait();
```

In the code example, we have defined that every successful response should be passed to the `storeInDatabase` method. We have also defined that any exceptions that are thrown should be passed to the `logException` method. This allows us to easily define what should happen when a successful response is returned and what should happen when an exception is thrown. Thus, the `storeInDatabase` method would be called six times if we received six successful responses. Similarly, if we were to receive four successful responses and two error responses, the `storeInDatabase` method would be called four times, and the `logException` method would be called two times.

Middleware

Sometimes, you may want to perform additional logic before sending requests to an API. For example, to add a header to the request, generate a unique request ID for debugging, or generate a signature that should be appended to the request headers. These are all things that can be achieved using "middleware".

Middleware in Saloon is very similar to middleware in Laravel. It's essentially a piece of code (a class or a closure) that allows us to tap into the requests or responses and make changes we want.

Saloon provides several ways to add middleware to your integrations. So you can choose an approach that best suits your feature's needs. Let's look at a few ways you'll likely use middleware in your integrations.

Imagine we want to generate a signature for each request sent to the API. Assume the API service requires this signature to be present so they can verify the request is coming from us and has not been tampered with.

Using the Connector's "boot" Method

One approach we can use would be to add the logic to the connector class's `boot` method. Logic added to the `boot` method will execute for every request sent using the connector, which may not be suitable for all cases. However, it's a good approach to use if you want to add a header to every request that is sent using the connector.

Let's look at an example of how we could do this:

```php
use Saloon\Http\Connector;
use Saloon\Http\PendingRequest;

final class GitHubConnector extends Connector
{
    public function boot(PendingRequest $pendingRequest): void
    {
        $pendingRequest->headers()->add(
            'X-Signature',
            $this->buildSignature($pendingRequest),
        );
    }

    // ...
}
```

As we can see in the code example, we're calling a `buildSignature` method (which would build and return a signature) and then adding the signature to the request headers.

Using Closures

A more flexible approach you may take rather than using the `boot` method is to define the middleware outside the connector. You can do this by defining the middleware logic inside a closure and passing it to the connector's `middleware()->onRequest()` method.

Let's see how we can take our previous example and use a closure instead:

```php
use App\Http\Integrations\GitHub\GitHubConnector;
use Saloon\Http\PendingRequest;

$connector = new GitHubConnector();

$connector->middleware()
    ->onRequest(function (PendingRequest $pendingRequest): void {
        $pendingRequest->headers()->add(
            key: 'X-Signature',
            value: $this->buildSignature($pendingRequest)
        );
    });

// Send requests here...
```

In the code example, we're passing a closure to the `onRequest` method. This closure will be executed for every request sent using the connector. However, you may want to execute the middleware only for a specific request. To do this, call the `middleware()->onRequest()` method on the request object itself, like so:

```php
use App\Http\Integrations\GitHub\GitHubConnector;
use App\Http\Integrations\GitHub\Requests\GetRepo;
use Saloon\Http\PendingRequest;

$connector = new GitHubConnector();
$request = new GetRepo('laravel', 'framework');

$request->middleware()
    ->onRequest(function (PendingRequest $pendingRequest): void {
        $pendingRequest->headers()->add(
            key: 'X-Signature',
            value: $this->buildSignature($pendingRequest)
        );
    });

$response = $connector->send($request);
```

In this case, the middleware will only be executed for that `GetRepo` request, and the middleware will not be executed for any other requests sent using the connector.

Using Invokable Classes

As your integrations grow, middleware might become large and complex. In this case, consider extracting middleware logic from the closure into a dedicated class to keep your code clean and maintainable. This can be done by creating an invokable class (a class that implements the `__invoke` method) that implements the `Saloon\Contracts\RequestMiddleware` interface and then passing it to the `middleware()->onRequest()` method of our connector or request.

Let's look at how we can update our previous example to use an invokable middleware class.

We'll create a new `AddSignatureHeader.php` file in the `app/Http/Integrations/GitHub/Middleware` directory and add the following code:

```
namespace App\Http\Integrations\GitHub\Middleware;

use Saloon\Contracts\RequestMiddleware;
use Saloon\Http\PendingRequest;

class AddSignatureHeader implements RequestMiddleware
{
    public function __invoke(PendingRequest $pendingRequest)
    {
        $pendingRequest->headers()->add(
            key: 'X-Signature',
            value: $this->buildSignature($pendingRequest),
        );
    }
}
```

In the code example, we've created a new class that implements the `RequestMiddleware` interface and the `__invoke` method. Inside this method, we're adding the `X-Signature` header to the request with a signature that we're generating using the `buildSignature` method (which we haven't created, but assume it builds and returns a signature).

If we wanted to use this middleware with our connector, we could do so like this:

```php
use App\Http\Integrations\GitHub\GitHubConnector;
use App\Http\Integrations\GitHub\Middleware\AddSignatureHeader;
use Saloon\Http\PendingRequest;

$connector = new GitHubConnector();

$connector->middleware()->onRequest(new AddSignatureHeader());

// Send requests here...
```

Now, every request sent through that connector will have the `X-Signature` header added.

Similarly, if we wanted to use this middleware with our `GetRepo` request, we could do so like this:

```php
use App\Http\Integrations\GitHub\GitHubConnector;
use App\Http\Integrations\GitHub\Middleware\AddSignatureHeader;
use App\Http\Integrations\GitHub\Requests\GetRepo;
use Saloon\Http\PendingRequest;

$connector = new GitHubConnector();
$request = new GetRepo('laravel', 'framework');

$request->middleware()->onRequest(new AddSignatureHeader());

$response = $connector->send($request);
```

In this case, only the `GetRepo` request will have the `X-Signature` header added.

Plugins

Saloon allows you to add functionality to your integrations using "plugins". Plugins are essentially traits that you can add to your connector classes and request classes to abstract away common functionality.

You can create plugins; we won't cover that in this book, but we'll look at the plugins that ship out of the box with Saloon.

AcceptsJson

The `AcceptsJson` plugin adds the `Accept: application/json` header to the request. This is useful if you're consuming an API that supports multiple response types and want to ensure you always receive JSON responses. It's one you'll likely use in a lot of integrations.

Here's how you might use this plugin a connector class:

```php
namespace App\Http\Integrations\GitHub;

use Saloon\Http\Connector;
use Saloon\Traits\Plugins\AcceptsJson;

final class GitHubConnector extends Connector
{
    use AcceptsJson;

    // ...
}
```

We added the `AcceptsJson` plugin to our connector class so that when we send a request using this connector, the `Accept: application/json` header will be added to the request.

AlwaysThrowOnError

The `AlwaysThrowOnError` plugin is handy, automatically throwing an exception if the request fails (such as receiving a `4xx` or `5xx` HTTP status code). Without this plugin, you must manually check the response status code and throw an exception yourself. This plugin saves you from having to do that.

I use this plugin often on connectors to ensure any unsuccessful requests throw an exception. This reduces my chances of trying to act on the response data when the request fails.

Let's look at how the `AlwaysThrowOnError` plugin might be used in one of your connector classes:

```
namespace App\Http\Integrations\GitHub;

use Saloon\Http\Connector;
use Saloon\Traits\Plugins\AlwaysThrowOnErrors;

final class GitHubConnector extends Connector
{
    use AlwaysThrowOnErrors;

    // ...
}
```

We've added the `AlwaysThrowOnError` plugin to our connector class. This means that whenever we send a request using this connector, an exception will be thrown if the request is unsuccessful.

HasTimeout

The `HasTimeout` plugin allows you to define the connection timeout and request timeout for your requests. This is useful if you're consuming an API with a slow response time and you want to avoid any errors thrown if the request takes longer than the default timeout.

Let's look at how the `HasTimeout` plugin might be used in one of your connector classes:

```
namespace App\Http\Integrations\GitHub;

use Saloon\Http\Connector;
use Saloon\Traits\Plugins\HasTimeout;

final class GitHubConnector extends Connector
{
    use HasTimeout;

    protected int $connectTimeout = 10;

    protected int $requestTimeout = 30;

    // ...
}
```

Adding the `HasTimeout` plugin allowed us to add the `connectTimeout` (to define the timeout for connecting to the API server) and the `requestTimeout` (to define the timeout for the request itself) properties to our connector. These properties will be used when sending requests via this connector.

Error Handling

When consuming APIs, errors are practically inevitable for many reasons:

- Rate-limiting
- A service is down
- Authentication issues
- Mistakes in a request, like an invalid request body
- Conflicts, like trying to create a resource that already exists

When errors occur, you must handle them correctly and efficiently. You might be okay with the request failing and throwing an exception, which presents an error page, but you should usually catch the error to show a more user-friendly error message. These things depend on your use case and the feature you're building using the API.

Saloon's Exceptions

By default, Saloon ships with the following exceptions which are all located in the `Saloon\Exceptions` namespace:

- `SaloonException`
    - `Request\FatalRequestException` (Connection errors)
    - `Request\RequestException` (Request errors)
        - `Saloon\Exceptions\Request\ServerException` (5xx errors)
            - `Request\Statuses\InternalServerErrorException` (500)
            - `Request\Statuses\ServiceUnavailableException` (503)
            - `Request\Statuses\GatewayTimeoutException` (504)
        - `Request\ClientException` (4xx errors)
            - `Request\Statuses\UnauthorizedException` (401)
            - `Request\Statuses\ForbiddenException` (403)

- `Request\Statuses\NotFoundException` (404)
- `Request\Statuses\MethodNotAllowedException` (405)
- `Request\Statuses\RequestTimeOutException` (408)
- `Request\Statuses\UnprocessableEntityException` (422)
- `Request\Statuses\TooManyRequestsException` (429)

These exceptions can either be triggered manually or automatically. Let's look at how to trigger them manually.

Manually Handling Errors

By default, Saloon won't throw an exception if an error occurs when sending a request. Instead, you can assess the request's status using these methods, which check if the HTTP status code of the response falls within specific ranges:

- `$response->successful()` - Code 200-299 (Success)
- `$response->ok()` - Code 200 (OK)
- `$response->redirect()` - Code 300-399 (Redirection)
- `$response->failed()` - Code 400-599 (Client or Server Error)
- `$response->clientError()` - Code 400-499 (Client Error)
- `$response->serverError()` - Code 500-599 (Server Error)

Using a combination of these methods, you can determine whether an error occurred and handle it accordingly. For example, you could use the following code:

```php
use App\Http\Integrations\GitHub\GitHubConnector;
use App\Http\Integrations\GitHub\Requests\GetRepo;

$connector = new GitHubConnector();
$response = $connector->send(new GetRepo('laravel', 'framework'));

if ($response->failed()) {
    // Handle the error here.
}

// The request was successful. Continue as normal.
```

Similarly, you may want to use the response's `onError` method to define some logic that is run if the request is unsuccessful. For example, you could use the following code:

```php
use App\Http\Integrations\GitHub\GitHubConnector;
use App\Http\Integrations\GitHub\Requests\GetRepo;
use Saloon\Http\Response;

$connector = new GitHubConnector();
$response = $connector->send(new GetRepo('laravel', 'framework'));

$response->onError(function (Response $response) {
    // Handle the error here.
});

// Continue as normal.
```

However, there may be times when you want to throw an exception if an error occurs. To do this, you can use the `throw` method on the response like so:

```
use App\Http\Integrations\GitHub\GitHubConnector;
use App\Http\Integrations\GitHub\Requests\GetRepo;

$connector = new GitHubConnector();

$response = $connector->send(
    new GetRepo('laravel', 'framework')
)->throw();

// Continue as normal.
```

In the code example, an exception will be thrown if the request fails. Otherwise, the code will continue to run as normal.

Automatically Handling Errors

You can manually handle errors, but this can be tedious and cumbersome, especially in a large integration with many request classes. You may also forget to handle the errors in some places.

For this reason, you'll likely want to use Saloon's `AlwaysThrowOnError` plugin, as discussed. This plugin automatically throws an exception whenever an error occurs, so you don't have to handle errors manually. Instead, exceptions will be thrown based on the response's status code.

To use the plugin, add the plugin's trait to your connector like so:

```php
namespace App\Http\Integrations\GitHub;

use Saloon\Http\Connector;
use Saloon\Traits\Plugins\AlwaysThrowOnErrors;

final class GitHubConnector extends Connector
{
    use AlwaysThrowOnErrors;

    // ...
}
```

Using Your Own Exceptions

As mentioned in this book, we want to abstract Saloon away as much as possible to keep our integration flexible and maintainable. Thus, we may want to throw our own custom exceptions instead of Saloon's.

Let's take this example:

```php
use App\Http\Integrations\GitHub\GitHubConnector;
use App\Http\Integrations\GitHub\Requests\GetRepo;
use Saloon\Exceptions\Request\RequestException;


try {
    $connector = new GitHubConnector();

    $response = $connector->send(
        new GetRepo('laravel', 'framework')
    )->throw();
} catch (RequestException $exception) {
    // Handle the exception here.
}
```

In this code example, we're catching Saloon's `RequestException` exception. However, what would happen if we decided to stop using Saloon? That exception wouldn't exist or be thrown anymore. We'd have to update our application code to listen for a different exception instead, which we would rather avoid. This is where custom exceptions come in.

Let's start by creating a base `GitHubException` that our GitHub exceptions will extend from. If needed, this will allow us to catch all our GitHub exceptions using a single exception class.

We can create the `GitHubException` by running the following Artisan command:

```
php artisan make:exception Integrations/GitHub/GitHubException
```

This will create a new `GitHubException` class in the

`app/Exceptions/Integrations/GitHub` directory that looks like this:

```
namespace App\Exceptions\Integrations\GitHub;

use Exception;

class GitHubException extends Exception
{

}
```

For this book, we'll create two new exceptions that extend from the `GitHubException` class:

- `NotFoundException` - Thrown if a 404 error occurs.
- `UnauthorizedException` - Thrown if a 403 error occurs.

We can create these exceptions with the following Artisan commands:

```
php artisan make:exception Integrations/GitHub/NotFoundException
```

```
php artisan make:exception Integrations/GitHub/UnauthorizedException
```

We'll need to ensure both exceptions extend the `GitHubException` class. For example, our `NotFoundException` class will look like this:

```php
namespace App\Exceptions\Integrations\GitHub;

class NotFoundException extends GitHubException
{

}
```

Now that we've created our exceptions, we can instruct Saloon to throw these exceptions instead of its own exceptions. To do this, we can add the `getRequestException` method to our connector like so:

```php
use App\Exceptions\Integrations\GitHub\GitHubException;
use App\Exceptions\Integrations\GitHub\NotFoundException;
use App\Exceptions\Integrations\GitHub\UnauthorizedException;
use Saloon\Http\Connector;
use Saloon\Http\Response;
use Throwable;

final class GitHubConnector extends Connector
{
    // ...

    public function getRequestException(
        Response $response, ?Throwable $senderException
    ): ?Throwable {
        return match ($response->status()) {
            403 => new UnauthorizedException(
                message: $response->body(),
                code: $response->status(),
```

```
                previous: $senderException,
            ),
            404 => new NotFoundException(
                message: $response->body(),
                code: $response->status(),
                previous: $senderException,
            ),
            default => new GitHubException(
                message: $response->body(),
                code: $response->status(),
                previous: $senderException,
            ),
        };
    }
}
```

We have used the `match` expression to return the correct exception based on the response's status code. If the response's status code is `403`, we'll return an `UnauthorizedException`. If the response's status code is `404`, we'll return a `NotFoundException`. Otherwise, we'll return a `GitHubException`. Whichever exception is returned will be thrown by Saloon.

Let's look at two methods in a controller to get some context of where these exceptions could be caught.

Firstly, we might want to catch any `GitHubException` exceptions that are thrown when trying to create a new repository. We can do this like so:

```php
namespace App\Http\Controllers;

use App\Exceptions\Integrations\GitHub\GitHubException;
use App\Http\Requests\GitHub\StoreRepoRequest;
use App\Interfaces\GitHub;
use Illuminate\Http\RedirectResponse;

final class GitHubController extends Controller
{
    public function store(
        StoreRepoRequest $request,
        GitHub $gitHub
    ): RedirectResponse {
        try {
            $repo = $gitHub->createRepo($request->toDto());
        } catch (GitHubException $exception) {
            return redirect()
                ->route('github.repos.create')
                ->with('error', $exception->getMessage());
        }

        return redirect()
            ->route('github.repos.show', [$repo->owner, $repo->name])
            ->with('success', 'Repo created successfully');
    }
}
```

In this example, we're catching any `GitHubException` exceptions that are thrown when trying to create a new repository. If an exception is thrown, we'll redirect the user to the create repository page and display the exception's message. Otherwise, we'll redirect the user to a success page.

Secondly, we might want to listen to individual exceptions and tailor the response based on the exception. For example, we might want to listen for any `UnauthorizedException` or `NotFoundException` exceptions and redirect the user to a different page. We can do this like so:

```
namespace App\Http\Controllers;

use App\Exceptions\Integrations\GitHub\NotFoundException;
use App\Exceptions\Integrations\GitHub\UnauthorizedException;
use App\Interfaces\GitHub;
use Illuminate\Http\RedirectResponse;

final class GitHubController extends Controller
{
    public function destroy(
        string $owner,
        string $name,
        GitHub $gitHub
    ): RedirectResponse {
        try {
            $gitHub->deleteRepo(
                owner: $owner,
                repoName: $name,
            );
        } catch (UnauthorizedException) {
            return redirect()
                ->route('github.repos.show', [$owner, $name])
                ->with(
```

```
                'error',
                'You do not have permission to delete this repo.'
            );
        } catch (NotFoundException) {
            return redirect()
                ->route('github.repos.show', [$owner, $name])
                ->with('error', 'The repo does not exist.');
        }

        return redirect()
            ->route('github.repos.index')
            ->with('success', 'Repo deleted successfully');
    }
}
```

In the code example, we're listening for any `UnauthorizedException` or `NotFoundException` exceptions. If either of these exceptions is thrown, we'll redirect the user back to the repository's show page and display a message that is determined based on the exception. Otherwise, we'll redirect the user to the index page and display a success message.

Changing the Exception Logic

There may be times when you're consuming an API that doesn't use the conventional HTTP status codes to represent the response's status. For example, the API may return a `200` status code for both successful and unsuccessful requests.

In such cases, Saloon won't be able to detect errors and throw exceptions for us, so you'll need to change the logic determining which exception is thrown.

Take this JSON response from a successful call for deleting a user from an imaginary API:

```
{
  "status": "success",
  "message": "User deleted successfully"
}
```

And take this JSON response from an unsuccessful call for deleting a user from the same imaginary API:

```
{
  "status": "error",
  "message": "User does not exist"
}
```

Ideally, the error response should return a `404` status code. However, in this case, we'll assume the API returns a `200` status code for both successful and unsuccessful requests.

Let's configure our Saloon connector so that it can determine when the API returns an error response. We can do this by adding a `hasRequestFailed` method to our connector like so:

```php
namespace App\Http\Integrations\GitHub;

use Saloon\Http\Connector;
use Saloon\Http\Response;

final class GitHubConnector extends Connector
{
    // ...

    public function hasRequestFailed(Response $response): bool
    {
        return $response->json('status') === 'error';
    }
}
```

In this method, we're stating that if the response body's `status` field is `"error"` we should throw an exception. Otherwise, we should not throw an exception and assume the request was successful.

If you choose to use this approach and override the exceptions that are thrown (like we've shown in this section), then you'll also need to update the logic that determines which exception is thrown.

Retrying Requests

When consuming APIs, requests will inevitably fail. The reasons range from problems out of your control (e.g., the API is down) to problems within your control (e.g., the API rate limit was exceeded).

Therefore, you must have a strategy in place for handling these failures. In the previous chapter, we covered how to handle these failures by using exceptions based on the HTTP status code of the response. However, there may be times when you want to retry a request first instead of throwing an exception.

A rule I follow is that if the request fails but can be successful if retried, then retry the request; otherwise, throw an exception. But what does this mean in practice? Imagine you're trying to send a request to the GitHub API, and you receive a `422 Unprocessable Entity` response. In this case, the data you're sending in the request is invalid. Therefore, retrying the request will not make a difference. So, in this case, you should throw an exception.

However, imagine receiving a `500 Server Error` or `503 Service Unavailable` response. In these cases, it indicates an issue with the API itself. Therefore, retrying the request may be successful. In this case, you should retry the request. There's no guarantee that any retries will succeed, but it's worth doing in case the problem is temporary.

Retry a Request

Saloon provides a handy `sendAndRetry` method to send a request and retry it if it fails. Imagine we want to make a request to the GitHub API to fetch details of a repository. We'll specify that if the request fails, we want to retry it up to two times more, with a three-second delay between each retry. We can do this like so:

```php
$connector = new GitHubConnector();

$response = $connector->sendAndRetry(
    request: new GetRepo('laravel', 'framework'),
    maxAttempts: 3,
    interval: 3000, // 3 seconds
);
```

If the request is successful during any of the three attempts, the response will be returned as expected. However, an exception will be thrown if the request fails during all three attempts.

Customize the Retry Logic

As mentioned, we only want to retry requests with a chance of succeeding. So, we should not retry the request if we receive a client error response (e.g., `400 Bad Request` or `422 Unprocessable Entity`). However, we should retry the request if we receive a server error response (e.g., `500 Server Error` or `503 Service Unavailable`).

To do this, we can pass a closure to the `sendAndRetry` method that determines whether the request should be retried. If the closure returns `true`, then the request will be retried. Otherwise, the request will not be retried.

Let's update our previous example to only retry if we receive a server error response. We can do this like so:

```php
use App\Http\Integrations\GitHub\GitHubConnector;
use App\Http\Integrations\GitHub\Requests\GetRepo;
use Saloon\Exceptions\Request\FatalRequestException;
use Saloon\Exceptions\Request\RequestException;

$connector = new GitHubConnector();

$response = $connector->sendAndRetry(
    request: new GetRepo('laravel', 'framework'),
    maxAttempts: 3,
    interval: 3000,
    handleRetry: fn(FatalRequestException|RequestException $exception): bool =>
        $exception instanceof FatalRequestException
        || $exception->getResponse()->serverError()
);
```

Let's break down what's happening in the code example. We're passing a closure to the `handleRetry` parameter that expects either a `Saloon\Exceptions\Request\FatalRequestException` or `Saloon\Exceptions\Request\RequestException`. These are the exceptions thrown when a request fails. If we received a `FatalRequestException`, we could not connect to the API at all. If we receive a `RequestException`, this indicates we received a response from the API, but the request failed for some reason.

So, we specified in our closure that if we receive a `FatalRequestException`, we should retry the request. We also specified that we should retry the request if we receive a server error (with a `5xx` HTTP status code).

It's important to note that Saloon will only attempt to retry requests if a `FatalRequestException` or `RequestException` is thrown. If any other exception is thrown, then the request will not be retried. Therefore, if you're overriding the exceptions that are thrown (like we've shown in this chapter), you'll likely want to update your exceptions to extend the `Saloon\Exceptions\Request\FatalRequestException` or `Saloon\Exceptions\Request\RequestException` exceptions.

For example, you may want to create a base `App\Exceptions\Integrations\GitHubException` that extends `\Exception`. You may then want to create an `App\Exceptions\Integrations\GitHubRequestException` that extends `Saloon\Exceptions\Request\RequestException`. Your request exceptions (such as `App\Exceptions\GitHub\NotFoundException`) could then extend the `App\Exceptions\Integrations\GitHubRequestException` exception. This allows you to continue using your own custom exception classes and use them with Saloon's retry logic.

Handling API Rate Limits

A large majority of APIs enforce some sort of rate limiting and throttling to limit the number of requests you can make in a given timeframe, so it's something you must handle. Let's clarify what rate limiting is and how you can handle it in your code using Saloon.

What is Rate Limiting?

Rate limiting is a technique that limits the number of requests that can be made to an API in a given timeframe. For example, the API might impose various limits, such as:

- Maximum of 10 requests per second
- Maximum of 60 requests per minute
- Maximum of 1000 requests per day
- Maximum of 10,000 requests per month

The limits may be imposed for several reasons:

- **Prevent API overload** - The API provider may want to prevent their API from being overloaded with requests and causing strain on their application's infrastructure. Putting too much strain on the API could cause it to slow down or even crash.
- **Subscription-level limits** - If the API service provides multiple subscription levels, they might want to enforce limits based on the user's subscription level. For example, a free subscription might have a limit of 100 requests per day, whereas a paid subscription might have a limit of 10,000 requests per day.
- **Prevent API abuse** - For public and free APIs, the API provider may want to prevent someone from making too many simultaneous requests. Enforcing limits can reduce the chance of someone attempting to use the API for malicious purposes.

How limits are imposed depends on the API. For example, some APIs might impose a limit for an account (or API key) to all routes in the API. Other APIs might impose a limit for an account (or API key) to a specific route in the API. Some APIs impose a limit based on the IP address of the machine making the request. It's important to read the documentation for the API you're consuming to understand how limits are imposed. You don't want to release code to your production application that may hit the API rate limits.

If a request is made to an API and the rate limit is exceeded, the API will usually respond with a `429 Too Many Requests` response. The response will usually contain headers providing information about the rate limits so you can know when to make another request.

Strategies for Working with Rate Limited APIs

In general, there are two strategies you can use when working with rate-limited APIs:

- Avoid hitting the rate limit altogether
- Retry the request if the rate limit is hit

Avoiding Hitting the Rate Limit

Depending on the number of requests you're sending, avoiding hitting rate limits is usually the best strategy. This may involve caching responses, delaying requests, batching requests, or using a queue to send requests.

Caching responses allows you to avoid making requests to the API if you already have the needed data. However, this isn't always possible. Delaying requests is also a useful tactic that you can use. For example, you may delay requests by a few seconds to reduce the chances of hitting any second-based or minute-based API limits. This usually works well with queued jobs as you can also delay the job from being processed.

Some APIs support "batching", meaning you can perform multiple actions in one request. A perfect example of a service that supports batching is Mailgun, which is used for sending emails. Imagine you want to send 1,000 emails using Mailgun. Typically, you might make an individual API request for each email you want to send. However, Mailgun allows you to send 1,000 emails in a single API request. Reducing 1,000 API requests to a single request will reduce the chance of hitting the API limits — and significantly improve performance.

Although batching can be handy, it's not something every API supports. You'll need to check the documentation for the API you're consuming. The API endpoint and request body may look different depending on whether you're sending a single or batched request, too, so you must ensure you're sending the correct data.

Most APIs implementing throttling provide information in the response headers about the rate limits. Let's look at the typical response headers from a Laravel project using Laravel's built-in rate-limiting middleware.

If the rate limit hasn't yet been hit, the response will contain the two following headers:

```
X-RateLimit-Limit: 100
X-RateLimit-Remaining: 30
```

The `X-RateLimit-Limit` header specifies the total number of requests allowed within a timeframe (e.g., per minute). The `X-RateLimit-Remaining` header shows how many requests you can still make before hitting this limit. In the example above, the API allows 100 requests in the timeframe, and there are 30 requests remaining before the limit is hit, meaning we've already sent 70 requests.

In the event that the rate limit is hit, the response will contain the following four headers:

```
Retry-After: 40
X-RateLimit-Limit: 100
X-RateLimit-Remaining: 0
X-RateLimit-Reset: 1692900371
```

As we can see, the `X-RateLimit-Remaining` header is now `0`, meaning we've hit the rate limit. There's also an `X-RateLimit-Reset` header, which gives us the time that the rate limit will reset so that we can retry sending our request (we'll look at retrying requests next). We can only send requests once the rate limit resets. In this case, the rate limit will reset at `1692900371`, the Unix timestamp representation for Thursday, 24th August 2023 18:06:11 GMT. The `Retry-After` header also gives us the number of seconds we should wait before retrying the request. In this case, we should wait 40 seconds before retrying the request.

You can use the information in these headers to avoid hitting the rate limits or to display a message to the user if the rate limit is hit.

Retrying Requests

Although it's best to avoid hitting rate limits altogether, there may be times you do. This could be due to an unexpected spike in traffic to your application or a bug causing more requests than expected. No matter the reason, it's important to know how to retry the failed requests.

If the rate limit is hit, the API usually responds with a `429 Too Many Requests` response. The response will usually contain headers with information about the rate limits so you can know when to make another request.

It's important to ensure you don't try sending more requests until the rate limit has reset. If you do, it will waste system resources because you'll need to wait for the limit to reset or temporarily store requests in your queue to be processed later.

Installing the Saloon Rate Limit Plugin

To start rate limiting in Saloon, you must first install Saloon's rate limit plugin. You can do this using Composer by running the following command:

```
composer require saloonphp/rate-limit-plugin
```

After this, the rate limit plugin will be available with Saloon.

Configuring the Rate Limits

Next, we'll need to configure our connector so it uses the rate limit plugin and knows what the limits are. We can use the `Saloon\RateLimitPlugin\Traits\HasRateLimits` trait in our connector class. This trait contains two abstract methods we must implement in our connector class.

Let's add the trait and the two abstract methods to our connector class:

```php
namespace App\Http\Integrations\GitHub;

use Saloon\Http\Connector;
use Saloon\RateLimitPlugin\Contracts\RateLimitStore;
use Saloon\RateLimitPlugin\Traits\HasRateLimits;

final class GitHubConnector extends Connector
{
    use HasRateLimits;

    // ...

    protected function resolveLimits(): array
    {

    }

    protected function resolveRateLimitStore(): RateLimitStore
    {

    }
}
```

Here, we defined two new methods: `resolveLimits` and `resolveRateLimitStore`. The `resolveLimits` method should return an array of `Saloon\RateLimitPlugin\Limit` objects that define how many requests can be made in a given time frame. The `resolveRateLimitStore` method should return an instance of a class that implements the `Saloon\RateLimitPlugin\Contracts\RateLimitStore` interface. This class will define how the limits are stored and read so Saloon can track how many requests have been made in a given timeframe.

Let's look at what these two methods should look like.

Defining the Rate Limits

Saloon provides many helper methods we can use to define our rate limits in a human-readable way. Let's see an example of how to define our rate limits for our `GitHubConnector` connector class. Imagine that the API only allows us to make ten requests a second and a maximum of 500 an hour. We can define these limits using the following code:

```
namespace App\Http\Integrations\GitHub;

use Saloon\Http\Connector;
use Saloon\RateLimitPlugin\Limit;
use Saloon\RateLimitPlugin\Traits\HasRateLimits;

final class GitHubConnector extends Connector
{
    // ...

    protected function resolveLimits(): array
    {
        return [
            Limit::allow(requests: 10)->everySeconds(seconds: 1),
            Limit::allow(requests: 500)->everyHour(),
        ];
    }
}
```

In the `resolveLimits` method, we've defined our two rate limits in a human-readable way. Saloon also provides several other helper methods to write our rate limits:

- `Limit::allow(60)->everySeconds(seconds: 1)`
- `Limit::allow(60)->everyMinute()`
- `Limit::allow(60)->everyFiveMinutes()`
- `Limit::allow(60)->everyThirtyMinutes()`
- `Limit::allow(60)->everyHour()`
- `Limit::allow(60)->everySixHours()`
- `Limit::allow(60)->everyTwelveHours()`
- `Limit::allow(60)->everyDay()`
- `Limit::allow(60)->everyDayUntil('6pm')`
- `Limit::allow(60)->untilMidnightTonight()`
- `Limit::allow(60)->untilEndOfMonth()`

Defining the Rate Limit Store

In the `resolveRateLimitStore`, we need to return an instance of a class that implements the `Saloon\RateLimitPlugin\Contracts\RateLimitStore` interface. The returned object will instruct Saloon on storing and reading the rate limits to track how many requests have been made in a given timeframe.

Although Saloon allows you to create your own stores if you'd like, it supports drivers out of the box that store limits in the following ways:

- **Memory** - In an in-memory array on the connector. The limits will be lost when the connector is destructed (e.g., at the end of your Laravel application's request lifecycle).
- **File** - In a file on the local filesystem.
- **Redis** - In Redis, using PHP's `Redis` extension.
- **Predis** - In Redis, using the `predis/predis` package.
- **PSR Cache Store** - In a PSR-16 cache store provided by the `psr/simple-cache` library.

- **Laravel Cache Store** - In any of Laravel's cache disks.

For this example, we will use the Laravel cache store so the limits are stored in the same cache store as the rest of our application. To do this, we can configure the `resolveRateLimitStore` method to return an instance of the `Saloon\RateLimitPlugin\Stores\LaravelCacheStore` class:

```
namespace App\Http\Integrations\GitHub;

use Illuminate\Support\Facades\Cache;
use Saloon\Http\Connector;
use Saloon\RateLimitPlugin\Contracts\RateLimitStore;
use Saloon\RateLimitPlugin\Stores\LaravelCacheStore;
use Saloon\RateLimitPlugin\Traits\HasRateLimits;

final class GitHubConnector extends Connector
{
    // ...

    protected function resolveRateLimitStore(): RateLimitStore
    {
        return new LaravelCacheStore(Cache::store(config('cache.default')));
    }
}
```

In the code example, we defined that we want to use the default cache store configured in our Laravel application.

Rate Limiting by Key

In our GitHub example, we've assumed that our application will only ever make requests using an API key stored in our `.env` file. However, this isn't always the case. Sometimes, we may want to make requests on behalf of a user using their own API key. They might have manually input the API key into our application, or we might have generated one using OAuth.

We might want to apply separate rate limits to each API key in this scenario. We wouldn't want to apply the same rate limits to all API keys, as this would mean that if one user made many requests, it would affect the other users.

By default, Saloon will track the rate limits using the following naming convention:

```
{ConnectorClassName}:{RequestsAllowed}_every_{Seconds}
```

For example, if we were only permitted to make 50 requests per minute using our `GitHubConnector` connector class, Saloon would store the rate limit using the following key:

```
GitHubConnector:50_every_60
```

However, we can override this behaviour to create separate rate limit keys per user. For our example, assume we've passed an `App\Models\User` model to our connector class and that we're sending requests on behalf of that user. We can override the default naming convention by overriding the `getLimiterPrefix` method:

```php
namespace App\Http\Integrations\GitHub;

use ReflectionClass;
use Saloon\Http\Connector;

final class GitHubConnector extends Connector
{
    // ...

    protected function getLimiterPrefix(): ?string
    {
        return (new ReflectionClass($this))->getShortName()
            .':user_'
            .$this->user->id;
    }
}
```

In the `getLimiterPrefix`, we updated the naming convention so the prefix of the rate limit key includes the user's ID. For example, if the user's ID were `123`, the rate limit key would be:

```
GitHubConnector:user_123:50_every_60
```

This means we can now apply separate rate limits to each user.

Sending the Requests

Now that our connector class is set up and ready to handle rate limits, we can start sending requests to the API. We do this just as we would before we added rate limiting to our connector class:

```
use App\Http\Integrations\GitHub\GitHubConnector;
use app\Http\Integrations\GitHub\Requests\GetRepo;

$connector = new GitHubConnector();
$response = $connector->send(new GetRepo('laravel', 'framework'));
```

Before Saloon sends the request, it checks whether the connector has any rate limits defined. If it does, it will check to ensure that we've stayed within all of them. If no limits have been exceeded, the request will be sent. However, if Saloon detects that a limit has been exceeded and that the request would result in an HTTP `429 Too Many Requests` response, it will throw a `Saloon\RateLimitPlugin\Exceptions\RateLimitReachedException` exception.

In this scenario, we have several options for handling the exception:

- We can catch the exception and handle it ourselves.
- We can allow Saloon to catch the exception and retry the request for us automatically.
- If we're making the request inside a queued job, we can push the job back onto the queue and retry later.

Let's take a look at each of these options in more detail.

Catching the Exception

Depending on where and why you're making the request, you may want to catch the exception using a try-catch block. This can be very handy if you'd like to handle the exception in a specific way. For example, you can log the exception, email the user to inform them that they've exceeded their rate limit, or display the error to the user in a webpage.

To demonstrate, imagine we are trying to make a request to the GitHub API. If the rate limit has been exceeded, we want to redirect the user to their dashboard and display an error message. Otherwise, we want to display a view containing information about the repository. The code may look something like this:

```
namespace App\Http\Controllers;

use App\Interfaces\GitHub;
use Saloon\RateLimitPlugin\Exceptions\RateLimitReachedException;

final class GitHubController extends Controller
{
    public function show(
        string $owner,
        string $name,
        GitHub $gitHub,
    ) {
        try {
            $repo = $gitHub->getRepo(
                owner: $owner,
                repoName: $name,
            );
        } catch (RateLimitReachedException $exception) {
            $seconds = $exception->getLimit()->getRemainingSeconds();
```

```
            return redirect(route('dashboard'))
                ->with(
                    'error',
                    'Rate limit exceeded. Please try again in '
                        .$seconds
                        .' seconds.',
                );
        }

        return view('repos.show')->with([
            'repo' => $repo,
        ]);
    }

    // ...
}
```

As you can see in the example, we can call `getLimit` on the exception to get access to the `Saloon\RateLimitPlugin\Limit` object that represents the exceeded rate limit. We can then use this to get the number of seconds until the limit resets.

Silently Waiting and Retrying the Request

Another approach to retrying a request when the rate limit has been exceeded is to allow Saloon to silently retry the request without throwing an exception. To do this, you can use the `sleep` method on the `Saloon\RateLimitPlugin\Limit` you define. For example, if we wanted to wait until the rate limit resets, we could do something like so:

```php
namespace App\Http\Integrations\GitHub;

use Saloon\Http\Connector;
use Saloon\RateLimitPlugin\Limit;
use Saloon\RateLimitPlugin\Traits\HasRateLimits;

final class GitHubConnector extends Connector
{
    // ...

    protected function resolveLimits(): array
    {
        return [
            Limit::allow(requests: 10)->everySeconds(seconds: 3)->sleep(),
        ];
    }
}
```

In the code example, we've defined that only ten requests can be made every three seconds. If we exceed this limit, Saloon will wait until the limit resets (a maximum of three seconds) before sending the request. Otherwise, it will be sent straight away.

This approach is handy for rate limits over a small timeframe, such as "X requests every second". The `sleep` method delays the sending of the request, so if we only need to wait for a couple of seconds until the limit resets, it will just increase our wait time by a couple of seconds. For instance, imagine we are making an API request inside a queued job, and the maximum time we need to wait before we can retry the request is one second. It would be much easier (and likely less strain on the application infrastructure) to just wait one second before retrying the request rather than pushing the job back onto the queue and waiting for it to be processed again.

However, we can't use this same approach for rate limits over a longer timeframe, such as "X requests every five minutes". If we exceed this limit, we must wait up to 5 minutes before the request is sent. This is not ideal as it would attempt to keep our Laravel application's lifecycle open for up to five minutes. Not only would this likely result in a request timeout, it would mean we couldn't provide any visual feedback to the user if it were done in a web request. If your application were also using a serverless infrastructure, the serverless function would be attempted to be kept alive for 5 minutes, likely resulting in a higher cost than simply ending the request and retrying again later.

Retrying the Request in a Queued Job

Saloon provides a very handy `Saloon\RateLimitPlugin\Helpers\ApiRateLimited` Laravel job middleware. This middleware can be placed on any queued jobs you use to make API requests and will automatically push your job back onto the queue if the rate limit has been exceeded.

Imagine we have a `SyncRepoInfo` queued job that makes a request to the GitHub API to fetch information about a repository and store it in the database. The job class may look something like this:

```php
namespace App\Jobs\GitHub;

use Illuminate\Contracts\Queue\ShouldQueue;
use Saloon\RateLimitPlugin\Helpers\ApiRateLimited;

class SyncRepoInfo implements ShouldQueue
{
    // ...

    public function middleware(): array
    {
        return [new ApiRateLimited()];
    }
}
```

In this code example, we've registered the `Saloon\RateLimitPlugin\Helpers\ApiRateLimited` middleware on the job. Imagine the job runs and a `Saloon\RateLimitPlugin\Exceptions\RateLimitReachedException` exception is thrown because the rate limit has been exceeded and doesn't reset for another 60 seconds. In this case, the job will be pushed back onto the queue and won't be retried for at least 60 seconds. Theoretically, this means that when the job is pulled off the queue for running next time, the rate limit will have reset, and the request will be sent successfully.

If you choose to use this approach in a queued job that runs any code before the API request is made, remember that the code will run again when the job is retried. This may be fine, as the code may just be something like a database query. However, if you're doing something that causes a change, like writing to the database, this write will also be run on the code retry. You'll need to keep this in mind to decide whether to add a clean-up process that should run if the request (and, therefore, the job) fails.

Catching 429 Error Responses

Although you should be able to rely on Saloon to prevent making requests to rate limited APIs, there may be times when you still hit an API rate limit. For example, this may be due to you not configuring your Saloon limits correctly, the API provider changing their limits without you knowing, or your application receiving a sudden spike in traffic you weren't expecting.

If this happens, you'll receive an HTTP `429 Too Many Requests` response from the API. This response should contain a `Retry-After` header that will tell you how many seconds you need to wait before you can make another request. If this happens, Saloon will automatically detect this and throw a `Saloon\RateLimitPlugin\Exceptions\RateLimitReachedException` exception (or delay and retry the request if you used `sleep` on the limit).

Saloon tries to determine how long to wait using the `Retry-After` header before making another request. If it can't calculate this, it will default to 60 seconds. As a result, future requests sent through the connector class will automatically be prevented by Saloon until the limit has been reset.

This approach is a handy fallback that can generate limits on the fly for us if we accidentally make a request when we shouldn't have. Since, under the hood, Saloon is just creating a `Saloon\RateLimitPlugin\Limit` instance automatically for us, we'll be able to handle request failures in the same way we would if we had defined the limits ourselves (as shown above).

Setting Your Own Rate Limit Thresholds

As just discussed, Saloon can automatically create limits for us if it detects an HTTP `429 Too Many Requests` response from the API. However, you can set your own rate limit thresholds to reduce the chances of hitting the API's rate limits.

For example, imagine an API allows 1,000 requests a day. You may want to set your limit like so:

```
Limit::allow(requests: 1000)->everyDay();
```

Theoretically, this means the 1,001st request would be prevented by Saloon rather than the API. However, you might want to be a bit more cautious and set your limit like so:

```
Limit::allow(requests: 1000, threshold: 0.9)->everyDay();
```

In this code example, we've set a `threshold` value. This can be an integer between 0 and 1 representing a percentage of the limit. In this case, we set the threshold to `0.9`, so Saloon will prevent the request if it detects that you've made 90% of the requests you're allowed. This means you'll have a 10% buffer before hitting the API's rate limit. So, if we were to make 900 requests in a day, the 901st request would be prevented by Saloon.

This helps you be confident you'll never hit the API's rate limit just in case you accidentally make more requests than you should.

Caching Responses

When consuming APIs in your Laravel application, you may want to cache the responses to your requests. This can be useful for a number of reasons:

- It can improve the performance of your application by reducing the number of requests made to the API. Retrieving data from a cache (such as Redis) is usually much faster than making a request to an API.
- It can reduce the chances of hitting API rate limits because fewer requests are being made.
- It can reduce the risk of your application breaking if the API is down.

You won't always want to cache responses to your requests. For example, you wouldn't want to cache the response to a request that creates a new resource. However, you may want to cache the response to a request that fetches a list of resources. For example, imagine you're consuming an exchange rates API. Say you want to fetch the exchange rate between two currencies on a given date. This data won't change soon, so you could cache the response to prevent needing to make the same request again shortly.

To highlight the performance improvements of caching responses, let's look at the results of a basic comparison. We'll make ten requests to the GitHub API to fetch all the authenticated users' repositories. We'll then cache the results of the requests and attempt to fetch the repositories again (which will be fetched from the cache). The average time of each approach is as follows:

- Fetching from the API: 6,675ms
- Fetching from the cache: 18ms

The performance improvements are massive!

Note that the results of this comparison are purely for demonstration purposes. The tests were run on a local machine using Laravel Valet and a local Redis instance. These results will vary depending on your machine and the environment in which you're running your application. However, this should give you an idea of the performance improvements you can expect.

Installing the Cache Plugin

Before we can start caching our requests' responses, we'll need to install the `saloonphp/cache-plugin` package. This package provides a plugin we can use to cache the responses to our requests.

You can install it using Composer by running the following command in your terminal:

```
composer require saloonphp/cache-plugin
```

The plugin should now be installed and ready to use.

How to Cache Responses

To enable caching for a request, you must update your request class or connector class so they implement the `Saloon\CachePlugin\Contracts\Cacheable` interface. This interface requires adding a `resolveCacheDriver` method and `cacheExpiryInSeconds` method. You must also ensure that the class uses the `Saloon\CachePlugin\Traits\HasCaching` trait.

Imagine we wanted to update our paginated `GetAuthRepos` request class we looked at in the "Pagination" section earlier in this chapter. We could update it to implement the `Saloon\CachePlugin\Contracts\Cacheable` interface and add the methods and trait like so:

```php
namespace App\Http\Integrations\GitHub\Requests;

use Illuminate\Support\Facades\Cache;
use Saloon\CachePlugin\Contracts\Cacheable;
use Saloon\CachePlugin\Contracts\Driver;
use Saloon\CachePlugin\Drivers\LaravelCacheDriver;
use Saloon\CachePlugin\Traits\HasCaching;
use Saloon\Http\Request;

final class GetAuthUserRepos extends Request implements Cacheable
{
    use HasCaching;

    // ...

    public function resolveCacheDriver(): Driver
    {
        return new LaravelCacheDriver(Cache::store(config('cache.default')));
    }

    public function cacheExpiryInSeconds(): int
    {
        return 3600; // 1 hour
    }
}
```

In this request class, we use the `resolveCacheDriver` method to specify that we want to use the Laravel cache driver. This allows us to use the same cache driver we use for the rest of our application. We also use the `cacheExpiryInSeconds` method to specify that we want to cache the response for 3600 seconds (1 hour). However, depending on your requirements, you may use a different cache driver or cache expiry time.

This now means the response will be cached when the request is first made. If the request is made again, the response will be fetched from the cache instead of making a new request to the API.

Saloon provides the ability to check whether the response was fetched from the cache or not. You can do this by calling the `isCached` method on the response. For example, if we wanted to check whether the response was fetched from the cache or not, we could do something like this:

```
$connector = new GitHubConnector();
$response = $connector->send(new GetRepo('laravel', 'laravel'));

$response->isCached(); // false

$response = $connector->send(new GetRepo('laravel', 'laravel'));

$response->isCached(); // true
```

As we can see, the first time we make the request, the response is not fetched from the cache. However, the second time we make the request, the response is fetched from the cache.

Disabling and Invalidating the Cache

Sometimes, you'll want to disable the cache for a specific request or flush the response from the cache altogether. Imagine a page in your application displays a list of a user's GitHub repositories. On each page load, you wouldn't want to make a request to the API to fetch the repositories. Instead, you should fetch the repositories from the cache whenever possible. However, you may want to allow the user to refresh the repositories and re-fetch them all from GitHub. This would allow new repositories to be displayed on the page. In this case, you should disable the cache for the request that fetches the repositories.

To flush the response from the cache, you can call the `invalidateCache` on your request class before sending it. For example, if we wanted to flush the response from the cache for the `GetRepo` request, we could do something like this:

```
$connector = new GitHubConnector();
$request = new GetRepo('laravel', 'laravel');

$request->invalidateCache();

$response = $connector->send($request);
```

Doing this will fetch the response from the API instead of the cache. The new response will then be cached for future requests, assuming the cache hasn't been disabled and the response was successful.

Similarly, if you'd like to disable the cache for a request, you can call the `disableCaching` method on your request class before sending it. For example, if we wanted to disable the cache for the `GetRepo` request, we could do something like this:

```
$connector = new GitHubConnector();
$request = new GetRepo('laravel', 'laravel');

$request->disableCaching();

$response = $connector->send($request);
```

This will fetch the response from the API instead of the cache. The response will not be cached for future requests, which is handy if you'd like to bypass the cache when debugging or testing your application.

Testing API Integrations

Now that we've covered how to use Saloon in your Laravel application to consume an API, let's look at how to test our API integrations.

Benefits of Testing

Writing tests for your API integration is an important part of the development process and shouldn't be overlooked. While tests can't guarantee that your code is bug-free, they can greatly impact the quality of your code and your confidence in it. Following is an overview of some key benefits of tests.

Help Spot Bugs Early

Be honest: how often have you written code, run it once or twice and then committed it? I'll hold my hand up — I've done it myself. You think, "It looks right and seems to run; I'm sure it'll be fine".

Every time I did this, either my pull requests were rejected or bugs were released into production. By writing tests, you can spot bugs before committing your work and have more confidence when you release it to production.

Make Future Work and Refactoring Easier

Imagine you build an API integration for your Laravel application. You write the code, test it, and then release it into production. A few months later, you need to add new functionality to the integration. As part of adding this new functionality, you might need to change some existing code.

If you have a good-quality test suite for your integration, you can use it to ensure that your changes haven't broken any existing functionality. This is known as regression testing. It's a great way to make sure your changes caused issues. This is also extremely useful for other developers who may not have seen the code before. They can be more confident that their changes haven't broken anything they may not be aware of.

Without automated tests, you must manually test new functionality to ensure it works, as well as all existing functionality. This is a tedious, time-consuming process, so it's easy to miss something, and it's unlikely you'll want to test all the minutia of your code every time you make a small change.

Change the Way You Approach Writing Code

When I first learned about testing and started writing tests (for a Laravel app using PHPUnit), I quickly realized my code was pretty difficult to write tests for. It was hard to mock classes, prevent third-party API calls, and make certain assertions. To write code in a way that can be tested, you must look at the structure of your classes and methods from a slightly different angle than before.

Learning to write code that can be tested drastically changes how you approach writing code — at least it did for me. When writing any code, I think, "Am I going to be able to write tests for this easily?". If the answer is "No", it might indicate that I need to rethink the structure of my code.

The easier a piece of code is to test, the more likely you are to write tests for it. The more tests you have, the more confident you can be in your code. But if your code is difficult to test, you're less likely to write tests for it because it can be a tedious and painful process.

Act as Living Documentation for Your Code

A huge benefit of writing tests for your code is that it can act as a form of living documentation. If you're working on a project that has a lot of tests, you can use them to get a good understanding of how the code works.

For example, imagine we have the following method in our API integration that deletes a repository from GitHub:

```
public function deleteRepo(string $owner, string $name): bool
{
    // ...
}
```

We might want to write tests with the following names:

- `true_is_returned_when_a_repo_is_deleted_successfully`
- `UnauthorizedException_is_thrown_when_the_user_is_not_authorized`
- `NotFoundException_is_thrown_when_the_repo_does_not_exist`
- `GitHubException_is_thrown_when_an_unexpected_error_occurs`

By looking at these test names, we can get a quick, high-level understanding of the expected behaviour of the `deleteRepo` method. To provide even more context to the developer, the tests themselves will provide even more detail about the expected behaviour.

This can be useful for reminding yourself how a piece of code works. It can also be useful for other developers working on the same project as you. If the developer has never touched this piece of code before, they'll be able to use a mixture of the code itself, any documentation, and the tests to understand how it works.

Should We Make Real Requests?

A much-debated topic in the world of software testing is whether or not tests should make real requests to the API. To summarize, there are two main approaches to testing API integrations:

- **Mocking** - We create a fake version of the API response and use this in our tests to simulate what would be returned if we made the response to the API.
- **Making the Actual Request** - We make the actual request to the API and use the response in our tests.

These approaches have pros and cons, and both have their place in your test suite.

Mocking

By mocking a response, we avoid the need to make an actual request to the API. This allows tests to run faster and we don't need to worry about authentication, rate limits, and caching.

For example, if you imagine you're going to be running your tests on each commit or push to your repository, you'll want them to run as quickly as possible. Doing this may also lead to hitting the API rate limit, which could cause your tests to fail.

Therefore, you can use mocking to avoid these issues. You can create a fake version of the API response and use this in your tests. For instance, you can mock successful and failed responses to test both scenarios.

Although this can be beneficial in terms of performance, it does have some downsides. Creating all the mock responses for your integration can be tedious, especially for a larger integration. There's a chance of creating a mock incorrectly that doesn't realistically represent a response from the API. You'll also need to ensure that your mock responses are up-to-date with the API. If the API changes, you'll need to update your mock responses to reflect this. Otherwise, you could have tests that pass when your integration doesn't work.

Making the Actual Request

The other approach to testing is to make actual requests to the API. This way, you don't need to worry about creating mock responses and keeping them up-to-date. You can just make requests to the API and use the responses in your tests.

This can be beneficial because if the API changes, your tests will fail, and you'll immediately know you need to update your integration. This helps ensure your integration is always up-to-date with the API. Therefore, you should do this with some mission-critical parts of your system. For example, if you have a payment integration, you may want to make the actual request to the Stripe API to ensure your application can correctly take payments from users.

In projects I've worked on, sending real requests to the API has worked well for the team, ensuring our integration was always up-to-date with the API and giving us confidence that our integration would work in production. However, hitting the API isn't always ideal. It can be slow, you may hit the API rate limit, and you may need to worry about authentication and caching.

Some third-party services provide "test credentials" or "sandboxes" for this purpose. For example, Stripe provides test credentials to make requests to their API without actually taking payments. This is a good way to test your integration without affecting production data. However, not every service provides this, so you may not be able to use this approach for every integration.

Another downside to making actual requests is that it can be challenging to test certain scenarios. For example, if you want to test a scenario where the API returns a `500` error, you may be unable to do this with the actual API. You may also not be able to test scenarios where the API is down or slow. In these situations, you'll likely want to use mocking instead. It's important to remember that you don't need to use one approach or the other exclusively — you can use a mix of both in your test suite.

Another downside to making actual requests to the API is that it can be difficult for other developers to run your tests. If you're using a third-party service that requires authentication, you'll likely need to share your credentials with other developers so they can run your tests. Or, if you're each using your own accounts on the API service, you'll need to provide instructions (either automated or manual) that other developers can use to set up their accounts for the tests to run. Adding this extra friction to running tests can be a pain for other developers and may dissuade them from wanting to use the test suite at all, so you want to keep this process as painless as possible.

If you write some tests that make real requests to the API, consider only running these tests in your continuous integration (CI) environment, such as GitHub Actions. This means you don't need to worry about sharing credentials with other developers. It also means you can run your faster tests locally and then run the slower tests in CI. This can be a good way to get the best of both worlds.

As an example, imagine we have a test that is making a request to the GitHub API to fetch a repository. The outline of the test may look something like this:

```
namespace Tests\Feature\Services\GitHub\GitHubService;

use PHPUnit\Framework\Attributes\Group;
use PHPUnit\Framework\Attributes\Test;
use Tests\TestCase;

final class GetRepoTest extends TestCase
{
    #[Test]
    #[Group('Api')]
    public function repo_can_be_returned(): void
    {
        // ...
    }
}
```

Here, we've added the `Api` group to the test. This means we can exclude this group when running our tests locally. We can then run the tests in the `Api` group in CI instead. To run the tests locally and exclude the `Api` group, we can run the following command that uses the `--exclude-group` flag:

```
./vendor/bin/phpunit --exclude-group=Api
```

If we only wanted to run the tests in the `Api` group, we could run the following command that uses the `--group` flag:

```
./vendor/bin/phpunit --group=Api
```

If we wanted to run all the tests, such as when we're running them in CI, we can just run the following command without either of the flags:

```
./vendor/bin/phpunit
```

What Should We Test?

In this book, we're mainly mocking responses for our integration tests rather than making the actual requests to the API. But what exactly should we be testing?

To explain what we should test, consider an example use case where we might interact with an API. Let's stick with our previous examples and imagine we're building a Laravel application that allows users to manage their GitHub repositories. We might have a method in a controller that allows us to fetch a single repository from GitHub. The method may look like this:

```php
namespace App\Http\Controllers;

use App\Interfaces\GitHub;
use Illuminate\Contracts\View\View;

public function show(string $owner, string $name, GitHub $gitHub): View {
    $repo = $gitHub->getRepo(
        owner: $owner,
        repoName: $name,
    );

    return view('repos.show')->with([
        'repo' => $repo,
    ]);
}
```

In this example, we inject an `App\Interfaces\GitHub` interface into the controller. In our case, we'll assume that whenever we try to resolve a `GitHub` instance from the container, we'll get an instance of the `App\Services\GitHub\GitHubService` class that uses Saloon to make requests to the GitHub API.

At this stage, you may be tempted to write a test for the controller method that mocks the response from the GitHub API. However, I'd recommend against this. Although this would allow testing the entire flow of the request, it would also mean we're testing the implementation details of the service class. This tightly couples the test to the implementation of the service class and Saloon, so if we replaced Saloon with a different package, we'd need to update our tests. We want to avoid this.

Imagine we also created an Artisan command or queued job that allows us to fetch a repository from the GitHub API. If we used this same approach of only mocking the response, our

`GitHubService` class would still run in the requests. Thus, tests for controllers, commands, and queued jobs would all test the same functionality of the `GitHubService` class. While you might want this to increase confidence that your code works correctly, such redundancy can make maintaining tests cumbersome.

Instead, I'd recommend using a different approach to writing the tests. As covered in this book, we've abstracted Saloon away from the rest of our application code as much as possible. To do this, we've used our `App\Interfaces\GitHub` interface and Laravel's service container to swap out the interface implementation easily. Theoretically, this means that no matter how we're making requests to the GitHub API (using Saloon or another package), we should be able to pass arguments to the public methods of the bound class and get back the same response.

With this in mind, we should isolate our tests a little more. Instead of our controller tests testing that the request was made, we can test that the correct arguments were passed to the `getRepo` method. We can then write a separate test for the `GitHubService` class that tests that the request was made. This means we're testing the implementation details of the `GitHubService` class in the tests for that class, and we're testing the public API of the `GitHubService` class in the controller tests.

After all, our controller tests shouldn't care what's happening under the hood and how we're making the requests. The controller tests should just care that the correct arguments are being passed to the `getRepo` method and that the expected result is being passed to view.

Instead, we can take this approach to writing our tests:

- Write tests for the `GitHubController` to assert that the correct arguments are being passed to which class is bound to the `GitHub` interface and that the returned result is being passed to the view.
- Write tests for the `GitHubService` to assert that the correct request is being made to the GitHub API and that the correct response is being returned.

Using a Test Double

Now that we know how we can approach isolating the tests and making them more "unit-style" tests, let's see how we can achieve this.

If you've already written tests for your Laravel applications before, you may already be familiar with the concepts of test doubles and fakes (even without realizing it).

You might have seen the `Mail::fake()` method or `Queue::fake()`. These methods allow us to fake the mail and queue drivers to test that the correct emails are sent, and the correct jobs are dispatched. Generally, these fakes work by adding your mail classes and queued jobs to an array or Collection rather than actually sending or executing them. This means you can then make assertions (such as `Mail::assertSent()` and `Queue::assertPushed()`) in your tests to check that the correct emails were sent or the correct jobs were dispatched. We're going to use this same approach and create our own test double that we can use to fake the `GitHub` interface.

We'll start by creating a `GitHubServiceFake` class in the `app/Services/GitHub` directory and updating it to implement the `App\Services\GitHub\GitHubService` interface. The class should look something like this at first:

```
declare(strict_types=1);

namespace App\Services\GitHub;

use App\Collections\GitHub\RepoCollection;
use App\DataTransferObjects\GitHub\NewRepoData;
use App\DataTransferObjects\GitHub\Repo;
use App\DataTransferObjects\GitHub\UpdateRepoData;
use App\Interfaces\GitHub;
```

```php
final class GitHubServiceFake implements GitHub
{
    public function __construct(
        private readonly string $token,
    ) {}

    public function getRepos(): RepoCollection
    {
        throw new \Exception('Not implemented');
    }

    public function getRepo(string $owner, string $repoName): Repo
    {
        throw new \Exception('Not implemented');
    }

    public function getRepoLanguages(string $owner, string $repoName): array
    {
        throw new \Exception('Not implemented');
    }

    public function createRepo(NewRepoData $repoData): Repo
    {
        throw new \Exception('Not implemented');
    }

    public function updateRepo(
        string $owner,
        string $repoName,
        UpdateRepoData $repoData
    ): Repo {
```

```php
        throw new \Exception('Not implemented');
    }

    public function deleteRepo(string $owner, string $repoName): void
    {
        throw new \Exception('Not implemented');
    }
}
```

The class looks like any other class we might use in our application code. Notice that I've thrown an exception in each method. I like to do this when creating a test double to show which methods I still need to implement. As I write tests for each method, I'll replace the exception with test code. You don't need to do this, but I find it useful.

Let's start implementing the `getRepos` method with a simple implementation that returns a `RepoCollection`. We'll add it to the class and then look at what's happening:

```php
namespace App\Services\GitHub;

use App\Collections\GitHub\RepoCollection;
use App\DataTransferObjects\GitHub\Repo;
use App\Interfaces\GitHub;
use Faker\Generator;

final class GitHubServiceFake implements GitHub
{
    private Generator $faker;

    // ...
```

```php
    public function getRepos(): RepoCollection
    {
        return RepoCollection::make([
            $this->fakeRepo(),
            $this->fakeRepo(),
        ]);
    }

    private function fakeRepo(string $owner = null, string $name = null): Repo
    {
        $faker = app(Generator::class);

        $owner ??= $faker->word;
        $name ??= $faker->word;

        return new Repo(
            id: $faker->randomNumber(),
            owner: $owner,
            name: $name,
            fullName: $owner.'/'.$name,
            private: $faker->boolean(),
            description: $faker->sentence,
            createdAt: now(),
        );
    }
}
```

In the code example, we've added a simple implementation to the `getRepos` method that returns an `App\Collections\GitHub\RepoCollection` containing two `App\DataTransferObjects\GitHub\Repo` objects. We've also added a `fakeRepo` method to create a fake Repo object. This method will come in handy for future tests, too.

Now that we've got a simple implementation of the getRepos method, let's look at how this could fit into a test for a controller. Imagine we have the following basic controller method:

```
declare(strict_types=1);

namespace App\Http\Controllers;

use App\Interfaces\GitHub;
use Illuminate\Contracts\View\View;

final class GitHubController extends Controller
{
    public function index(GitHub $gitHub): View
    {
        return view('repos.index')->with([
            'repos' => $gitHub->getRepos(),
        ]);
    }

    // ...
}
```

Let's write a test for the controller method that uses the GitHubServiceFake class we've just created. To start, we'll create an IndexTest.php file in the tests/Feature/Controller/GitHubController directory. Where you write your tests is a personal preference. I prefer writing my tests in a directory structure that matches that of my application code. I then ensure each public method has its own test class (e.g., IndexTest, ShowTest, StoreTest, etc.) so I can easily find the tests for a particular class and method.

We'll take a look at the `tests/Feature/Controller/GitHubController/IndexTest` file and then discuss what's happening:

```
namespace Tests\Feature\Controllers\GitHubController;

use App\Collections\GitHub\RepoCollection;
use PHPUnit\Framework\Attributes\Test;
use Tests\TestCase;
use App\Interfaces\GitHub;
use App\Services\GitHub\GitHubServiceFake;

final class IndexTest extends TestCase
{
    #[Test]
    public function view_can_be_returned_with_repos(): void
    {
        $gitHubServiceFake = new GitHubServiceFake(
            config('services.github.token')
        );

        // Swap the implementation of the GitHub interface.
        $this->swap(GitHub::class, $gitHubServiceFake);

        // Make a request to the route and ensure the correct view is returned.
        $this->get(route('github.repos.index'))
            ->assertOk()
            ->assertViewIs('repos.index')
            ->assertViewHas(
                'repos',
                fn (RepoCollection $repoCollection)
```

```
                    => $repoCollection->count() === 2
            );
    }
}
```

In our test, we start by creating an instance of our `GitHubServiceFake` class. We then use the `swap` method that Laravel provides us. This method allows us to swap out the implementation of a class with another implementation. In this case, we're telling Laravel, "In the AppServiceProvider, we told you to give us an instance of GitHubService when we ask for the GitHub interface. But for this test, give us an instance of GitHubServiceFake instead." This powerful ability highlights why we use interfaces and the service container in our application code.

So if we were to run `app(GitHub::class)` in this test, we'd get an instance of `App\Services\GitHub\GitHubServiceFake`. This means we don't need to worry about the `App\Services\GitHub\GitHubService` class at all.

The rest of the test is a simple test that calls the controller method (available through the `github.repos.index` named route) and asserts that the correct response code is returned, the correct view is returned, and the view has correct data. We're using a closure to assert that the `repos` variable in the view is a `RepoCollection` that contains two `Repo` objects.

In our test, we've kept the assertions relatively simple. We may also want to write extra tests to simulate scenarios, such as when the GitHub API returns the following:

- An empty array of repositories
- An error
- A rate limit error

Our example above should highlight the process of using a fake service class. You can then build on this to create more complex tests.

Extracting Test Helpers Into Traits

As your test suite grows, you might find things repeated in your tests that could be extracted into a single place. In our case, we'll swap out our `GitHub` implementation with the `GitHubServiceFake` class in multiple tests using this code:

```
$gitHubServiceFake = new GitHubServiceFake(
    config('services.github.token')
);

// Swap the implementation of the GitHub interface.
$this->swap(GitHub::class, $gitHubServiceFake);
```

When building API integrations, I like to create traits I can use in my tests that contain helper methods related to specific API services. I follow a consistent naming convention for `InteractsWith{ServiceName}` traits. For example, `InteractsWithGitHub`, `InteractsWithSpotify`, `InteractsWithFacebook`, and so on. This means I can keep any common test code related to a specific API service in a single place.

I highly recommend adding any helpers like this to your tests. It'll make your tests easier to read and maintain. As mentioned, removing resistance to writing tests makes you more likely to write them.

As an example, let's create an `InteractsWithGitHub` trait we can use in our tests. We'll create a new `InteractsWithGitHub` trait in the `tests/Traits` directory. We'll then add a new `fakeGitHub` method to the trait that we can use in our tests:

```php
namespace Tests\Traits;

use App\Interfaces\GitHub;
use App\Services\GitHub\GitHubServiceFake;

trait InteractsWithGitHub
{
    private function fakeGitHub(): GitHubServiceFake
    {
        $gitHubServiceFake = new GitHubServiceFake(
            config('services.github.token')
        );

        $this->swap(GitHub::class, $gitHubServiceFake);

        return $gitHubServiceFake;
    }
}
```

In the `fakeGitHub` method, we're swapping out our `GitHub` implementation like before, but we're then returning the `GitHubServiceFake` object. We're doing this because we'll be adding assertions to the class in the next section, so we must be able to access the test double in our tests.

We can then update our `IndexTest` test to make use of the new trait:

```php
namespace Tests\Feature\Controllers\GitHubController;

use App\Collections\GitHub\RepoCollection;
use PHPUnit\Framework\Attributes\Test;
use Tests\TestCase;
use Tests\Traits\InteractsWithGitHub;

final class IndexTest extends TestCase
{
    use InteractsWithGitHub;

    #[Test]
    public function view_can_be_returned_with_repos(): void
    {
        $this->fakeGitHub();

        // Make a request to the route and ensure the correct view is returned.
        $this->get(route('github.repos.index'))
            ->assertOk()
            ->assertViewIs('repos.index')
            ->assertViewHas(
                'repos',
                fn (RepoCollection $repoCollection)
                    => $repoCollection->count() === 2
            );
    }
}
```

As we can see in the code, we're now using the `InteractsWithGitHub` trait and the `fakeGitHub` method at the beginning of our test. This makes our test more readable and keeps the focus on the main components of the test.

Adding Assertions to Your Test Double

The `GitHubServiceFake` test double we've created so far is very basic. It's only returning a fixed number of repositories for us. This is fine for some tests, but we can take this a step further and add some helper methods to our tests that we can use for assertions.

Imagine we want to write a test for the following controller method:

```php
namespace App\Http\Controllers;

use App\Exceptions\Integrations\GitHub\GitHubException;
use App\Http\Requests\GitHub\StoreRepoRequest;
use App\Interfaces\GitHub;
use Illuminate\Http\RedirectResponse;

final class GitHubController extends Controller
{
    // ...

    public function store(
        StoreRepoRequest $request,
        GitHub $gitHub
    ): RedirectResponse {
        try {
            $repo = $gitHub->createRepo($request->toDto());
        } catch (GitHubException $exception) {
            return redirect()
                ->route('github.repos.create')
                ->with('error', $exception->getMessage());
        }

        return redirect()
            ->route('github.repos.show', [$repo->owner, $repo->name])
            ->with('success', 'Repo created successfully');
    }
}
```

Before writing any tests, let's break down what's happening in this controller method. The method is used for creating a new repository in GitHub. We know that the `App\Interfaces\GitHub` interface expects an instance of `App\DataTransferObjects\GitHub\NewRepoData` to be passed to it. So we'll assume that the `toDto` method on the `App\Http\Requests\GitHub\StoreRepoRequest` class returns an instance of `App\DataTransferObjects\GitHub\NewRepoData`. If the call is successful and we can make a new repository in GitHub, we'll redirect the user to the "show" page for the repository. But if an `App\Exceptions\Integrations\GitHub\GitHubException` is thrown, we'll redirect the user back to the "create" page and display an error message.

So we can use this intended behaviour to build out the tests we want to write:

- The user is redirected to the "show" page when a repository is successfully created.
- The user is redirected to the "create" page when an exception is thrown.

Let's update the `createRepo` method in the `GitHubServiceFake` class and then delve into what's being done:

```
namespace App\Services\GitHub;

use App\DataTransferObjects\GitHub\NewRepoData;
use App\DataTransferObjects\GitHub\Repo;
use App\Exceptions\Integrations\GitHub\GitHubException;
use App\Interfaces\GitHub;
use Illuminate\Support\Collection;

final class GitHubServiceFake implements GitHub
{
    private Collection $reposToCreate;

    private GitHubException $failureException;
```

```php
    public function __construct(
        private readonly string $token,
    ) {
        $this->reposToCreate = new Collection();
    }

    public function createRepo(NewRepoData $repoData): Repo
    {
        if (isset($this->failureException)) {
            throw $this->failureException;
        }

        $this->reposToCreate->push($repoData);

        return $this->fakeRepo('owner-here', $repoData->name);
    }

    public function shouldFailWithException(GitHubException $exception): self
    {
        $this->failureException = $exception;

        return $this;
    }

    // ...
}
```

In our `createRepo` method, we now check to see if a `failureException` property has been set in the class. I'll explain later why we've done this, but we can use the `shouldFailWithException` method to set this property to simulate an error being returned from the API. If the property has been set, we throw an exception. Otherwise, we continue with the method normally. This consists of us adding the `NewRepoData` DTO that we've just passed to a `reposToCreate` property on the class. We then return a fake `Repo` object.

Adding the `repoData` object to the Collection means that later in our test, we can make assertions based on what we expected would happen.

There are two things that we may want to simulate in our tests:

- A repository was created with the correct data.
- A repository is not created when something goes wrong.

We can add two methods to our `GitHubServiceFake` class to help us with these assertions: `assertNoReposCreated` and `assertRepoCreated`. Depending on how you interact with the API, you may also want to write more in-depth assertions, such as checking that a specific repo was not created with a given set of data. However, we'll keep it simple.

We can add our two assertions to the `GitHubServiceFake` class:

```
namespace App\Services\GitHub;

use App\Exceptions\Integrations\GitHub\GitHubException;
use App\Interfaces\GitHub;
use Faker\Generator;
use Illuminate\Support\Collection;
use PHPUnit\Framework\Assert;

final class GitHubServiceFake implements GitHub
{
    private Collection $reposToCreate;
```

```php
    // ...

    public function assertNoReposCreated(): void
    {
        Assert::assertEmpty(
            $this->reposToCreate,
            'Repos were created.'
        );
    }

    public function assertRepoCreated(
        string $name,
        string $description,
        bool $isPrivate
    ): void {
        $repoIsToBeCreated = $this->reposToCreate
            ->where('name', $name)
            ->where('description', $description)
            ->where('isPrivate', $isPrivate)
            ->isNotEmpty();

        Assert::assertTrue(
            $repoIsToBeCreated,
            'Repo was not created.'
        );
    }
}
```

This means we can now make assertions in our tests that a repository was created with the correct data, or that no repositories were created at all. If either of these assertions fails, the test will fail.

The `assertNoReposCreated` method checks that the `reposToCreate` field is empty. If it is, this simulates that no repositories were created. If it's not empty, the assertion will fail, thus making the test fail.

The `assertRepoCreated` accepts several arguments we can use to filter items in the `reposToCreate` field. If we can find an item that matches the arguments passed, we know that a repository was created with the correct data. If we can't find an item, the assertion will fail, causing the test to fail.

Let's write a test that asserts a user is redirected to the "show" page when a repository is successfully created:

```
namespace Tests\Feature\Controllers\GitHubController;

use PHPUnit\Framework\Attributes\Test;
use Tests\TestCase;
use Tests\Traits\InteractsWithGitHub;

final class StoreTest extends TestCase
{
    use InteractsWithGitHub;

    #[Test]
    public function repo_can_be_created(): void
    {
        $gitHubFake = $this->fakeGitHub();

        $postBody = [
            'name' => 'test-repo',
```

```
            'description' => 'test-description',
            'is_private' => true,
        ];

        // Make a request to the route and ensure the correct view is returned.
        $this->post(route('github.repos.store'), $postBody)
            ->assertRedirect(route(
                'github.repos.show',
                ['owner-here', 'test-repo']
            ))
            ->assertSessionHas('success', 'Repo created successfully');

        $gitHubFake->assertRepoCreated(
            name: $postBody['name'],
            description: $postBody['description'],
            isPrivate: $postBody['is_private'],
        );
    }
}
```

In the test, we start by faking our GitHub implementation. We then build an array (`postBody`) representing the data we'll send to the controller. The `postBody` is then passed in the request to the controller, and we're asserting that the user is redirected to the correct route with the correct success message.

Following this, we use our new `assertRepoCreated` method in our `GitHubServiceFake` to assert that the correct data would have been passed to the GitHub API.

Note that we only pass some basic arguments to the `assertRepoCreated`, but if you want to make more in-depth assertions, consider changing the `assertRepoCreated` to accept a closure like so:

```
public function assertRepoCreated(\Closure $callback): void
{
    $repoIsToBeCreated = $this->reposToCreate
        ->filter($callback)
        ->isNotEmpty();

    Assert::assertTrue(
        $repoIsToBeCreated,
        'Repo was not created.'
    );
}
```

You would then be able to call the method like so in your tests:

```
$gitHubFake->assertRepoCreated(fn(NewRepoData $repo): bool =>
    $repo->name === $postBody['name']
    && $repo->description === $postBody['description']
    && $repo->isPrivate === $postBody['is_private']
);
```

Now that we've tested a successful API call, we can also test an API call that would fail. Let's add the test and then discuss what's happening:

```
namespace Tests\Feature\Controllers\GitHubController;
```

```php
use App\DataTransferObjects\GitHub\NewRepoData;
use App\DataTransferObjects\GitHub\Repo;
use App\Exceptions\Integrations\GitHub\GitHubException;
use PHPUnit\Framework\Attributes\Test;
use Tests\TestCase;
use Tests\Traits\InteractsWithGitHub;

final class StoreTest extends TestCase
{
    use InteractsWithGitHub;

    // ...

    #[Test]
    public function user_is_redirected_back_if_an_error_occurs(): void
    {
        $gitHubFake = $this->fakeGitHub()->shouldFailWithException(
            new GitHubException('Test error message')
        );

        $postBody = [
            'name' => 'test-repo',
            'description' => 'test-description',
            'is_private' => true,
        ];

        $this->post(route('github.repos.store'), $postBody)
            ->assertRedirect(route('github.repos.create'))
            ->assertSessionHas('error', 'Test error message');

        $gitHubFake->assertNoReposCreated();
```

```
    }
}
```

This test looks very similar to the previous one, but there are a few differences. Firstly, we're now calling the `shouldFailWithException` method on the fake we added earlier. This method accepts an exception we want to be thrown when the API call is made. In this case, we're passing a `GitHubException` with an example dummy message of "Test error message". This simulates what would happen if the GitHub API returned an error. We've passed a `GitHubException` for the example, but you want to pass a more specific exception to simulate specific scenarios, such as receiving an HTTP `403` response.

We then call the controller and assert that the user is redirected back to the "create" page with the correct error message.

Next, we use our new `assertNoReposCreated` method in our `GitHubServiceFake` to assert that no repositories were created.

Adding helper methods for these types of assertions can drastically improve your confidence in your tests. They can allow you to simulate different scenarios and make assertions on them. This can be especially useful when you're testing error handling.

We've kept our assertions relatively simple and barebones in this example purely so we can highlight the thought process behind them. However, you may want to add more assertions to your fakes for testing different scenarios. If you choose to do this, I recommend keeping your assertions as simple as possible. If you start making assertion methods too complex, it may lead to you adding bugs in your tests, which could lead to incorrect test results.

Mocking HTTP Responses

So far, we've been writing tests that make assertions against the input and output of our service class. However, we still need to test what's actually happening inside the service class itself. This is where we can write tests that make assertions against the HTTP requests being made.

Thankfully, Saloon provides testing features that allow us to mock HTTP responses to make this process easier. Before we continue writing tests, let's look at how we can mock responses in Saloon.

At the beginning of our tests, we can use the `Saloon::fake()` method to tell Saloon we should fake any HTTP requests. We can then pass an array of mocked responses (using the `MockResponse::make()` method) that should be returned when a request is made. Let's look at an example:

```
use Saloon\Http\Faking\MockResponse;
use Saloon\Laravel\Facades\Saloon;

Saloon::fake([
    MockResponse::make(['message' => 'Success'], 200),
    MockResponse::make(['message' => 'Forbidden'], 403),
    MockResponse::make(['message' => 'Error'], 500),
]);

// Make Saloon HTTP calls now...
```

In the code example, we've mocked three responses. This means the first HTTP request will return a `200` response with the body of `{"message": "Success"}`. The second HTTP request will return a `403` response with the body of `{"message": "Forbidden"}`. The third HTTP request will return a `500` response with the body of `{"message": "Error"}`. This is useful for testing multiple HTTP calls in the same test.

This approach will return the mocked responses in the order they're defined. But there may be times when you want to return a specific response for a specific request. Let's look at an example:

```
use App\Http\Integrations\GitHub\Requests\GetAuthUserRepos;
use App\Http\Integrations\GitHub\Requests\GetRepo;
use Saloon\Http\Faking\MockResponse;
use Saloon\Laravel\Facades\Saloon;

Saloon::fake([
    GetRepo::class => MockResponse::make([
        'single-repo-response-body-here'
    ]),
    GetAuthUserRepos::class => MockResponse::make([
        'multiple-repos-response-body-here'
    ]),
]);
```

This now means that any HTTP requests made to the `GetRepo` request will return the body of `"single-repo-response-body-here"`. Any HTTP requests made to the `GetAuthUserRepos` request will return the body of `"multiple-repos-response-body-here"`.

There may also be times when you want to return a response for a specific request URI. Let's look at an example:

```
use Saloon\Http\Faking\MockResponse;
use Saloon\Laravel\Facades\Saloon;

Saloon::fake([
    'github.com/repos/laravel/framework' => MockResponse::make([
        'laravel-framework-repo-data-here'
    ]),
    'github.com/repos/*' => MockResponse::make(['dummy-repo-data-here']),
    '*' => MockResponse::make(['catch-all-data-here']),
]);
```

In the code example, we state that any requests from Saloon made directly to `github.com/repos/laravel/framework` should return the body of `['laravel-framework-repo-data-here']`.

We then use wildcards in the other request URIs so we don't need to write the exact matches. For example, `github.com/repos/*` would match request URIs such as `github.com/repos/ash-jc-allen/short-url` and `github.com/repos/saloonphp/saloon`. Using wildcards is handy if your tests don't require being specific about the request URIs.

Finally, we're using a catch-all wildcard (`*` on its own) to match any request URIs that haven't been matched by the previous two.

Now that we know how to mock some of the responses for Saloon requests, let's write a test that uses this.

We'll start by writing a test for the `createRepo` method in the `App\Services\GitHub\GitHubService` class. Let's remind ourselves of the method:

```php
namespace App\Services\GitHub;

use App\DataTransferObjects\GitHub\NewRepoData;
use App\DataTransferObjects\GitHub\Repo;
use App\Http\Integrations\GitHub\Requests\CreateRepo;
use App\Interfaces\GitHub;

final readonly class GitHubService implements GitHub
{
    // ...

    public function createRepo(NewRepoData $repoData): Repo
    {
        return $this->connector()
            ->send(new CreateRepo($repoData))
            ->dtoOrFail();
    }
}
```

The `createRepo` method expects a `NewRepoData` object to be passed in. This object contains the data that should be used to create the repo. The method then uses the `GitHubConnector` (returned via the `connector` method) to send a `CreateRepo` request to GitHub. This request is then converted into a `Repo` data transfer object and returned. If the request fails, an instance of `App\Exceptions\Integrations\GitHub\GitHubException` is thrown.

Let's write a test for a successful request first and then discuss what's happening:

```php
namespace Tests\Feature\Services\GitHub\GitHubService;
```

```
use App\DataTransferObjects\GitHub\NewRepoData;
use App\Http\Integrations\GitHub\Requests\CreateRepo;
use App\Services\GitHub\GitHubService;
use Saloon\Enums\Method;
use Saloon\Http\Faking\MockResponse;
use Saloon\Laravel\Facades\Saloon;
use Tests\TestCase;

final class CreateRepoTest extends TestCase
{
    #[Test]
    public function repo_can_be_created_in_github(): void
    {
        // Fake a response for the request to create a repo.
        Saloon::fake([
            'user/repos' => MockResponse::make([
                'id' => 123456789,
                'name' => 'repo-name-here',
                'owner' => [
                    'login' => 'owner-name-here',
                ],
                'full_name' => 'owner-name-here/repo-name-here',
                'description' => 'description goes here',
                'private' => true,
                'created_at' => '2022-05-18T18:00:07Z'
            ]),
        ]);

        // Attempt to create a new repo.
        $repoData = new NewRepoData(
            name: 'repo-name-here',
```

```
        description: 'description goes here',
        isPrivate: true,
    );

    $repo = (new GitHubService('token'))->createRepo($repoData);

    // Assert the correct repo data was returned.
    $this->assertEquals(123456789, $repo->id);
    $this->assertEquals('owner-name-here', $repo->owner);
    $this->assertEquals('repo-name-here', $repo->name);
    $this->assertEquals('owner-name-here/repo-name-here', $repo->fullName);
    $this->assertTrue($repo->private);
    $this->assertEquals('description goes here', $repo->description);
    $this->assertEquals(
        '2022-05-18T18:00:07'
        $repo->createdAt->toDateTimeLocalString()
    );

    // Assert the correct request was sent to the GitHub API.
    Saloon::assertSent(static fn(CreateRepo $request): bool =>
        $request->resolveEndpoint() === '/user/repos'
            && $request->method() === Method::POST
            && $request->body()->all() === [
                'name' => 'repo-name-here',
                'description' => 'description goes here',
                'private' => true,
            ]
    );
}
```

At the beginning of the test, we instruct Saloon that if a request is made to `github.com/user/repos`, we should return the specified body as JSON. Note that in this test, we only specified the fields in the response we will use to build the `Repo` DTO. This is purely for brevity in this book. If possible, it is ideal to mock the full response body in your tests. Not only will this make your mock response more realistic, but it will also help in the future if you need to add more fields to the DTO and have to update your tests.

After this, we built our `NewRepoData` DTO and passed it to the `createRepo` method in our `GitHubService` class. Following this, we've made assertions to check that the properties in the DTO are correct, which ensures the DTO is built correctly from the response body.

Finally, we've asserted that the correct request was sent to the GitHub API. We've done this using the `Saloon::assertSent` method. This method can accept a closure as its argument. This closure is passed the request that was sent to the API. In the closure, we assert that the request's endpoint is `/user/repos`, the method is `POST`, and the body contains the correct data.

We can also write tests to simulate our request failing. Let's write a test to simulate the user not being able to create a repository because one already exists with the same name:

```php
namespace Tests\Feature\Services\GitHub\GitHubService;

use App\DataTransferObjects\GitHub\NewRepoData;
use App\Exceptions\Integrations\GitHub\GitHubException;
use App\Http\Integrations\GitHub\Requests\CreateRepo;
use App\Services\GitHub\GitHubService;
use Saloon\Http\Faking\MockResponse;
use Saloon\Laravel\Facades\Saloon;
use Tests\TestCase;

final class CreateRepoTest extends TestCase
{
```

```php
    #[Test]
    public function exception_is_thrown_if_the_user_cannot_create_the_repo()
    {
        $this->expectException(GitHubException::class);

        // Fake an error response for the request to create a repo.
        Saloon::fake([
            'user/repos' => MockResponse::make([
                'message' => 'Repository creation failed.',
                'errors' => [
                    [
                        'resource' => 'Repository',
                        'code' => 'custom',
                        'field' => 'name',
                        'message' => 'name already exists on this account',
                    ],
                ],
            ], 422),
        ]);

        // Attempt to create a new repo.
        $repoData = new NewRepoData(
            name: 'ashallendesign',
            description: 'description goes here',
            isPrivate: true,
        );

        (new GitHubService(config('services.github.token')))
            ->createRepo($repoData);
    }
}
```

In this test, we prepare our test using the `expectException` method. This instructs PHPUnit to expect a `GitHubException` to be thrown in the test at some point. If the exception is thrown, the assertion will pass. But if one isn't thrown, the test will fail.

We then mocked the response we would receive from the GitHub API if a repository already existed with the same name.

After that, we called the `createRepo` method with a `NewRepoData` object passed to it.

You may have noticed we're not inspecting the request body in this test. That's because we can use the assertions from our previous test to assume that the request body is correct. We're only interested in testing the error handling in this test.

Recording HTTP Responses

So far, we've manually written out the responses we want to return from our fake requests. This is perfectly fine for simple responses, and it's probably the easiest approach. However, manually writing mock response can have several issues:

- **Time-consuming** - Writing out the response body for each request takes time, especially if the response body is large.
- **Higher likelihood of errors** - You may make mistakes when writing the response body, like typos, missing fields/headers, or incorrect HTTP status codes. This could lead to tests failing and spending time debugging the issue.

To help, Saloon provides a way to record the responses of actual API requests so that they can be replayed in your tests. This means you don't have to manually write out the response body for each request.

Let's look at how recording responses work in Saloon and how to use them in your tests. To record a response, you can use the following in your code:

```php
use Saloon\Http\Faking\MockResponse;
use Saloon\Laravel\Facades\Saloon;

Saloon::fake([
    MockResponse::fixture('GitHub/Repo/laravel/framework'),
]);
```

As you can see, it looks very similar to how we mock the responses, as we're using `Saloon::fake()`. However, instead of using `MockResponse::make()`, we're using `MockResponse::fixture()`. In this fixture we've passed the path where we want to store the request's response and read it from. By default, the fixtures are stored in your project's `tests/Fixtures` directory. So our above response (which we assume is returned from the GitHub API with data about the `laravel/framework` repository) would be stored in `tests/Fixtures/GitHub/Repo/laravel/framework.json`. The JSON file stores the response body, headers, and status code.

When you run your tests, if you attempt to send a request, Saloon first checks to see whether the fixture exists. If it does, it won't make a request to the API. Instead, it'll return the response from the fixture. If the fixture doesn't exist, it'll make a request to the API and store the response in the fixture.

This means that to use fixtures, you must have made a request to the API at least once. Where you choose to do this is up to you. There are two approaches that I typically use for recording responses:

- If the API is publicly available and doesn't require authentication, I'll allow the test to make the request to the API the very first time I run it.
- If the API requires authentication or any complex data to send the request and get a realistic response, I'll temporarily add the `Saloon::fake()` call to my application code and make the request outside of the test (e.g., acting as a user in the web browser). This

records the response for me to use in my tests. I can then delete the `Saloon::fake()` call from my application code. It's extremely important that you remember to delete the `Saloon::fake()` call from your application code if you choose this approach. It will lead to your application code in production using the fake responses rather than making actual requests to the API. We definitely don't want this to happen!

Consider creating a fixture class that can be used to redact sensitive data from the response. For example, if you record your response from your application code outside a test, your response may include some personal data. To do this, you can create a class that extends the `Saloon\Http\Faking\Fixture` class. Let's create a basic example class that redacts the 'name' from the `laravel/framework` repository API response to show you how this works:

```
namespace Tests\Fixtures\Saloon\GitHub\Repos\Laravel\Framework;

use Saloon\Http\Faking\Fixture;

class RepoFixture extends Fixture
{
    protected function defineName(): string
    {
        return 'GitHub/Repos/Laravel/Framework/repo';
    }

    protected function defineSensitiveJsonParameters(): array
    {
        return [
            'name' => 'REDACTED',
        ];
    }
}
```

Using the `defineName` method, we specified where the response should be stored after it's been fetched. In this case, the file will be stored at `tests/Fixtures/GitHub/Repos/Laravel/Framework/repo.json`. We've then used the `defineSensitiveJsonParameters` method to specify that we want to redact the 'name' field from the response. This means that when the response is stored in the fixture, the 'name' field will be replaced with 'REDACTED'.

You can also add `defineSensitiveHeaders` and `defineSensitiveRegexPatterns` methods to your fixture class. These can redact sensitive headers or use regular expressions to redact sensitive data from the response body.

Once you have your fixture class, you can register it as a fake response like so:

```
use Saloon\Http\Faking\MockResponse;
use Saloon\Laravel\Facades\Saloon;
use Tests\Fixtures\Saloon\GitHub\Repos\Laravel\Framework\RepoFixture;

Saloon::fake([
    new RepoFixture(),
]);
```

Now that we know how to configure fixtures for recording responses, let's see how to use them in our tests. Imagine we're writing a test for the `getRepos` method in our `GitHub` class that uses paginated responses to get the repositories for a user. It may look something like this:

```
namespace Tests\Feature\Services\GitHub\GitHubService;

use App\DataTransferObjects\GitHub\Repo;
use App\Http\Integrations\GitHub\Requests\GetAuthUserRepos;
use App\Services\GitHub\GitHubService;
```

```php
use PHPUnit\Framework\Attributes\Test;
use Saloon\Http\Faking\MockResponse;
use Saloon\Laravel\Facades\Saloon;
use Tests\TestCase;

final class GetReposTest extends TestCase
{
    #[Test]
    public function repos_can_be_returned_from_paginated_response(): void
    {
        // Mock the responses for each page.
        Saloon::fake([
            MockResponse::fixture('GitHub/Repos/All/Page1'),
            MockResponse::fixture('GitHub/Repos/All/Page2'),
            MockResponse::fixture('GitHub/Repos/All/Page3'),
            MockResponse::fixture('GitHub/Repos/All/Page4'),
        ]);

        $gitHubService = new GitHubService(config('services.github.token'));

        $repos = $gitHubService->getRepos();

        // Assert the correct number of repos were returned.
        $this->assertCount(94, $repos);
        $repos->ensure(Repo::class);

        // Assert that all 4 requests were made with the correct query
        // parameters.
        foreach ([1,2,3,4] as $pageNumber) {
            Saloon::assertSent(static fn(GetAuthUserRepos $request): bool =>
                $request->query()->all() === [
```

```
                    'per_page' => 30,
                    'page' => $pageNumber,
                ]
            );
        }
    }
}
```

In the test, we start by faking the responses for the calls to be made to the API. Four requests will be made to the API, so we've registered four separate fixtures (one for each page). We've then created a new instance of our `GitHubService` class and called the `getRepos` method.

We've then asserted that the intended number of repositories have been returned and are all instances of our `Repo` data transfer object.

Finally, we've used a `foreach` loop to assert that all requests were sent with the correct query parameters to get the expected pages. This allows us to have more confidence that we're parsing the paginated responses correctly to determine the number of pages that need to be fetched.

Conclusion

In this chapter, we've covered what Saloon is, alternative approaches to using Saloon, and how to use it in your Laravel application. We went over features such as authentication, pagination, concurrent requests, plugins, error handling, API rate limits, caching, and testing. You should now feel confident enough to start using Saloon in your own applications to consume APIs.

In the next chapter, we'll be taking a look at OAuth. After understanding what OAuth is, we'll explore how to use Saloon to consume an OAuth API.

OAuth

So far, this book has covered how to consume APIs when we have direct access to API keys, like in our project's `.env` file or when a user inputs them. But what if we want to consume an API and don't already have these keys? What if we want to make requests to an API on a user's behalf? Or, allow users to sign in to our apps using third-party accounts (e.g., Twitter, Google, or GitHub)?

This section covers how we do this using OAuth. We'll explore what OAuth is, how it works, and how we can use it in our Laravel apps. We'll look at the benefits and drawbacks of using OAuth, the different flows in the OAuth 2.0 specification, and how you can use it to authorize user access via third-party services. We'll also step through how to use Saloon and the "authorization code grant" with Spotify so we can make requests to the Spotify API on behalf of a user. Following this, we'll examine how you can write tests for your OAuth integration.

What is OAuth?

The abstract from the original RFC (request for comments) for OAuth 2.0 gives an excellent overview of what OAuth is:

"The OAuth 2.0 authorization framework enables a third-party application to obtain limited access to an HTTP service, either on behalf of a resource owner by orchestrating an approval interaction between the resource owner and the HTTP service, or by allowing the third-party application to obtain access on its own behalf. This specification replaces and obsoletes the OAuth 1.0 protocol described in RFC 5849."

Essentially, OAuth (**O**pen **Auth**orization) is a way for a user or machine to grant access to their account on a third-party service to another application. This allows the application to make requests to the third-party service on behalf of the user or machine.

There are various "flows" that OAuth can use to achieve this. One that you'll likely have come across when using web applications is the "Authorization Code" flow. This is usually used when you sign in to a web application using a third-party service, like when you see a "Sign in with Google" button.

Note that not every service provides an OAuth 2.0 implementation to authorize users. Some services may still use OAuth 1.0 (which has been superseded by OAuth 2.0, so we won't cover it) or might not provide any OAuth implementation. If you're looking to add OAuth to your application, you'll need to check whether the service you want to integrate with provides an OAuth implementation and, if so, which version of OAuth it uses. This may affect your decision on whether to use OAuth or not for the feature you're adding to your Laravel application.

At the time of writing, OAuth 2.0 is the current specification, so most OAuth implementations you'll come across will likely be built to adhere to this specification. However, the specification for OAuth 2.1 is publicly available and currently in draft. Most of the OAuth 2.1 specification is the same as the OAuth 2.0 specification. Still, there are some changes, such as removing the "Implicit" flow and the "Resource Owner Password Credentials" flow, which are both deprecated in

OAuth 2.0. Security improvements include requiring PKCE (Proof Key for Code Exchange) for the "Authorization Code" flow rather than recommending it.

Use Cases for OAuth

As a result of the number of flows that OAuth supports, it provides several use cases. Some of the most common use cases are:

Single-Sign-On (SSO)

You can use OAuth to allow users to identify themselves on your application using a third-party service. This is sometimes called "social sign-in" and is a common feature of many web applications. You may have encountered this when signing in to a web application, and you're presented with a "Sign in with Google" or "Sign in with Twitter" button.

This can benefit users because they don't have to remember a new set of credentials for your application when signing in. Instead, they can use existing credentials from a third-party service. It can also reduce friction for users signing up for your application for the first time because they don't have to fill out a registration form.

It can also benefit you as a developer because you don't have to handle the authentication of a user directly. Instead, you can let the third-party service handle this, so you don't have to worry about storing passwords securely or handling password resets.

Third-Party API Access

You can use OAuth to make API requests to third-party services on behalf of your application's users. Imagine you have a booking system application. Building an OAuth integration would allow your users to connect their account on your application to their account on a third-party service, in this case, an accounting service such as Xero or QuickBooks. This would allow you to make requests to the accounting service on behalf of the user, such as automatically recording sales data whenever bookings are made.

Authenticating on Smart Devices

Although you'll unlikely encounter this use case in your Laravel applications, you can use OAuth for authenticating on smart devices.

Using the "Device Code" flow (which we'll cover in more detail later), you can authenticate on devices with limited input capabilities or can't easily display a web page. This is useful for devices such as smart TVs and apps on gaming consoles or streaming devices.

For example, you may have come across this when you've tried to sign in to YouTube or Netflix on a smart TV. Instead of being presented with a web page to sign in, you're instead presented with a code you must enter on another device (such as your phone or computer) to authenticate. This uses the "Device Code" flow and is a great example of how OAuth can be used to authenticate on devices with limited input capabilities. Typing out a long password with uppercase letters, lowercase letters, numbers, and symbols on a TV remote is a nightmare!

Server-to-Server Authorization

Another use case for OAuth is for server-to-server communication, particularly in internal applications. This is often referred to as "machine-to-machine" communication. This type of communication differs from the other use cases we've looked at because it doesn't involve a user. Instead, it's used to allow one application to make requests to another application on behalf of itself.

This type of communication is typically carried out using the "Client Credentials" grant, covered later in this section. For example, suppose we have an application that books flights. The application may need to make an API call to another server to fetch the available flights. No one "owns" the flights, so we don't need to act on behalf of a user to access them. As a result, this means we can use the Client Credentials grant to get an access token that we can then use to access the list of flights.

OAuth Terminology

If you've never worked with OAuth before, the terminology may be overwhelming. So, let's look at some common terms you'll come across and what they mean.

OAuth Roles

OAuth revolves around four main roles. Each role plays a part in the OAuth flow. These roles are:

- **Resource Owner** - The user authorizing the application to access their account on the external service.
- **Client** - The application that wants to access the user's account on the external service.
- **Resource Server** - The server on the external service that hosts the user's account or data we're trying to access.
- **Authorization Server** - The server on the external service that verifies the user's identity and issues tokens back to the "client" application.

To give these roles more context, let's look at an example. Imagine you are building a web application allowing users to sign in using their Twitter account. In this example, the roles would be:

- **Resource Owner** - The user signing into your application using their Twitter account.
- **Client** - Your application.
- **Resource Server** - Twitter.
- **Authorization Server** - Twitter.

It's worth noting that in diagrams and literature, the authorization server and resource server are often shown as being two separate entities. However, in practice, this isn't always the case. Depending on which service you're integrating with, the authorization and resource servers may be the same. In general, this shouldn't affect how you build your integration because you shouldn't need to know what the service's infrastructure looks like. You only need to know the endpoints that you need to make requests to. But you should keep this in mind if you wish to build your own OAuth service.

Flows and Grants

In the OAuth 2.0 specification, the term "flow" is used to describe the process of how a user authorizes an application to access their data. The term "grant" describes the credentials used in the flow. However, in practice, these terms are often used interchangeably.

The flows available in the OAuth 2.0 specification are:

- Authorization Code
- Authorization Code with Proof Key for Code Exchange (PKCE)
- Client Credentials
- Device Code
- Refresh Token
- Implicit Flow
- Password Grant

We'll delve into each of these flows later in this section.

Tokens

In OAuth, tokens play a huge role in the authorization process. There are generally three types of tokens that are used in OAuth:

- **Authorization code** - A typically short-lived token used to verify a user has authorized an application to access their account on the external service. This is also called "authorization token". This token is usually only used once and is then exchanged for an access token.

- **Access token** - A token used to make requests to the external service on behalf of the user (usually sent as a bearer token in HTTP request headers). It's typically short-lived and usually lasts several hours or days, depending on the service. This token is usually used until it expires, at which point it may be refreshed.
- **Refresh token** - A long-lived token used to refresh the access token when it expires in some flows, such as the Authorization Code flow. This token is usually only used once and is exchanged for a new access token.

Note that not every flow uses all three of these tokens. For example, the Authorization Code flow can use all three tokens, whereas the Client Credentials flow only uses the access token.

Client ID and Client Secret

You'll often come across two terms in OAuth: "client ID" and "client secret". These are like a username and password for your application. Let's delve into these.

Say you're building a Laravel application and want to allow users to connect GitHub accounts to your app. Before you can start writing any code, you must go to GitHub and create a new "OAuth app". Depending on which third-party service you're trying to build the integration for, you might also see these referred to as "applications", "integrations", and so on. To create this OAuth app, you'll have to provide information such as the name of your application, a description, and a URL to your application's homepage. This is used on the website of the third-party service when it presents something like "[APP NAME] wants to access your [THIRD PARTY SERVICE] account. Do you want to grant them access?". This allows the user to know which application they're authorizing.

After creating your OAuth app, you'll be provided with a client ID. If your application is a "confidential client", you'll also be provided with a client secret. These credentials aren't for your account but for the app you've just created. When you make API requests to the authorization server to generate access tokens (covered later), you'll need to pass these credentials — one or both, depending on the grant type you're using).

You'll want to ensure that if you are building separate applications, you create separate "OAuth apps" in your third-party service for each application. For example, say you want to add Google OAuth integrations for two applications you own: a booking system application and a CRM application. You'll want to create separate OAuth apps in Google for each application. Even if the use cases for the applications are very similar, you'll still want to keep them separate.

By separating the apps, you'll reduce the amount of confusion for users. If the user were trying to connect their Google account to the booking system, they would expect to see a message saying something along the lines of "[BOOKING SYSTEM] wants to access your Google account", not "[CRM] wants to access your Google account".

As well as this, if the user has an account on both systems and decides to revoke access to one of them, they should still be able to use the other. However, if both applications use the same OAuth app, this would revoke access to both applications, which is not likely what they'd want.

Public and Confidential Clients

The OAuth 2.0 specification defines two types of clients: public and confidential. The main difference between the two is that confidential clients can securely store their credentials and keep the client secret a secret, whereas public clients cannot.

For instance, if you're building an OAuth integration in a Laravel app and storing your OAuth credentials on your server, this would be considered a confidential client because no one else can access your server and view your credentials. Since confidential clients can securely store their credentials, they can use the following flows:

- Authorization Code
- Authorization Code with Proof Key for Code Exchange (PKCE)
- Resource Owner Password Credentials
- Client Credentials
- Refresh Token

On the other hand, if you're building a JavaScript application that runs in the browser and doesn't have a server-side component, this would be considered a public client because anyone can view your application's source code and see your credentials. Since public clients cannot securely store their credentials, they can only use the following flows:

- Authorization Code with Proof Key for Code Exchange (PKCE)
- Implicit
- Refresh Token

Scopes

In OAuth, the term "scope" refers to the abilities the client requests from the user. Think of them as permissions you're allowing the application to have.

For example, GitHub provides a number of scopes you can request when using their OAuth integration. If a user were to use the Authorization Code flow to sign in to your application using their GitHub account, they would be presented with a screen that asks whether the application can access their GitHub account and lists the scopes the application is requesting. The user can then allow or deny the application access to their account.

By using scopes and limiting what the tokens can be used for, we can reduce the risk of a malicious application gaining access to a user's account and doing something the user didn't intend. It can also help to give the user peace of mind that the application isn't going to do anything they don't want it to do. For instance, you wouldn't want to give an application access to all your private repositories on GitHub if you only want it to access your public repositories or use it to sign in to your account.

OAuth 2.0 Flows

With a basic understanding of the OAuth terminology, let's look at some of the OAuth flows.

We'll go into more depth with the Authorization Code flow, which you will most likely come across when building Laravel applications. However, we'll also look at other flows to understand how they work and what they aim to achieve.

Authorization Code Grant

The "Authorization Code" flow is the one you'll likely come across the most when using and building web applications. Whenever you see a button such as "Sign in with Google" or "Connect to Twitter", this is usually used behind the scenes. Later in this section, we'll look at how to use Saloon to connect to a user's account using the Authorization Code flow and then fetch their private repositories.

The Authorization Code flow revolves around making a request to an authorization server to create an "authorization code" and then exchanging this code for an "access token" that can be used to make any future API requests.

To get a better understanding of how this flow works, let's look at a diagram that shows the steps involved:

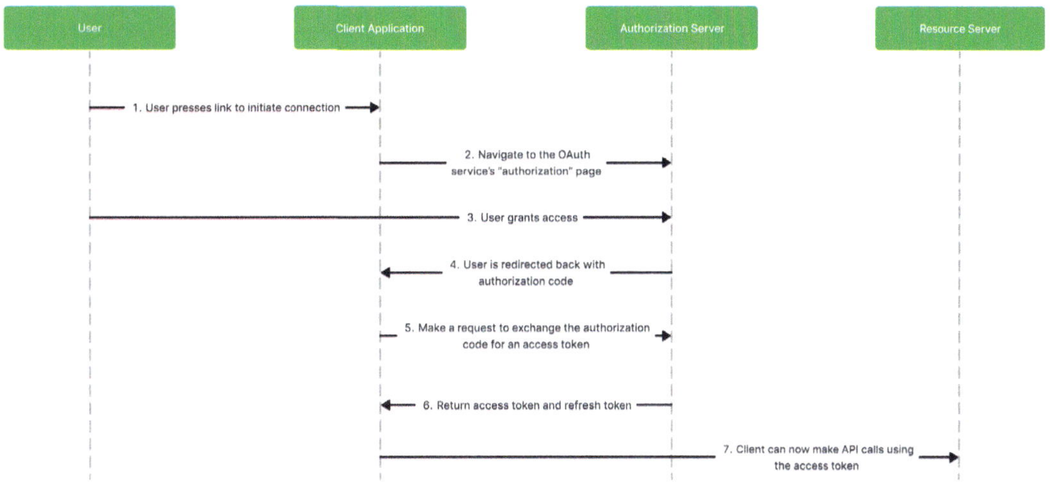

Let's break down the individual steps that are being taken and how they work:

1. Request Authorization from the User

The user first starts by clicking a link (such as "Connect to GitHub") in the client application, which redirects them to the authorization server's "authorization endpoint" (in this example, that's `https://app.com/oauth/authorize`) using a URL such as the following:

```
https://app.com/oauth/authorize?response_type=code
    &client_id=CLIENT_ID
    &redirect_uri=https://example.com/oauth/callback
    &scope=read
    &state=xyz
```

In the above URL, we're passing the following query parameters:

- `response_type` - By specifying the value of `code`, we're telling the authorization server to use the Authorization Code flow and expect an authorization code when the user is redirected back to the client application.
- `client_id` - The client ID of the OAuth integration generated when you created your OAuth app in the third-party service.
- `redirect_uri` - The URL you want the user to be redirected back to after they have authorized the application. This URL must match one of the redirect URIs you have pre-registered in your OAuth app settings. For this example, we've specified that the user should be redirected back to `https://example.com/oauth/callback`.
- `scope` - Specifies the permissions that the client is requesting from the user.
- `state` - A cryptographically secure string used to prevent CSRF (Cross-Site Request Forgery) attacks. This will be stored in the user's session and compared against the value returned by the authorization server to ensure that the request is legitimate. The field is optional, but it's highly recommended that you always use it.

2. Redirect Back to the Client Application

At this stage, the user should be presented with a screen asking something like, "Do you want to allow [CLIENT_NAME] to access your account?". After the user clicks "Allow", the authorization server will redirect the user back to the client application using the `redirect_uri` field that was originally passed. An example response that the server may return to redirect the user could be:

```
HTTP/3 302 Found
Location:
https://example.com/oauth/callback?code=SplxlOBeZQQYbYS6WxSbIA&state=xyz
```

This redirect URL will contain the following query parameters:

- `code` - The authorization code generated by the authorization server we will use to exchange for an access token.
- `state` - The same state we passed in the original request. We'll compare this to the `state` field stored in the user's session to verify that the request is legitimate.

3. Generate an Access Token

Now that the client application has an authorization code, it's time to exchange it for an access token that can be used to make API requests. To do this, a `POST` request is made to the authorization server's "token endpoint" (in this example, `https://app.com/oauth/token`) using the following request structure:

```
POST oauth/token HTTP/3
Host: example.com
Authorization: Basic Q0xJRU5UX0lEOkNMSUVOVF9TRUNSRVQ=

grant_type=authorization_code
&code=Splxl0BeZQQYbYS6WxSbIA
&redirect_uri=https://example.com/oauth/callback
```

In the above request, we're passing the following parameters:

- `grant_type` - The type of grant that we're using. In this case, we're using the "authorization_code" grant type to indicate that we're using the Authorization Code flow.
- `code` - The authorization code we received in the previous step.
- `redirect_uri` - The same redirect URI passed in the original request, used to verify the request is legitimate and has not been tampered with.

You may have also noticed the request contains an `Authorization` header. This header contains the client ID and client secret, concatenated as `client_id:client_secret` then base-64 encoded. This is a recommendation of the OAuth 2.0 specification and is used to authenticate the client application with the authorization server.

After receiving the above `POST` request, the authorization server should respond with an HTTP response similar to the following:

```
HTTP/3 200 OK

{
    "access_token":"2YotnFZFEjr1zCsicMWpAA",
    "token_type":"Bearer",
    "expires_in":3600,
    "refresh_token":"tGzv3JOkF0XG5Qx2TlKWIA",
}
```

The response should contain the following fields:

- `access_token` - The access token used to make API requests on behalf of the user.
- `token_type` - The type of token being returned. In this case, it's a "Bearer" token.
- `expires_in` - The number of seconds for which the access token is valid. In this case, it's valid for 3600 seconds (1 hour).
- `refresh_token` - A refresh token that can be used to generate a new access token when the current one expires. We'll discuss this in more detail later in this section.

Now that the client has the `access_token`, the application can make requests on the user's behalf.

You might have noticed that we needed to pass the client secret in the request to the token endpoint. So what happens if you're building a public client (such as a native application) where you can't securely store your client secret? That's where the "Proof Key for Code Exchange" (PKCE) extension comes in. Let's look at how that works next.

Authorization Code Grant with PKCE

The Authorization Code Grant with Proof Key for Code Exchange (PKCE) is an extension to the Authorization Code Grant that has an extra step to increase the security of the flow. Using PKCE (usually pronounced "pixie") in the Authorization Code flow is recommended for public clients that cannot securely store client secrets.

Although PKCE is a security feature initially intended for public clients (such as single-page apps and native applications), the OAuth 2.0 specification recommends you implement it in confidential clients, too. The OAuth 2.1 specification defines that PKCE will be mandatory for all Authorization Code grants. However, it's important to note that PKCE is not a replacement for the client secret. If you're building a confidential client, you should still use a client secret and pass it to the authorization server when making a request for an authorization token. It's just another layer of security. And the more layers you can add, the better.

Let's take a look at the steps involved in the Authorization Code with PKCE flow:

1. Request Authorization from the User

Similar to the traditional Authorization Code grant, we make a `GET` request to the authorization server's "authorization endpoint" (in this case `https://app.com/oauth/authorize`) to request the user's permission to access their account. The URL may look something like this:

```
https://app.com/oauth/authorize?response_type=code
    &client_id=CLIENT_ID
    &redirect_uri=https://example.com/oauth/callback
    &scope=read
    &state=xyz
    &code_challenge=CODE_CHALLENGE
    &code_challenge_method=S256
```

You may have noticed that the request data differs slightly from the traditional Authorization Code grant. The Authorization Code with PKCE flow includes two additional fields: `code_challenge` and `code_challenge_method`. These fields are integral to the PKCE extension, so let's examine how they work.

Before the client makes a request to the authorization server, the client must first generate a cryptographically secure string between 43 and 128 characters long that can use uppercase letters, lowercase letters, numbers, hyphens (-), periods (.), underscores (_), and tildes (~). This string is referred to as the "code verifier". The client then generates a hash of the code verifier using a hashing algorithm such as SHA-256. This hash is referred to as the "code challenge". At this stage, the client will need to temporarily store the code verifier string because it will need to be passed to the authorization server when exchanging the authorization code for an access token later. So, it may be stored in a cookie, local storage, cache, or database.

The code challenge is then base64-encoded and passed in the authorization request in the `code_challenge` field. The hashing method is passed in the `code_challenge_method` field. For example, if we used the SHA-256 hashing algorithm, we would pass `S256` in the `code_challenge_method` field.

2. Redirect Back to the Client Application

After the user has granted the client application permission to access their account, the authorization server will redirect the user back to the client application in the same way as the traditional Authorization Code grant. The redirect may look like this:

```
HTTP/3 302 Found
Location: https://example.com/cb?code=Splxl0BeZQQYbYS6WxSbIA&state=xyz
```

3. Generate an Access Token

Similar to the traditional Authorization Code grant, now that the client application has an authorization code, a `POST` request can be made to the authorization server's "token endpoint" (in this case `https://app.com/oauth/token`) to exchange the authorization code for an access token. However, the only difference here is that we must also pass the original code verifier string generated in step 1 in the `code_verifier` field.

If the request is made using a public client (where the client secret cannot be stored correctly), the client ID can be passed in the request body. The request may look like this:

```
POST /oauth/token HTTP/3
Host: app.com

grant_type=authorization_code
&code=AUTHORIZATION_CODE
&redirect_uri=https://example.com/oauth/callback
&client_id=CLIENT_ID
&code_verifier=CODE_VERIFIER
```

However, suppose the request is made using a confidential client (where the client secret can be stored securely). In that case, the client ID and client secret can both be passed in the concatenated, base-64 encoded format in the `Authorization` header. The request may look like this:

```
POST /oauth/token HTTP/3
Host: app.com
Authorization: Basic Q0xJRU5UX0lEOkNMSUVOVF9TRUNSRVQ=

grant_type=authorization_code
&code=AUTHORIZATION_CODE
&redirect_uri=https://example.com/oauth/callback
&code_verifier=CODE_VERIFIER
```

The authorization server now has the original code verifier string, the hashing method used, and the expected hashed value. This means the authorization server can attempt to hash the code verifier string and see if the hashes match the hashed value we had originally passed in the `code_challenge` field. If the hashes match, the server can be confident the request was made by the client that made the original authorization request, so an access token can be generated and returned. However, if the hashes don't match, the request is invalid and potentially from a malicious application that may have intercepted the initial request or response. Therefore, an access token won't be generated or returned.

If the request is valid and the token exchange is successful, the authorization server should return the following response:

```
HTTP/3 200 OK

{
    "access_token":"2YotnFZFEjr1zCsicMWpAA",
    "token_type":"Bearer",
    "expires_in":3600,
    "refresh_token":"tGzv3JOkF0XG5Qx2TlKWIA",
}
```

This response is the same as the response from the traditional Authorization Code grant and can be used to access the API on the user's behalf.

Refresh Token Grant

Another grant type defined in the OAuth 2.0 specification is the "Refresh Token" grant. The Refresh Token grant works slightly differently from the other grants discussed in this book. All the other grants are typically used to fetch an access token on behalf of the resource owner after they've authorized the client. However, the Refresh Token grant is used to fetch a new access token after the previous one has expired. You'll typically see it used with the Authorization Code grant, Device Code grant, and Resource Owner Password Credentials grant.

As mentioned, access tokens are usually short-lived. They can have a lifetime ranging from a few hours to several weeks. This is done to improve the user's security by ensuring that if the token is compromised, it can only be used for a short time. However, what happens when this token expires? It would be incredibly frustrating if the user had to re-authorize the client whenever their access token expired. This is where the Refresh Token grant comes in.

As we saw in the Authorization Code grant, when the authorization server returns the access token, it also returns a refresh token.

You would typically store the refresh token in a secure location, such as your application's database. When the access token expires, you can pass the refresh token to the authorization server to get a new access token and refresh token. Then, when that new access token expires, you can repeat the process with your new refresh token. And so on.

Since the access token is continuously passed around in requests, it could be intercepted or stolen. However, the refresh token is typically only ever transmitted twice: once when it's issued and once when it's used to get a new access token. This means the chances of compromising a refresh token are much lower.

Here is a diagram giving a high-level overview of the steps involved in the Refresh Token flow:

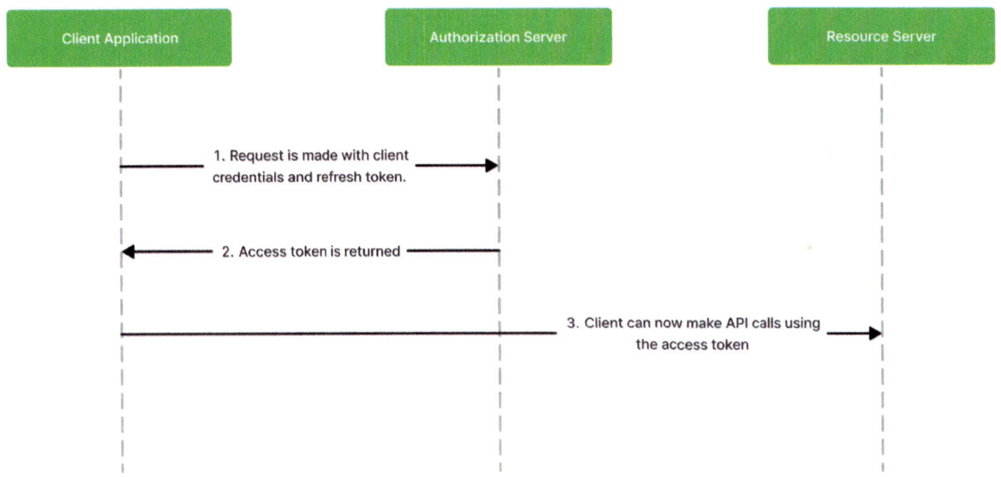

When the Refresh Token grant is used, new scopes can't be requested. Instead, the refresh token can only be used to fetch a new access token with the same (or fewer) scopes as the previous one.

Assuming that the client is a public client (meaning it cannot store the client secret securely) and has a valid refresh token, the request to the authorization server may look like this:

```
POST /oauth/token HTTP/3
Host: app.com

grant_type=refresh_token
&refresh_token=REFRESH_TOKEN
&client_id=CLIENT_ID
```

However, if the client is a confidential client (meaning it can store the client secret securely), we can pass the client ID and client secret in concatenated, base-64 encoded format using the `Authorization` header the request may look like so:

```
POST /oauth/token HTTP/3
Host: app.com
Authorization: Basic Q0xJRU5UX0lEOkNMSUVOVF9TRUNSRVQ=

grant_type=refresh_token
&refresh_token=REFRESH_TOKEN
```

As you may have noticed, the request is very similar to the request for the Authorization Code grant. The only difference is that the `grant_type` is set to `refresh_token`, and the `refresh_token` field is set to the refresh token we want to use to get a new access token.

At this stage, the authorization server may use additional security measures to ensure the refresh token is valid. These measures can include:

- Ensuring the refresh token belongs to the client ID
- Ensuring the refresh token hasn't been revoked
- Ensuring the refresh token hasn't expired
- (Optional) Ensuring the refresh token hasn't already been used
- (Optional) Attempting to prove that the request is coming from the client that originally requested the refresh token (using techniques such as "Mutual Transport Layer Security" (mTLS) method or the "OAuth 2.0 Demonstrating Proof-of-Possession at the Application Layer" (DPoP) method).

If all the security checks pass, the authorization server will return a response in the same format as the response from the Authorization Code grant. An example response may look like so:

```
HTTP/3 200 OK

{
    "access_token":"kF0XG5QxGzv325Qx2T",
    "token_type":"Bearer",
    "expires_in":3600,
    "refresh_token":"tG0XWIG5QxJOkF2Tlzv3KA",
}
```

At this stage, the client application can then store and use the new access token to access the API on the user's behalf. The client can also store the new refresh token to use when the access token expires.

Client Credentials Grant

Another flow defined in the OAuth 2.0 specification is the Client Credentials grant. The Client Credentials grant is slightly different from the other grant types we've discussed so far in that it does not typically involve a user. Instead, the Client Credentials grant is used for machine-to-machine communication (such as between multiple servers) where the client requests access to resources that it owns rather than acting on behalf of a user.

For example, imagine we are building an application that aggregates data about the weather. We may need an API to fetch the weather data from another server or machine to aggregate it. We could use the Client Credentials flow to get an access token that we can use to access the weather API. The weather API would be the resource server, and our application would be the client and resource owner.

Since the Client Credentials grant is typically used for server-to-server API calls, it can only be used in confidential clients. The grant involves the client passing their client ID and client secret to the authorization server to retrieve an access token. So, this flow does not use any authorization codes and involves a single HTTP request to get an access token.

As we've already covered, the Authorization Code grant can use refresh tokens so that the user isn't required to regularly re-authorize the application. However, since the Client Credentials grant doesn't involve a user, there's no need to use refresh tokens. Instead, the client can just request a new access token whenever the old one expires.

Here is a diagram giving a high-level overview of the steps involved in the Client Credentials flow:

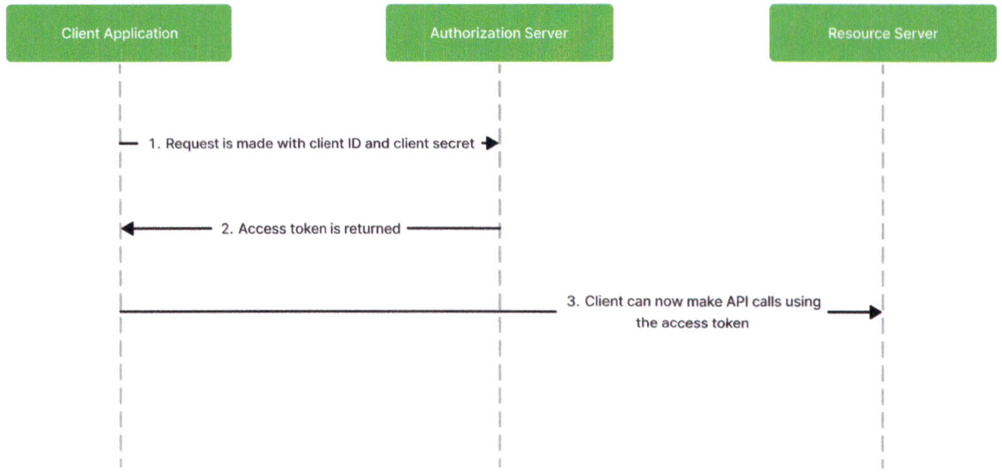

Let's look at the steps in the Client Credentials grant in more detail.

The client application starts by making a request to the authorization server's token endpoint (in this example, `https://app.com/oauth/token`). The request may look like this:

```
POST /oauth/token HTTP/3
Host: app.com
Authorization: Basic Q0xJRU5UX0lEOkNMSUVOVF9TRUNSRVQ=

grant_type=client_credentials
&scope=read
```

As we can see above, the request only contains two parameters:

- `grant_type` - Set to `client_credentials` to indicate we want to use the Client Credentials grant.
- `scope` - An optional parameter that can be used to request specific scopes. In this example, we're requesting the `read` scope.

You may have also noticed that the request also uses the `Authorization` header. As with other flows we've covered, the value of this header is the client ID and client secret concatenated and base-64 encoded.

Assuming that the request is valid, the authorization server can then return a response containing the access token like so:

```
HTTP/3 200 OK

{
    "access_token":"kF0XG5QxGzv325Qx2T",
    "token_type":"Bearer",
    "expires_in":3600,
}
```

As we can see above, the response is very similar to the response from the Authorization Code grant. The only difference is that the response does not contain a refresh token. This is because the Client Credentials grant does not involve a user, so there's no need to use refresh tokens, as we've already discussed. When the current access token expires, the client can simply request a new one using the above HTTP request.

Device Code Grant

The Device Code grant is a special OAuth flow that enables devices with no web browser or limited input capability to obtain an access token. As mentioned, the Device Code grant is used on devices like smart TVs, game consoles, and streaming devices to enable users to sign in to applications without needing to use an onboard browser.

You may have already used this grant type — for example, if you sign in to Netflix or YouTube on your TV, you may see a screen that either allows you to enter your username and password or generate a code (perhaps a PIN or QR code). If you don't want to go through the cumbersome process of typing your username and password on a TV remote, you can visit a specified URL on another device (like your phone) to sign in and enter the code you see on your TV. After, you'll be signed in to your account on your TV.

This flow is useful because it allows you to use devices with better input capabilities and access your device's password manager. (*You are using a password manager, right?*) This means you don't need to use the clunky onboard keyboard on the streaming device or smart TV to enter a long password comprised of mixed-case letters, numbers, and symbols. The Device Code Grant flow can add complexity to the sign-in process because multiple devices and the authorization server are involved.

Here is a diagram giving a high-level overview of the steps involved in the Device Code flow:

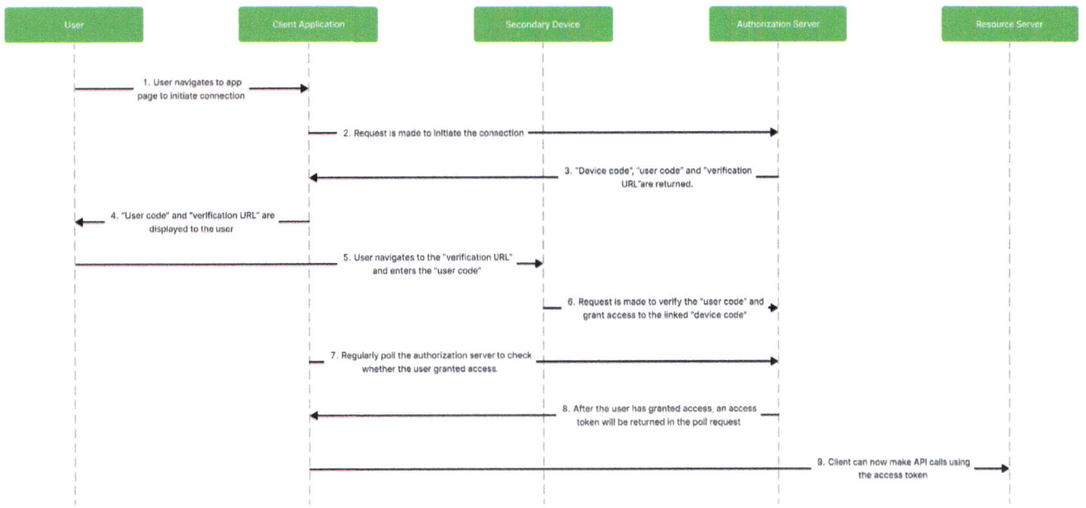

Let's look at the steps involved in the Device Code grant.

The first step is for the client application, running on the device, to make a `POST` request to the authorization server's device authorization endpoint (in this example `https://app.com/oauth/authorize`). The request may look like this:

```
POST /oauth/authorize HTTP/3
Host: app.com

response_type=device_code
&client_id=CLIENT_ID
```

As we can see, the request contains the following fields:

- `response_type` - Set to `device_code` to indicate we want to use the Device Code grant.

- `client_id` - The client ID of the client application.

The authorization server will then return a response to the device like this:

```
HTTP/3 200 OK

{
    "device_code":"kF0XG5QxGzv325Qx2T",
    "verification_uri":"https://app.com/verify",
    "user_code":"5Qx25Qx2",
    "expires_in":3600,
    "interval":5
}
```

The response contains the following data:

- `device_code` - A code the device can use to poll the authorization server to check if the user has signed in.
- `verification_uri` - A URL the user can visit on another device to sign in. This URL will usually be displayed on the page at this stage, typically as a link, short URL, or QR code.
- `user_code` - A code the user can enter on another device to sign in. This code will usually be displayed on the device at this stage.
- `expires_in` - The number of seconds for which the device code is valid.
- `interval` - The number of seconds the device should wait before polling the authorization server to check if the user has signed in. In this case, the device should poll the authorization server every 5 seconds to see if the user has signed in on the other device.

At this stage, the user would now navigate to the `verification_uri` on another device, such as a phone or computer. The user may need to sign in to their account using their username and password. Once the user is signed in, they can enter the code specified in the `user_code` field.

After the user has entered the code, the authorization server can associate the device code with the user's account and confirm that the user has signed in.

While the user is authorizing access on the other device, the original client application will regularly poll the authorization server to check if the user has signed in. The client application will make a `POST` request to the authorization server's token endpoint (in this example `https://app.com/oauth/token`). The request may look like this:

```
POST /oauth/token HTTP/3
Host: app.com

grant_type=device_code
&device_code=kF0XG5QxGzv325Qx2T
&client_id=CLIENT_ID
```

If the user has not yet signed in, the authorization server will return a response that looks like this:

```
HTTP/3 400 Bad Request

{
    "error":"authorization_pending",
}
```

By returning this response, the client application on the device knows the user has not yet signed in and should continue to poll the authorization server. Once the user has authorized access through the secondary device, the authorization server will return a response to the polling request that looks like this:

```
HTTP/3 200 OK

{
    "access_token":"kF0XG5QxGzv325Qx2T",
    "token_type":"Bearer",
    "expires_in":3600,
    "refresh_token":"tG0XWIG5QxJ0kF2Tlzv3KA",
}
```

As we can see, the response contains access and refresh tokens. These can then be used to make requests to the resource server on behalf of the user.

You might wonder, "Wait! There's no PKCE, client secret, or state involved here?". That's correct. Firstly, PKCE is used in conjunction with the Authorization Code grant because that flow involves redirecting the user, so there's potential for the authorization code to be stolen from the URL. However, the Device Code grant does not involve redirecting the user, so PKCE would not be useful here. Secondly, the client secret cannot be used in the Device Code grant because the client application is deemed a public client, so the secret cannot be stored securely. Finally, the state parameter is not used because the Device Code grant does not involve redirecting the user, so there's no need to use the state parameter to prevent CSRF attacks.

Instead, a large portion of this flow's security comes from the fact that the user needs to sign in on a secondary device. As it is unlikely that both devices would be compromised, the security of the flow is increased.

Implicit Grant

Another flow in the OAuth 2.0 specification is the "Implicit" flow. This flow is not recommended, but it's worth being able to recognize it if you come across it when working on an existing application.

It's similar to the Authorization Code flow but has a missing step. With the Authorization Code flow, a request is made to get an authorization code; another request is then made with that code to exchange it for a token. With the Implicit flow, we don't have this extra step of exchanging the authorization code for an access token. Instead, in our first request, we get the access token back in response. This means there is never any use of the client secret or PKCE to protect the process.

The Implicit flow was created to support public clients, such as native apps and single-page applications (SPAs) written in JavaScript. At the time this flow was created, Cross-Origin Resource Sharing (CORS) wasn't widely supported. CORS is a mechanism that allows a web browser to make requests to a different domain than the one the application is hosted on. This meant browsers couldn't make a `POST` request to exchange an authorization token for an access token like in the Authorization Code flow. So, the Implicit flow was created to support these types of applications.

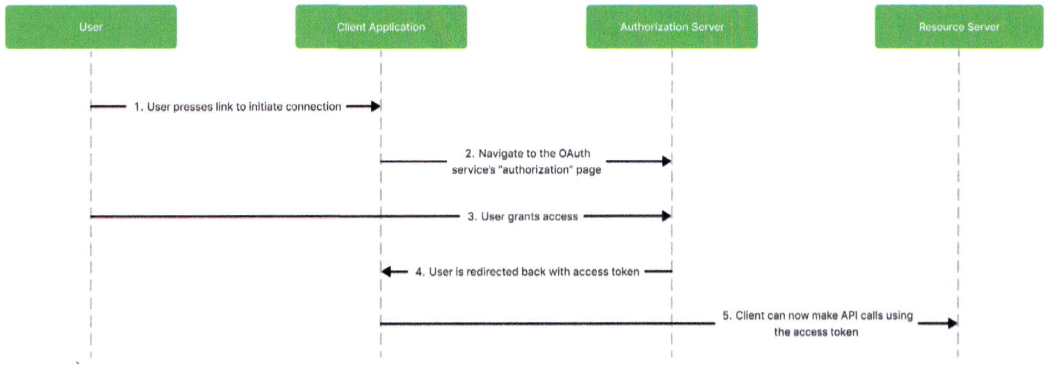

Let's take a look at the steps involved in the Implicit flow.

The client application starts by making a request to the authorization server's authorization endpoint (in this example, `https://app.com/oauth/authorize`). The URL may look like this:

```
https://app.com/oauth/authorize?response_type=token
    &client_id=CLIENT_ID
    &redirect_uri=https://example.com/oauth/callback
    &scope=read
    &state=xyz
```

The request contains the following parameters:

- `response_type` - Set to `token` to indicate we want to use the Implicit flow.
- `client_id` - The ID of the client application (this will have been automatically generated when you created the application in the third-party service).
- `redirect_uri` - The URI the authorization server will redirect the user to after logging in and authorizing the application. This will be a URI configured in your application.
- `scope` - The permissions the application is requesting access to.
- `state` - An optional parameter used to prevent CSRF attacks.

As with the Authorization Code grant, the authorization server will then redirect the user to the application's login page. After the user has permitted access, they'll be redirected back to the application with the following redirect:

```
HTTP/3 302 Found
Location: https://example.com/oauth/callback
          #access_token=2YotnFZFEjr1zCsicMWpAA
          &token_type=Bearer
          &state=xyz
          &expires_in=3600
```

Note the new lines have been to the `Location` header for readability purposes. The redirect would be on a single line in the actual response.

As we can see in the above redirect, all the information we need is in the URL itself. No more requests need to be made to the authorization server (as would be needed in the Authorization Code grant). Instead, the client can start making requests on behalf of the user straight away.

It's worth noting that the `access_token` is delivered as a fragment (using a `#`) rather than a query string. URL fragments aren't transmitted to the servers when making requests, so it helps to keep the token client-side only. Doing this can decrease the chance of the token being logged or cached on the server.

You may have also noticed that the response doesn't include a refresh token. That's because the Implicit flow is deemed not secure enough to allow refresh tokens to be issued. Therefore, if the access token expires, the user must go through the authorization flow again to generate a new access token.

The OAuth 2.0 specification acknowledges the security issues in the Implicit flow. Now that cross-origin requests are possible due to CORS being widely supported, it's strongly advised to avoid using the Implicit flow. Instead, it's advised that the Authorization Code with PKCE grant is used instead. The OAuth 2.1 specification does not include the Implicit flow at all.

Resource Owner Password Grant

Another grant type in the OAuth 2.0 specification is the "Resource Owner Password" (ROPC) grant. It's highly recommended by the OAuth specification that you don't use it due to security concerns, but you should be able to recognize this if you encounter it.

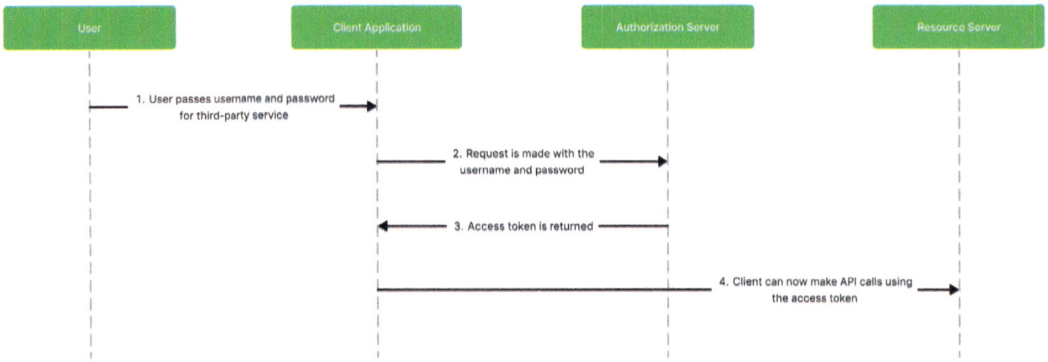

At its core, ROPC is a simple flow where the client application makes a `POST` request to the authorization server's "token endpoint" (in this example, `https://app.com/oauth/token`) using the user's username and password for the third-party service. The request looks like this:

```
POST /oauth/token HTTP/3
Host: app.com
Authorization: Basic Q0xJRU5UX0lEOkNMSUVOVF9TRUNSRVQ=

grant_type=password
&username=USERNAME
&password=PASSWORD
&scope=read
```

The request contains the following parameters:

- `grant_type` - Set to `password` to indicate that we want to use the ROPC grant.
- `username` - The username of the user's account on the third-party service.

- `password` - The password of the user's account on the third-party service.
- `scope` - The permissions the application is requesting access to.

As with the other grants we've covered, we include the client ID and client secret in the request's `Authorization` header as a Basic authentication header. The client ID and client secret are concatenated using `:` and base-64 encoded.

If the user's credentials are valid, the authorization server will then return the following response:

```
HTTP/3 200 OK

{
    "access_token":"kF0XG5QxGzv325Qx2T",
    "token_type":"Bearer",
    "expires_in":3600,
    "refresh_token":"tG0XWIG5QxJOkF2Tlzv3KA",
}
```

As with the flows we've covered, the access token can then be used to make requests to the API on behalf of the user. The refresh token can be used to request a new access token when the current one expires.

You may have noticed that this flow doesn't involve any user interaction on the OAuth applications part. For example, it doesn't require the user to accept that the application can access their account. Instead, all user interaction is carried out in the client application itself.

This grant type is not recommended because it exposes the user's third-party service credentials to the client application, which could store the user's credentials and use them to log in to the third-party service as the user. This is a huge security risk you should avoid at all costs. You should use the Authorization Code with PKCE grant type instead.

The ROPC grant type is discouraged by the OAuth 2.0 specification and will be removed from the OAuth 2.1 specification.

The Benefits of Using OAuth

OAuth can provide considerable benefits for your applications. These benefits can come in the form of user experience improvements for the users of your applications, as well as development improvements for you as a developer.

Let's look at some benefits of using OAuth to consume APIs from your Laravel applications.

Improved Security

When an OAuth flow is implemented correctly and securely, it can help to improve your users' security.

For example, if you use the Authorization Code Flow with PKCE to authorize with an external API, you'll typically be dealing with short-lived API tokens. Not only does this flow prevent the need for the user to share their credentials for third-party applications with you, but it also means that the tokens are scoped to specific resources and can only be used for what the user has granted access to.

For instance, if we want to access a user's profile information on GitHub, we could request the `read:user` scope. If the user grants us access, we can use the access token to make requests to the GitHub API to fetch their user profile data. However, we couldn't do anything else (such as creating new repositories or updating their user profile) because we didn't request any other scopes. Although scopes aren't specific to OAuth and could also be implemented as part of any other token generation system, OAuth encourages the use of scopes to provide a more granular level of access control that the user can understand and can explicitly grant or deny access to.

Additionally, if short-lived tokens are used, it reduces the risk of a token being compromised in case of a leak or breach compared to a long-lived token (or one that never expires).

Improved User Experience

Depending on the type of application you're building, your application's users may not know what an API is. So, asking them for an API token may alienate your users and make it more difficult to use your application.

Imagine you're building a recipe website where avid cooks and bakers share recipes. You want to provide the functionality for your users to share recipes with their friends and followers on Facebook. If you asked your users to sign in to their Facebook accounts and generate API keys, you wouldn't likely get many users to do it. A few users who fancy a challenge or are keen on sharing their recipes may try, but this would seem like an unnecessary and complicated step for a majority of users. However, providing a "Connect to Facebook" button would allow users to connect their Facebook account to your application. You'd likely see a much higher adoption rate as users don't need to know what an API is or how to generate API keys. They just need to click a button and grant your application access to their Facebook account.

On the other hand, if you're building a developer-focused application where users are likely to be developers who understand what an API is, asking them to generate an API key may be perfectly acceptable. This is something you need to decide on a project-by-project basis.

Common and Well-Supported Standard

Although OAuth 2.0 is a complex standard, it's generally well-supported and widely used by many platforms and services. While there may be a learning curve to using it and differences between how different providers implement it, it can provide a similar way to authenticate across many applications.

As a result, if you're using OAuth for social sign-in (such as "Sign in with Google"), it can simplify the process of adding new social providers in the future since they follow the same flow and use the same standard.

View and Revoke Access

A significant security benefit of using OAuth 2.0 in your application is that users can revoke access to their resources at any time. This can provide peace of mind that they can control and manage the access they've granted to third-party applications.

Say you built an application, and a user connected their "Twitter" account to it. If they no longer wanted your application to have access to their Twitter account, they could head to their Twitter account and revoke access to your application.

Likewise, depending on the service providing the OAuth integration, a user may also be able to view helpful information such as the date that access was granted, when the integration was last used to grant access, and the scopes that were granted. This can be useful for periodically reviewing what access you've granted to third-party applications.

The Drawbacks of Using OAuth

Although OAuth 2.0 can provide various benefits for your applications, it also has drawbacks you should be aware of.

Complexity

OAuth 2.0 can be a complex standard to implement, especially for developers who are new to the standard. The specification includes various grant types, flows, and token management techniques, which can be overwhelming and challenging to grasp.

Writing an integration that consumes an OAuth 2.0 API can be a complex task that can take a lot of time and effort to get right. This can sometimes be a barrier to entry for less-experienced developers who want to integrate their applications with third-party APIs.

Security Concerns

Correctly implementing OAuth 2.0 is crucial for ensuring security. Misconfigurations or improper implementation can lead to vulnerabilities, such as token leakage, man-in-the-middle attacks, or token replay attacks.

For this reason, consuming an OAuth 2.0 API can be a daunting task for developers who are new to the standard. Likewise, if you are creating your own OAuth 2.0 implementation for your API so other developers can use it to authorize using your service, it can potentially lead to security vulnerabilities in your application if it's not implemented and tested correctly.

Third-Party Dependency

This point isn't necessarily specific to OAuth and applies to APIs in general. But, if you're using an OAuth 2.0 service to authenticate your users (such as providing a "Sign in with Google" button), you're relying on that service to be available for your users to be able to sign in. This adds an external dependency to your application, which could become a point of failure and prevent your users from being able to sign in.

You'll need to be aware of this when deciding if you want to add a "Sign in with *Service Name*" button to your application. Do you trust that the service will be available when your users need it?

Also, if you're using OAuth to authenticate your users, you'll need to ensure you're keeping your integration up to date with the latest changes to the API. If the API changes and you don't update your integration, it could break your application and prevent your users from being able to sign in (especially if your application doesn't provide any other ways to sign in).

Potential for Inconsistent Implementations

OAuth 2.0 is a flexible framework, and there is room for multiple interpretations. Although the general concepts may remain the same, the implementation details can vary between different services and applications. So, if you already authorize with an external API using OAuth, you might be unable to simply copy your code and use it with another API. Your code may require some changes to work with the new API.

Possible Alienation of Users

Although we've mentioned that OAuth can help to improve the user experience by removing the need for users to create and handle API keys, OAuth can sometimes alienate users. Like most things in web development, OAuth is a tool that can solve a problem. But it's not always the right tool for the job.

For example, let's say you are building a web application for a local village's church, which we'll assume has a relatively older demographic that isn't very tech-savvy. Based on the fact that many aspects of everyday life require you to have an email address (such as getting e-receipts when shopping), we could assume that some of the users will have email addresses. But we could assume that even fewer users will have Facebook, TikTok, or Twitter/X accounts. If you only provided "Sign in with Facebook" to authenticate, it could alienate many users as they would need to sign up for Facebook just to be able to use your application.

For some applications, using email addresses and passwords as the sign-in method is sufficient. So, it's important to consider your target audience and the problem you're trying to solve when deciding if OAuth is the right tool for the job.

OAuth Best Practices

Although OAuth can provide great benefits for your application, you must follow some best practices to ensure you're using it correctly and securely. Let's look at some of these.

Use PKCE with the Authorization Code Flow

The OAuth 2.0 specification recommends using Proof Key for Code Exchange (PKCE) whenever using the Authorization Code flow. This is because the extension can significantly increase the security of the flow and can prevent certain attacks, such as a malicious browser extension or app intercepting the authorization code. The OAuth 2.1 specification states that PKCE will be required for the Authorization Code flow, including confidential clients, rather than just being a recommendation.

To recap the benefits of this flow, let's remind ourselves of how PKCE can improve security. PKCE involves the client creating a cryptographically secure string called a "code verifier". This string is then hashed using a hashing algorithm such as SHA-256 to create a "code challenge". The hashed string (code challenge) and hashing algorithm (code challenge method) are then passed to the authorization server when requesting an authorization code. This means that only the client knows the original string, and the authorization server only knows what the hashed string is and the algorithm they need to use to reproduce it. Then, when the client makes the next call to the authorization server to exchange the authorization code for the access token, the code verifier field will also be passed.

The authorization server will then be able to use that same hashing algorithm on its end to hash the code verifier. If their hashed string matches the hashed code challenge field we sent originally, the authorization server can be sure that the second request was made from the same client that made the first request.

Thus, if a malicious browser extension or app intercepted the authorization code, they couldn't exchange it for an access token because they would not know the original code verifier string.

Don't Use the Password Grant

As mentioned, the Password grant is a legacy grant that involves exchanging user credentials for an access token.

As of OAuth 2.0, the Password grant is no longer recommended and should be avoided. Furthermore, it's not included in the OAuth 2.1 specification at all. So, if you're building an OAuth integration, avoid using the Password grant and use the Authorization Code grant instead.

This is because the Password grant requires the user's credentials to be sent to the OAuth server, which can be a security risk and make it harder to use multi-factor authentication. It can also have a negative effect on the user because it can normalize the practice of entering credentials into third-party applications. Although this might not be an issue when using a trusted application, it can lead to users entering credentials into malicious applications and assuming that it's okay.

Use the Authorization Code Flow Instead of the Implicit Flow

As we've already discussed, the Implicit flow was primarily created as a workaround for the fact that JavaScript applications couldn't make requests to the OAuth authorization server due to the lack of CORS. However, now that web browsers universally support CORS, this is no longer an issue.

Therefore, it's recommended by the OAuth 2.0 specification that you use the Authorization Code with PKCE flow instead of the Implicit flow as it's much more secure. As of the OAuth 2.1 specification, the Implicit flow has been removed entirely.

Use Exact String Matching for Redirect URIs

As mentioned, when you create your integration on the third-party service to allow your application to authorize using OAuth, you'll be asked for a "redirect URI" (such as `https://example.com/oauth/callback`). This is the URI that the user will be redirected to after they have authorized access to your application.

As of the OAuth 2.0 specification, it's highly recommended that the OAuth server performs exact string matching on the redirect URI. This means that the redirect URI must match exactly, including the scheme, host, and path. For example, if you specify a redirect URI of `https://example.com/oauth/callback`, the OAuth server should only allow redirects to that exact URI. It should not allow redirects to URIs such as `https://*.example.com`, `https://example.com/*`, `https://example.com/oauth/callback/` or `https://example.com/oauth/callback?foo=bar`. The OAuth 2.1 specification states that exact string matching will be a requirement rather than a recommendation.

By forcing the user to pre-register the URI that the user may be redirected to, it prevents a malicious user from redirecting the user to a different URI that they control. For example, suppose an attacker finds your client ID in a public client (such as a mobile app) that is publicly available. In that case, they could create a malicious application that looks identical to yours to trick users into authorizing access to their application. To prevent this, forcing the API consumer to pre-register the redirect URI and using exact string matching prevents the attacker from redirecting the user to their own application.

For this reason, most of the services that provide OAuth integration will not allow you to define wildcard URIs (that use the `*` symbol) as the redirect URI. However, you may need to integrate with a service that does allow wildcard URIs or doesn't do exact string matching when validating the redirect URI. Although it may be tempting to use a wildcard URI in these scenarios, it's recommended that you don't do this and still use a specific URI.

Don't Use Access Tokens in Query Strings

As briefly covered when discussing the Implicit flow, you mustn't use access tokens in query strings. This is because query strings are often logged, whether by the browser, the server, or third-party services you include in your webpages, such as Google Analytics.

Whenever you make a request to another site, such as a CDN (content delivery network), to load some assets like JavaScript files, the request contains a `Referrer` HTTP header. This header contains the URL of the page that the request originated from, including any query parameters. Thus, the CDN servers will now have a copy of the access token in their logs. It's worth noting that this situation is unlikely to happen when using the Implicit grant because the access token is returned in the URL fragment (using a `#`), not the query string. However, it's unlikely you'll be using the implicit grant, and it's still a good practice to avoid using access tokens in URLs.

Instead, it's strongly advised to ensure you're only passing the access tokens as bearer tokens in the `Authorization` header of the request.

Use Sender-Constrained or One-Time Use Refresh Tokens

As mentioned, refresh tokens can be used in conjunction with other flows (such as the Authorization Code flow) to generate new access tokens as long as the refresh token is still valid and hasn't expired.

This removes the need for a user to manually re-authorize the application when the access token expires. However, since these refresh tokens are long-lived and act as bearer tokens to "identify" a client, they could be used to generate new access tokens and refresh tokens indefinitely if they're compromised. This would be a huge security risk, so the OAuth 2.0 specification recommends that refresh tokens are sender-constrained, one-time use, or both. Implementing these extra security measures can reduce the risk of a compromised refresh token being used to generate new access tokens. The OAuth 2.1 specification states that refresh tokens **must** be sender-constrained or one-time use.

One-Time Use Refresh Tokens

By allowing a refresh token to be used only once, the authorization server can reject any future requests to exchange the already-used refresh token for a new access token. Doing this means that if the authorization server detects a refresh token is being used after it's been invalidated, it can highlight a potential attack and that the refresh token has somehow been compromised. This can allow the API developers and API consumers (building the client application) to take action to prevent any further damage and investigate how the tokens were compromised.

This detection is sometimes referred to as "refresh token reuse detection". It works by checking whether a refresh token has been used before, and if it has, it will reject the request to exchange the refresh token for a new access token. But it will also do something quite interesting: it invalidates all descendant refresh tokens generated from the original compromised refresh token. Using this approach will essentially deny access for both the legitimate user and the malicious user, requiring the legitimate user to re-authorize the application from scratch. Although this may seem like a hassle, it means the malicious user can no longer access the user's resources.

Sender-Constrained Tokens Using mTLS and DPoP

Alternatively, the OAuth provider's authorization server can also allow tokens to be sender-constrained. This is a method of proving that the client attempting to use the refresh token is the same client that generated it rather than a malicious actor that may have compromised it somehow. This can be done through either the use of the "Mutual Transport Layer Security" (mTLS) method or the "OAuth 2.0 Demonstrating Proof-of-Possession at the Application Layer" (DPoP) method.

We won't delve into how mTLS works as it is a complex topic, but if you're interested in finding out more, I recommend checking out the OAuth 2.0 specification to find out how it is implemented under the hood. Essentially, mTLS is a method of using digital certificates to prove that the client is who they say they are by binding tokens to the TLS connection used between the client and authorization servers. mTLS is used in popular implementations of OAuth 2.0, such as Open Banking UK, which is a set of standards that financial institutions in the UK must adhere to when implementing their APIs and can allow banks to communicate with each other. However, it's not always implemented because of the extra infrastructure complexity that it adds.

The other approach to sender-constraining refresh tokens is to use DPoP. Although DPoP adds an extra level of security to the OAuth implementation, it doesn't add as much as mTLS. Whereas mTLs is implemented at the transport layer, DPoP is implemented at the application layer, making it much easier to include in an OAuth flow. In its simplest terms, DPoP works by having the client generate a key pair of public and private keys. The keys in this key pair are then used within different stages of the authorization flow and sent as JSON web tokens (JWT). Like mTLS, we won't delve into how DPoP works under the hood. But if you want to learn more about how it works, check out the OAuth 2.0 specification for more information.

Allow Users to Revoke Access

This measure can apply to both the API developer and the developer building the application consuming the API.

It's important that the API developer builds a way for users to revoke access to their resources without needing to access the client. For example, let's say you granted access to your GitHub account to a third-party application. If you want to revoke access to your GitHub account, you should be able to do so from your GitHub account settings without needing to access the third-party application.

Similarly, if you're building the client application using the OAuth service, it's important to implement a way for users to revoke access and "disconnect" their accounts from your application. This can be as simple as providing a button in your application that allows users to revoke access to the OAuth service. The OAuth service should provide you with an API endpoint you can make a request to from your application that revokes access to the user's resources. As an extra precaution, you should also delete any tokens you have stored against the user in your database.

Pass Credentials in the Authorization Header

When adding an OAuth integration to your Laravel applications, you may find multiple ways to send your client ID and client secret to the authorization server. For example, you could send them in the body of the request like so:

```
POST /oauth/token HTTP/3
Host: auth.example.com

grant_type=authorization_code
&client_id=CLIENT_ID_HERE
&client_secret=CLIENT_SECRET_HERE
```

However, as mentioned, the OAuth 2.0 specification recommends you send the client ID and client secret (concatenated together in the form of `client_id:client_secret`) as base-64 encoded credentials in the `Authorization` header of the request instead of using the `Basic` authentication type. Not all authorization servers will support this, but you should use it if it exists. This is because the `Authorization` header is generally not logged or cached, reducing the chance of the credentials being leaked compared to if they were in the body of the request.

For this example, assume our client ID and client secret concatenated to `CLIENT_ID:CLIENT_SECRET` is equal to `Q0xJRU5UX0lEOkNMSUVOVF9TRUNSRVQ=` when base-64 encoded. If we were to send this in the `Authorization` header, our request would look like this:

```
POST /oauth/token HTTP/3
Host: auth.example.com
Authorization: Basic Q0xJRU5UX0lEOkNMSUVOVF9TRUNSRVQ=

grant_type=authorization_code
```

Laravel Packages for OAuth

Laravel has two OAuth-related, first-party packages you can use in your applications. These are Laravel Socialite and Laravel Passport. Although we won't use these packages in this book, we'll briefly examine what they are and where they could fit into your application.

Laravel Socialite

Laravel Socialite is a package for consuming an OAuth service. It provides a simple API to authenticate users with an OAuth service and retrieve basic user information. It also provides a way to retrieve an access token for the user and use it to make requests to the OAuth service's API on behalf of the user.

At the time of writing, Laravel Socialite supports the following OAuth services:

- Facebook
- Twitter/X (OAuth 1.0)
- Twitter/X (OAuth 2.0)
- LinkedIn
- Google
- GitHub
- GitLab
- Bitbucket
- Slack

Many drivers for other providers are created and maintained by members of the Laravel community. These can be found at https://socialiteproviders.com.

You might be wondering, "If Laravel Socialite exists, why would I use Saloon for my OAuth integration?".

That's a totally valid question. If you are looking for a straight-to-the-point package to consume an OAuth integration, this might be the package for you — especially if your application needs to make API requests for other features. But if you want more control over your OAuth integration or intend to make other API requests, Saloon might be a better fit. For example, using Saloon, you can easily modify requests sent to OAuth servers and tailor them to your application's needs.

It's best not to view Saloon and Laravel Socialite as being in competition with each other. Instead, they're different packages used for different purposes. Socialite is purely for consuming an OAuth integration, whereas Saloon is used for sending HTTP requests and makes it easy to consume an OAuth integration.

Laravel Passport

Another first-party package you can use is Laravel Passport. This package differs from Socialite in that it doesn't allow you to consume an OAuth integration. Instead, it allows you to create your very own OAuth server. This means you can create your own OAuth integration other applications can use to authenticate their users.

This book is focused on consuming APIs rather than building our own. But if you're interested in building your own OAuth server using Laravel, check out Laravel Passport, as it's incredibly powerful and takes away some of the pain of building your own OAuth server.

OAuth2 with Saloon — Authorization Code Grant

Now that we've covered each of the flows let's look at how to use the Authorization Code flow in Saloon. We'll step through how to authorize a user with Spotify, then make a simple request to the Spotify API to retrieve the user's top artists. I use Spotify for this example because it supports PKCE for confidential clients, so we can demonstrate how to use PKCE with Saloon.

After creating our integration, we'll look at how to test our integration using techniques covered in the previous chapter.

Preparing the OAuth Integration

Before writing any code, we must head to https://developer.spotify.com and create a new OAuth app. We'll then need to fill in the form with the following details:

- **App name** - The name of your app. This will be displayed to users when they are authorizing your app.
- **App description** - The description of your app. This will be displayed to users when they are authorizing your app.
- **Website** - The website of your app. This can provide extra information about your application so the user can decide whether they want to authorize your app.
- **Redirect URI** - The URI the user will be redirected to after they authorize your app. This must be a URI that you control that is part of your Laravel application. Remember, this must be an exact match to the URI in your `redirect_uri` parameter when you are requesting an access token.

After you fill out the form and hit "Save", you can head to the "Settings" for your Spotify app and get your client ID and client secret. We'll add these to your Laravel app's `.env` file:

```
SPOTIFY_CLIENT_ID=your-client-id-here
SPOTIFY_CLIENT_SECRET=your-client-secret-here
```

We must then add these to our `config/services.php` config file so we can access them in our code:

```
return [

    // ...

    'spotify' => [
        'client_id' => env('SPOTIFY_CLIENT_ID'),
        'client_secret' => env('SPOTIFY_CLIENT_SECRET'),
    ],
];
```

Creating the OAuth Routes

With our credentials ready, we must create the routes to handle the OAuth flow. We need to create two separate routes:

- `redirect` - Where the user will go when beginning their authorization flow. For example, this might be where the user goes after clicking the "Connect with Spotify" button.
- `callback` - Where the OAuth service will redirect the user after they authorize (or deny access to) your application.

Assume we have created an `app/Http/Controllers/OAuth/SpotifyAuthController.php` controller containing `redirect` and `callback` methods. We'll examine this controller later.

Let's add our routes to the `routes/web.php` file:

```
use App\Http\Controllers\OAuth\SpotifyAuthController;
use Illuminate\Support\Facades\Route;

// ...

Route::middleware('auth')->group(function () {
    Route::controller(SpotifyAuthController::class)
        ->as('oauth.spotify.')
        ->group(function () {
            Route::get('oauth/spotify/redirect', 'redirect')->name('redirect');
            Route::get('oauth/spotify/callback', 'callback')->name('callback');
        });
});
```

In our `web.php` file, we defined the two routes we need. We also wrapped these routes in a `Route::middleware('auth')` group, so the user must be logged in to access these routes. This isn't a requirement for using OAuth. In fact, if you were using OAuth as a form of authentication (for example, "Sign in with Spotify"), you couldn't use this. However, for the sake of this example, we will use OAuth to connect our application's users to their Spotify accounts. This means that we need to know which user is connecting their account.

We're also using a controller group to define the controller for these routes, so we don't need to specify the controller for each route. We can also use the `as` method to define a prefix for the route names. Thus, we now have the following named routes: `oauth.spotify.redirect` and `oauth.spotify.callback`.

Preparing Your Connector For OAuth

We next create a connector for making requests to the Spotify API. As we'll need to configure some OAuth settings, we can use the `saloon:connector` Artisan command and pass the `--oauth` option. This creates a boilerplate connector class with the OAuth methods added for us. We'll do this by running the following Artisan command:

```
php artisan saloon:connector Spotify SpotifyConnector --oauth
```

This should create a new `app/Http/Integrations/Spotify/SpotifyConnector.php` file like:

```
namespace App\Http\Integrations\Spotify;

use Saloon\Helpers\OAuth2\OAuthConfig;
use Saloon\Http\Connector;
use Saloon\Traits\OAuth2\AuthorizationCodeGrant;
use Saloon\Traits\Plugins\AcceptsJson;

class SpotifyConnector extends Connector
{
    use AuthorizationCodeGrant;
    use AcceptsJson;

    public function resolveBaseUrl(): string
    {
        return '';
    }
```

```php
    protected function defaultOauthConfig(): OAuthConfig
    {
        return OAuthConfig::make()
            ->setClientId('')
            ->setClientSecret('')
            ->setRedirectUri('')
            ->setDefaultScopes([])
            ->setAuthorizeEndpoint('authorize')
            ->setTokenEndpoint('token')
            ->setUserEndpoint('user');
    }
}
```

Let's discuss what the different parts of this file do.

As seen in the previous chapter, the `resolveBaseUrl` method for the connector allows us to define the base URL for the API we're integrating with.

The `defaultOauthConfig` config allows us to define the default fields our connector will use to connect to the OAuth service. We can override these values when creating an instance of our connector, but it's useful to have some default values we can use. The methods allow us to do the following:

- `setClientId` - The client ID of the OAuth integration. This is provided by the OAuth service when you create an integration.
- `setClientSecret` - The client secret of the OAuth integration. This is provided by the OAuth service when you create an integration.
- `setRedirectUri` - The redirect URI that the OAuth service will redirect the user to after they authorized (or denied access to) your application. This is usually a route in your application that handles the callback from the OAuth service. Remember, this must be an

exact match to the redirect URI that you registered in the OAuth service when creating your OAuth integration.

- `setDefaultScopes` - The scopes you want to request from the OAuth service (such as 'user:read', 'user:write', etc.). You can override these when you create an instance of your connector if you'd like to request different scopes for a specific request.
- `setAuthorizeEndpoint` - The endpoint that the OAuth service uses to authorize a user. This is where your users will be navigated when they click the "Connect with Spotify" button on your application.
- `setTokenEndpoint` - The endpoint the OAuth service uses to exchange an authorization code for an access token. Our Laravel application will send a request to this URL when the user has authorized our application.
- `setUserEndpoint` - The endpoint we can use to fetch information about the user that just authorized access.

Now that we know what each of these fields is for, let's make updates to this method in our connector:

```php
namespace App\Http\Integrations\Spotify;

use Saloon\Helpers\OAuth2\OAuthConfig;
use Saloon\Http\Connector;

class SpotifyConnector extends Connector
{
    // ...

    protected function defaultOauthConfig(): OAuthConfig
    {
        return OAuthConfig::make()
            ->setClientId(config('services.spotify.client_id'))
            ->setClientSecret(config('services.spotify.client_secret'))
            ->setRedirectUri('https://example.com/oauth/spotify/callback')
            ->setAuthorizeEndpoint('https://accounts.spotify.com/authorize')
            ->setTokenEndpoint('https://accounts.spotify.com/api/token')
            ->setDefaultScopes(['user-top-read']);
    }
}
```

In our config, we're using the client ID and client secret we previously added to our `.env` to access it via the `config` helper. For the sake of this example, we assume our application is running on `https://example.com` and that our redirect URI is `https://example.com/oauth/spotify/callback`. We'll come back to this later when we create our routes.

We have set the authorization and token endpoints based on the information provided in the Spotify API documentation. The documentation also tells us that we must request the `user-top-read` scope to access the user's top artists.

Building the Interface and Classes

We'll create an interface for our Spotify integration as we did with the GitHub integration in the previous chapter. This defines the public methods available for our integration. We'll also create a class that implements this interface to handle the requests to the Spotify API. Doing so will make switching out our implementation (whether in application code or tests) much easier.

We want to be able to do three things with our Spotify class:

- Get the OAuth authorization URL
- Handle the OAuth callback
- Get the user's top artists

Thus, we create a `Spotify` interface in the `app/Interfaces` directory like so:

```php
namespace App\Interfaces;

use App\Collections\Spotify\ArtistCollection;
use App\DataTransferObjects\Spotify\AccessTokenDetails;
use App\DataTransferObjects\Spotify\AuthorizationCallbackDetails;
use App\DataTransferObjects\Spotify\AuthorizationRedirectDetails;
use App\Models\User;

interface Spotify
{
    public function getAuthRedirectDetails(): AuthorizationRedirectDetails;

    public function authorize(
        AuthorizationCallbackDetails $callbackDetails
    ): AccessTokenDetails;

    public function getTopArtists(User $user): ArtistCollection;
}
```

In our interface, notice that we're referencing some classes that don't exist yet:

- `App\DataTransferObjects\Spotify\AuthorizationRedirectDetails` - This DTO will contain the details needed to redirect the user to the OAuth authorization URL.
- `App\DataTransferObjects\Spotify\AccessTokenDetails` - This DTO will contain the access token, refresh token, and expiry time for the access token.
- `App\DataTransferObjects\Spotify\AuthorizationCallbackDetails` - This DTO will contain some details returned from the OAuth service when the user has authorized our application. We'll use these details to exchange the authorization code for an access token.
- `App\Collections\Spotify\ArtistCollection` - This collection will contain a collection of `App\Models\Spotify\Artist` DTOs we'll use to represent the user's top

artists.

Building the DTOs and Collection

We'll follow a similar setup process for our integration as in the previous chapter for our GitHub integration. Let's build these DTOs and the Collection next.

Building the AuthorizationRedirectDetails DTO

We'll first create our `AuthorizationRedirectDetails` DTO. This DTO will contain the details needed to redirect the user to the OAuth authorization URL.

We'll create this DTO in the `app/DataTransferObjects/Spotify` directory, and it will look like this:

```
namespace App\DataTransferObjects\Spotify;

final readonly class AuthorizationRedirectDetails
{
    public function __construct(
        public string $authorizationUrl,
        public string $state,
        public string $codeVerifier,
    ) {}
}
```

The `authorizationUrl` field is the actual URL the user will be redirected to.

`state` is a random string used to verify that the user is who they say they are when they return to our application. We'll store this in the user's session and then compare it during our OAuth callback.

`codeVerifier` is the plain-text string we use to generate the `code_challenge` field sent to the OAuth service. We'll store this in the user's session and then send it back to the OAuth service when we exchange the authorization code for an access token. This is part of the PKCE flow we'll use to secure our OAuth integration.

Building the AuthorizationCallbackDetails DTO

The `AuthorzationCallbackDetails` DTO will contain the details returned from the OAuth service when the user has authorized our application. We'll use these details to exchange the authorization code for an access token.

We'll create this DTO in the `app/DataTransferObjects/Spotify` directory, and it will look like this:

```
namespace App\DataTransferObjects\Spotify;

final readonly class AuthorizationCallbackDetails
{
    public function __construct(
        public string $authorizationCode,
        public string $expectedState,
        public string $state,
        public string $codeVerifier,
    ) {}
}
```

`authorizationCode` is the authorization code we'll exchange for an access token. Spotify will return this as a query parameter when the user is redirected to our callback URL.

`expectedState` is the state we stored in the user's session when we redirected them to the OAuth authorization URL. We'll compare this to the `state` field to verify that the user is who they say they are.

`codeVerifier` is the field we stored in the user's session when we redirected them to the OAuth authorization URL. We'll send this back to the OAuth service when we exchange the authorization code for an access token.

Building the AccessTokenDetails DTO

The `AccessTokenDetails` DTO will contain the access token, refresh token, and expiry time for the access token. This will be returned from our Spotify service class after we've successfully generated a new access token. We'll then store this information in our database and use it for future requests to the Spotify API.

We'll create this DTO in the `app/DataTransferObjects/Spotify` directory, and it will look like this:

```php
namespace App\DataTransferObjects\Spotify;

use DateTimeImmutable;

final readonly class AccessTokenDetails
{
    public function __construct(
        public string $accessToken,
        public string $refreshToken,
        public DateTimeImmutable $expiresAt,
    ) { }
}
```

`accessToken` is the access token we'll use to request the Spotify API.

`refreshToken` is the refresh token we'll use to refresh the access token when it expires.

`expiresAt` is the date and time the access token will expire. We'll be using this to determine whether we need to refresh the access token before making a request to the Spotify API.

Building the Artist DTO

To demonstrate how we can use the access token we generated to make requests to the Spotify API, we'll make a request to the Spotify API to get the user's top artists.

We'll create an `Artist` DTO to represent an artist in our Spotify integration in the `app/DataTransferObjects/Spotify` directory, and it will look like this:

```
namespace App\DataTransferObjects\Spotify;

final readonly class Artist
{
    public function __construct(
        public string $id,
        public string $name,
        public int $popularity,
    ) {}
}
```

Building the ArtistCollection

As our Spotify service returns a collection of `Artist` DTOs, we'll create an `ArtistCollection` collection class to hold these DTOs in the `app/Collections/Spotify` directory. It will look like this:

```
namespace App\Collections\Spotify;

use App\DataTransferObjects\Spotify\Artist;
use Illuminate\Support\Collection;

/** @extends Collection<int,Artist> */
final class ArtistCollection extends Collection
{

}
```

Preparing Our Model and Database

After the user authorizes our Laravel application to access their Spotify account, we'll have three pieces of information to store in our database: the access token, the refresh token, and the expiry time of the access token.

For this example, we'll store this information in the `users` table. To add these fields to our database table, we'll create a new migration by running the following command:

```
php artisan make:migration add_spotify_oauth_to_users_table --table=users
```

This creates a new migration file in the `database/migrations` directory. We can then update the migration like so:

```php
use Illuminate\Database\Migrations\Migration;
use Illuminate\Database\Schema\Blueprint;
use Illuminate\Support\Facades\Schema;

return new class extends Migration {
    public function up(): void
    {
        Schema::table('users', function (Blueprint $table) {
            $table->string('spotify_access_token', 1000)->nullable();
            $table->string('spotify_refresh_token', 1000)->nullable();
            $table->dateTime('spotify_expires_at')->nullable();
        });
    }

    public function down(): void
    {
        Schema::table('users', function (Blueprint $table) {
            $table->dropColumn([
                'spotify_access_token',
                'spotify_refresh_token',
                'spotify_expires_at',
            ]);
        });
    }
};
```

In the `up` method, we're specifying that when the `php artisan migrate` command is run, we should add three new columns to our `users` table: `spotify_access_token`, `spotify_refresh_token`, and `spotify_expires_at`.

You may have noticed we explicitly stated the max length for the `spotify_access_token` and `spotify_refresh_token` columns. This is because we'll encrypt the tokens before we store them in the database, and the encrypted tokens will be longer than the unencrypted tokens, so we need to ensure that the columns are long enough to store them in the encrypted format. We'll discuss the encryption in a moment.

In the `down` method, we specify that if this migration is ever rolled back (e.g., using the `php artisan migrate:rollback` command), we'll remove the three columns we added in the `up` method.

We can now run the migration to add the fields to our `users` table by running the following command:

```
php artisan migrate
```

We now want to make several changes to our `User` model. First, we'll add the three new fields to the model's `hidden` array, which means they won't be returned when we convert the model to an array or JSON. This prevents accidental exposure of the access token, refresh token, or expiry time to the front end of our application or in any API responses.

Our `User` model will now look like this:

```php
namespace App\Models;

use Illuminate\Foundation\Auth\User as Authenticatable;

class User extends Authenticatable
{
    protected $hidden = [
        'password',
        'remember_token',
        'spotify_access_token',
        'spotify_refresh_token',
        'spotify_expires_at',
    ];

    // ...
}
```

We'll also define casts for our model to specify that the `spotify_access_token` and `spotify_refresh_token` fields will be encrypted when stored in the database and decrypted when retrieved from it. By encrypting the fields, we drastically improve the security of our application. If someone were to gain access to the database, they wouldn't be able to see the access token or refresh token in plain text. They could only see the encrypted tokens.

It's important to remember that your Laravel application's APP_KEY is used to encrypt and decrypt the tokens. If someone obtained your APP_KEY, they could decrypt the tokens. So it's essential to keep your APP_KEY safe and secure. Likewise, if someone gained access to your application server, they could decrypt the tokens. This approach isn't perfect, but it's much better than storing tokens in plain text.

If you require a more secure approach, you may wish to explore different options for securely storing user tokens.

We'll add another cast for the `spotify_expires_at` field. This allows us to specify that the field should be cast to a `Carbon\Carbon` instance when retrieved from the database. This makes it easy to compare the expiry time to the current time.

Our model now looks like this:

```
namespace App\Models;

use Illuminate\Foundation\Auth\User as Authenticatable;

class User extends Authenticatable
{
    // ...

    protected $casts = [
        'spotify_access_token' => 'encrypted',
        'spotify_refresh_token' => 'encrypted',
        'spotify_expires_at' => 'datetime',
    ];

    // ...
}
```

We then want to make a final change to our `User` model and add two helper methods:

- One to update the model's access token, refresh token, and expiry time.
- One to check whether the user is connected to Spotify.

Let's add these methods and then explain what they're doing:

```
namespace App\Models;

use Illuminate\Foundation\Auth\User as Authenticatable;

class User extends Authenticatable
{
    // ...

    public function updateSpotifyOAuthDetails(
        string $accessToken,
        string $refreshToken,
        \DateTimeImmutable $expiresAt
    ): void {
        $this->spotify_access_token = $accessToken;
        $this->spotify_refresh_token = $refreshToken;
        $this->spotify_expires_at = $expiresAt;

        $this->save();
    }

    public function isConnectedToSpotify(): bool
    {
        return $this->spotify_access_token
            && $this->spotify_refresh_token
            && $this->spotify_expires_at;
    }
}
```

In the code, we can see that we've added an `updateSpotifyOAuthDetails` method. This accepts an access token, refresh token, and expiry time and then stores them in the database.

There's also an `isConnectedToSpotify` method that can be used to determine whether the user has completed the OAuth flow with Spotify and we have their access token.

Creating the Integration Service Class

We can now start creating our service class that will use Saloon. Let's create a `SpotifyService` class in the `app/Services/Spotify` directory that implements the `App\Interfaces\Spotify` interface. We won't add the implementations for the methods just yet, but we'll add the class and interface so we can start building out the class. The class may look like this:

```php
namespace App\Services\Spotify;

use App\Collections\Spotify\ArtistCollection;
use App\DataTransferObjects\Spotify\AccessTokenDetails;
use App\DataTransferObjects\Spotify\AuthorizationCallbackDetails;
use App\DataTransferObjects\Spotify\AuthorizationRedirectDetails;
use App\Interfaces\Spotify;
use App\Models\User;

final class SpotifyService implements Spotify
{
    public function getAuthRedirectDetails(): AuthorizationRedirectDetails
    {

    }

    public function authorize(
        AuthorizationCallbackDetails $callbackDetails
    ): AccessTokenDetails {

    }

    public function getTopArtists(User $user): ArtistCollection
    {

    }
}
```

Binding the Interface to the Concrete Implementation

As with our GitHub example in the previous chapter, we can now bind the `Spotify` interface to the `SpotifyService` class in the `App\Providers\AppServiceProvider` class. This allows type-hinting the `Spotify` interface in our controllers and other classes, and Laravel will automatically inject an instance of the `SpotifyService` class.

We'll update our `AppServiceProvider` class to look like this:

```
namespace App\Providers;

use App\Interfaces\Spotify;
use App\Services\Spotify\SpotifyService;
use Illuminate\Support\ServiceProvider;

class AppServiceProvider extends ServiceProvider
{
    public function register(): void
    {
        $this->app->bind(Spotify::class, SpotifyService::class);
    }
}
```

We have now prepared our application so we can start building our OAuth integration with Spotify.

Generating an Authorization URL

The first step in the Authorization Code flow is redirecting the user to an authorization URL, allowing them to grant access to our application. We must generate this URL and redirect the user to it.

Thankfully, Saloon provides a handy `getAuthorizationUrl` method to generate the URL via our connector class.

Let's update the `getAuthRedirectDetails` method in our `App\Services\SpotifyService` class, and then we'll delve into what's being done:

```
use App\DataTransferObjects\Spotify\AuthorizationRedirectDetails;
use App\Http\Integrations\Spotify\SpotifyConnector;
use App\Interfaces\Spotify;
use Illuminate\Support\Str;

final class SpotifyService implements Spotify
{
    public function getAuthRedirectDetails(): AuthorizationRedirectDetails
    {
        $codeVerifier = Str::random(random_int(43, 128));

        $codeChallenge = hash('sha256', $codeVerifier, true);
        $codeChallenge = strtr(base64_encode($codeChallenge), '+/', '-_');
        $codeChallenge = trim($codeChallenge, '=');

        $connector = $this->connector();

        $authorizationUrl = $connector->getAuthorizationUrl(
```

```
            additionalQueryParameters: [
                'code_challenge' => $codeChallenge,
                'code_challenge_method' => 'S256',
            ]
        );

        return new AuthorizationRedirectDetails(
            authorizationUrl: $authorizationUrl,
            state: $connector->getState(),
            codeVerifier: $codeVerifier,
        );
    }

    private function connector(): SpotifyConnector
    {
        return new SpotifyConnector();
    }
}
```

In the `getAuthRedirectDetails` method, we first generate a random string between 43 and 128 characters long. This will be the code verifier as part of the PKCE flow to improve security.

We then generate the code challenge by hashing the code verifier using the SHA256 algorithm. The code challenge is encoded using base64 and replacing the `+` and `/` characters with `-` and `_` respectively. Finally, we trim `=` characters from the end of the string. This is all done to ensure the code challenge is URL-safe and can be sent in the authorization URL.

Following this, we access our connector (which we abstract into a `connector` method) and call the `getAuthorizationUrl` method. This will generate the URL that we redirect the user to. You may have noticed we're also passing in some additional query parameters. These are the code challenge and code challenge methods we generated earlier and will be appended as query parameters in our URL.

Finally, we return an instance of the `App\DataTransferObjects\Spotify\AuthorizationRedirectDetails` DTO. This contains the authorization URL, state, and code verifier. We'll use the state and code verifier later in the flow to verify that the callback is legitimate and exchange the authorization code for an access token.

Let's look at how we might use this in our `SpotifyAuthController`:

```php
namespace App\Http\Controllers\OAuth;

use App\Http\Controllers\Controller;
use App\Interfaces\Spotify;
use Illuminate\Http\RedirectResponse;
use Illuminate\Http\Request;

final class SpotifyAuthController extends Controller
{
    public function redirect(Request $request): RedirectResponse
    {
        $redirectDetails = app(Spotify::class)->getAuthRedirectDetails();

        $request->session()->put('oauth_spotify_state', $redirectDetails->state);
        $request->session()->put(
            'oauth_spotify_code_verifier',
            $redirectDetails->codeVerifier
        );

        return redirect($redirectDetails->authorizationUrl);
    }

    // ...
}
```

In the `redirect` method of the controller, we're resolving an instance of the `Spotify` interface (thus giving us access to the `SpotifyService` class) and generating an authorization URL.

We're then storing the state and code verifier in the user's session to access them later in the flow when we receive the callback.

Finally, we're redirecting the user to the authorization URL, which takes the user to Spotify's authorization page. At this point, they'll be asked whether they want to grant access to our application and the scopes we've requested (in this case, the `user-top-read` scope).

Handling the Authorization Callback

Once the user has chosen to grant or deny access, they'll be redirected back to the redirect URL we specified when we registered our application with Spotify. This will be the `callback` method in our `SpotifyAuthController`:

Let's examine how we might implement this controller method, and then we'll delve into what's being done:

```
namespace App\Http\Controllers\OAuth;

use App\DataTransferObjects\Spotify\AuthorizationCallbackDetails;
use App\Exceptions\Integrations\Spotify\SpotifyException;
use App\Http\Controllers\Controller;
use App\Interfaces\Spotify;
use Illuminate\Http\RedirectResponse;
use Illuminate\Http\Request;

final class SpotifyAuthController extends Controller
{
    public function callback(Request $request): RedirectResponse
    {
        if ($request->input('error') === 'access_denied') {
            return redirect()
```

```
            ->route('dashboard')
            ->with('error', 'Spotify account connection denied.');
    }

    $hasRequiredFields = $request->filled(['code', 'state'])
        && $request->session()->has('oauth_spotify_state')
        && $request->session()->has('oauth_spotify_code_verifier');

    if (!$hasRequiredFields) {
        abort(400, 'Missing required fields.');
    }

    $callbackDetails = new AuthorizationCallbackDetails(
        authorizationCode: $request->input('code'),
        expectedState: $request->session()->pull('oauth_spotify_state'),
        state: $request->input('state'),
        codeVerifier: $request->session()
            ->pull('oauth_spotify_code_verifier'),
    );

    try {
        $accessDetails = app(Spotify::class)->authorize($callbackDetails);

        $request->user()->updateSpotifyOAuthDetails(
            accessToken: $accessDetails->accessToken,
            refreshToken: $accessDetails->refreshToken,
            expiresAt: $accessDetails->expiresAt,
        );
    } catch (SpotifyException) {
        return redirect()
            ->route('dashboard')
```

```
                ->with('error', 'Failed to connect to Spotify account.');
        }

        return redirect()
            ->route('dashboard')
            ->with('success', 'Spotify account connected successfully.');
    }
}
```

We first check whether the user has denied access to our application. We can do this by checking whether the request contains an `error` query parameter with the value of `access_denied`. If so, we redirect the user to the dashboard with an error message.

Next, we check whether the request contains all the fields required to continue with the flow. We need to check that the request contains the `code` (the authorization code we'll be exchanging for an access token) and the `state` field (we'll compare this to the state we stored in the user's session to ensure the callback is legitimate). We also need to check that the user's session contains the `oauth_spotify_state` and `oauth_spotify_code_verifier` fields we stored earlier. If any of these fields are missing, we return an HTTP `400 Bad Request` response.

If we have all the necessary fields, we can use them to build an instance of our `AuthorizationCallbackDetails` DTO. This DTO contains all the information needed to continue the flow and exchange the authorization code for an access token. To get the fields from the session, we're using the `$request->session()->pull()` method. The `pull` method retrieves the value from the user's session and then removes the field from the session after retrieving it. By doing this, it ensures that no values are left in the session in the event that something goes wrong.

We then call the `authorize` method on our `Spotify` interface (thus calling it on our `App\Services\Spotify\SpotifyService` class), passing in the callback details. This will exchange the authorization code for an access token and return an instance of the

`App\DataTransferObjects\Spotify\AuthorizationAccessDetails` DTO. We then use the data in this DTO to update the user's Spotify OAuth details in our database.

You may have noticed we've wrapped the authorization code exchange inside a try-catch block. This block will catch any `App\Exceptions\Integrations\Spotify\SpotifyException` exceptions that are thrown. We haven't shown this exception class here, but it's a custom exception class (similar to our `GitHubException` from the previous chapter). If any instances of this exception are thrown (for example, if we can't make a connection to the Spotify API), we'll redirect the user back to the dashboard with an error message.

Finally, if everything has gone well, we'll redirect the user back to the dashboard with a success message.

We've seen how we're completing the OAuth flow from the controller. So let's look at the `authorize` method in the `App\Services\Spotify\SpotifyService` class and see what's happening under the hood for us to be able to do this:

```
namespace App\Services\Spotify;

use App\DataTransferObjects\Spotify\AccessTokenDetails;
use App\DataTransferObjects\Spotify\AuthorizationCallbackDetails;
use App\Interfaces\Spotify;

final class SpotifyService implements Spotify
{
    // ...

    public function authorize(
        AuthorizationCallbackDetails $callbackDetails
    ): AccessTokenDetails {
        $tokenDetails = $this->connector()->getAccessToken(
```

```php
            code: $callbackDetails->authorizationCode,
            state: $callbackDetails->state,
            expectedState: $callbackDetails->expectedState,
            requestModifier: function (
                GetAccessTokenRequest $saloonRequest
            ) use ($callbackDetails) {
                $saloonRequest->body()->add(
                    'code_verifier',
                    $callbackDetails->codeVerifier,
                );
            }
        );

        return new AccessTokenDetails(
            accessToken: $tokenDetails->accessToken,
            refreshToken: $tokenDetails->refreshToken,
            expiresAt: $tokenDetails->expiresAt,
        );
    }

    // ...
}
```

In the `authorize` method, we call the `getAccessToken` method on the `SpotifyConnector` (accessed via the `connector` method). We pass the authorization code that Spotify returned to us, the state Spotify returned to us, the state we stored in the user's session, and a request modifier callback.

Saloon will check that the state we passed in matches the state Spotify returned. If it doesn't, an exception will be thrown. Otherwise, Saloon will make a request to the Spotify API to exchange the authorization code for an access token. We also pass a request modifier callback to the `getAccessToken` method. This callback can change the request (such as modifying headers or the request body) before it's sent to the Spotify API. We use this callback to add the `code_verifier` field to the request body. This is the code verifier we generated earlier and stored in the user's session. We must send this to Spotify so they can verify that our application is the one that initiated the authorization flow.

If the request is successful, Saloon will return an instance of `Saloon\Http\Auth\AccessTokenAuthenticator` containing the access token, refresh token, and expiry date. This class provides a `serialize` method that we could use to prepare this data for storing in the database against the user. You can use this method to return the serialized format of this data. However, as we're trying to keep Saloon abstracted away from our application code to keep our code decoupled, we'll instead create a new `App\DataTransferObjects\Spotify\AccessTokenDetails` DTO and pass the data from the `Saloon\Http\Auth\AccessTokenAuthenticator` instance into it. We'll then return this DTO from the `authorize` method.

Customizing the Access Token Request

Saloon ships with a request class (`Saloon\Http\OAuth2\GetAccessTokenRequest`) used by default to exchange the authorization code for the access token. In most cases, this request will be sufficient for your needs. However, there are a few minor changes we'd like to make to the structure of the request.

Saloon's `GetAccessTokenRequest` request class will send the `client_id` and `client_secret` fields in the request body. As mentioned in this chapter, the OAuth 2.0 specification recommends passing your client credentials using Basic authentication in the `Authorization` header if the service supports it. Thankfully, Spotify does support this method of passing credentials, so we'll update our code to use this approach and improve our integration's security.

We first need to create our own `GetAccessTokenRequest` class by running the following Artisan command:

```
php artisan saloon:request Spotify GetAccessTokenRequest
```

This command should create a new `app/Http/Integrations/Spotify/Requests/GetAccessTokenRequest.php` file. Let's update the request class and then take a look at what's happening:

```
use Saloon\Contracts\Body\HasBody;
use Saloon\Enums\Method;
use Saloon\Helpers\OAuth2\OAuthConfig;
use Saloon\Http\Request;
use Saloon\Traits\Body\HasFormBody;
use Saloon\Traits\Plugins\AcceptsJson;

final class GetAccessTokenRequest extends Request implements HasBody
{
    use HasFormBody;
    use AcceptsJson;

    protected Method $method = Method::POST;

    public function __construct(
        private readonly string $code,
        private readonly OAuthConfig $oauthConfig,
    ) {
        $this->withBasicAuth(
            $oauthConfig->getClientId(), $oauthConfig->getClientSecret()
```

```
        );
    }

    public function resolveEndpoint(): string
    {
        return $this->oauthConfig->getTokenEndpoint();
    }

    public function defaultBody(): array
    {
        return [
            'grant_type' => 'authorization_code',
            'code' => $this->code,
            'redirect_uri' => $this->oauthConfig->getRedirectUri(),
        ];
    }
}
```

Our request class implements the `HasBody` interface so Saloon knows to send a body in the request. We've also specified that the request should have the `Content-Type: application/x-www-form-urlencoded` and `Accept: application/json` headers, which are added via the `HasFormBody` and `AcceptsJson` plugins, respectively. We've also specified that the request should use the `POST` method.

We've used the same `__construct` method signature as Saloon's `Saloon\Http\OAuth2\GetAccessTokenRequest` request class. It accepts the authorization code and the OAuth config that will be coming from our connector. We then use the `withBasicAuth` method to add the client ID and client secret to the `Authorization` header.

Following this, we use the `resolveEndpoint` method to return the token endpoint from the OAuth config. Finally, we use the `defaultBody` method to return the default body that should be sent with the request. We pass the `grant_type`, `code`, and `redirect_uri` fields to the request body.

Now that our request class is prepared, we must register it in our `SpotifyConnector` class so Saloon knows to use our custom request class instead of the default one. We can do this by overriding the `resolveAccessTokenRequest` method in the connector like so:

```
namespace App\Http\Integrations\Spotify;

use App\Http\Integrations\Spotify\Requests\GetAccessTokenRequest;
use Saloon\Helpers\OAuth2\OAuthConfig;
use Saloon\Http\Connector;
use Saloon\Http\Request;

class SpotifyConnector extends Connector
{
    // ...

    protected function resolveAccessTokenRequest(
        string $code,
        OAuthConfig $oauthConfig
    ): Request {
        return new GetAccessTokenRequest($code, $oauthConfig);
    }
}
```

As a result, when we make the request to generate an access token, the client ID and client secret won't be passed in the request. Instead, they'll be passed in the request headers.

Making a Request Using the Access Token

Now that we know how to generate an access token and store it in the database, let's look at how to use it to make a basic request to the Spotify API. We'll fetch the user's top artists.

To get started, let's add an implementation for our `getTopArtists` method in our `SpotifyConnector` class:

```php
namespace App\Services\Spotify;

use App\Collections\Spotify\ArtistCollection;
use App\Exceptions\Integrations\Spotify\SpotifyException;
use App\Http\Integrations\Spotify\Requests\UserTopArtists;
use App\Interfaces\Spotify;
use App\Models\User;

class SpotifyService implements Spotify
{
    // ...

    public function getTopArtists(User $user): ArtistCollection
    {
        if (!$user->isConnectedToSpotify()) {
            throw new SpotifyException('User is not connected to Spotify.');
        }

        return $this->connectorForUser($user)
            ->send(new UserTopArtists())
            ->dtoOrFail();
    }
}
```

This method first calls `isConnectedToSpotify`, which we added to our `App\Models\User` model earlier. This ensures the user is connected to Spotify and that we have the relevant data needed to make the request. If the user isn't connected to Spotify, we throw an `App\Exceptions\Integrations\Spotify\SpotifyException` exception.

If the user is connected to Spotify, we first call the `connectorForUser` method (which we'll add in a moment) to fetch an instance of our `SpotifyConnector` class that is authenticated and has the user's access token ready to send in the request. As we've seen previously, we then call the `send` method on the connector and return an `ArtistCollection` containing the user's top artists. We've already seen how to build the request classes and map the response to DTOs in the previous chapter, so we won't focus on that here. Instead, we'll focus more on what's happening inside the `connectorForUser` method.

Let's look at this method and the others we must add to our `SpotifyConnector` class:

```
namespace App\Services\Spotify;

use App\DataTransferObjects\Spotify\AccessTokenDetails;
use App\Http\Integrations\Spotify\SpotifyConnector;
use App\Interfaces\Spotify;
use App\Models\User;
use Saloon\Http\Auth\AccessTokenAuthenticator;

class SpotifyService implements Spotify
{
    // ...

    private function connectorForUser(User $user): SpotifyConnector
    {
        $accessTokenDetails = $this->getSpotifyOAuthDetails($user);

        $connector = $this->connector()->authenticate($accessTokenDetails);

        if ($accessTokenDetails->hasExpired()) {
            $newAccessTokenDetails =
            $connector->refreshAccessToken($accessTokenDetails);
            $connector->authenticate($newAccessTokenDetails);
```

```php
            $this->updateSpotifyOAuthDetails($newAccessTokenDetails, $user);
        }

        return $connector;
    }

    private function getSpotifyOAuthDetails(User $user): AccessTokenAuthenticator
    {
        return new AccessTokenAuthenticator(
            $user->spotify_access_token,
            $user->spotify_refresh_token,
            $user->spotify_expires_at->toDateTimeImmutable(),
        );
    }

    private function updateSpotifyOAuthDetails(
        AccessTokenAuthenticator $newAccessTokenDetails,
        User $user
    ): void {
        $user->updateSpotifyOAuthDetails(
            $newAccessTokenDetails->getAccessToken(),
            $newAccessTokenDetails->getRefreshToken(),
            $newAccessTokenDetails->getExpiresAt(),
        );
    }
}
```

We have three different methods here. Let's work through the `connectorForUser` method and discuss what's happening.

The first thing we're doing is calling the `getSpotifyOAuthDetails` method. This method fetches the user's access token, refresh token, and expiry date from the database and returns an instance of `Saloon\Http\Auth\AccessTokenAuthenticator` that we can use to authenticate our connector. We then pass this authenticator to the `authenticate` method on the connector. This adds the access token to the request headers for any requests we make using this connector.

We then call `hasExpired` on the `AccessTokenAuthenticator` object to check if the access token has expired. If it has, we must refresh the token before making a request. We do this by running the `refreshAccessToken` method, which makes an API request to Spotify's "token" endpoint (that we specified in our connector) using the `refresh_token` grant type. Assuming the refresh token is valid, a new access token, refresh token, and expiry time will be returned to us.

We then pass these fresh tokens and expiry date to the `authenticate` method again to set the correct tokens. Finally, we call the `updateSpotifyOAuthDetails` method to update the user's access token, refresh token, and expiry date in the database.

Following this, we return our connector class so it can be used to make requests. Any requests made using this instance will contain the correct access token in the request headers.

Customizing the Refresh Token Request

As we did with the access token request, you may want to use a custom request class to refresh the access token. This will allow you to make changes to the request you need, such as passing the client ID and client secret in the request headers instead of the request body.

To do this, you can override your connector's `resolveRefreshTokenRequest` method and return your custom request class. You can then use the `refreshAccessToken` method on the connector to refresh the access token using your custom class.

Imagine we created our own

`App\Http\Integrations\Spotify\Requests\GetRefreshTokenRequest` request class. We could then use it in our connector like so:

```
namespace App\Http\Integrations\Spotify;

use App\Http\Integrations\Spotify\Requests\GetRefreshTokenRequest;
use Saloon\Helpers\OAuth2\OAuthConfig;
use Saloon\Http\Connector;
use Saloon\Http\Request;

class SpotifyConnector extends Connector
{
    // ...

    protected function resolveRefreshTokenRequest(
        OAuthConfig $oauthConfig,
        string $refreshToken
    ): Request {
        return new GetRefreshTokenRequest($oauthConfig, $refreshToken);
    }
}
```

Testing Your OAuth2 Integrations

Like any other part of your application, it's important to ensure your OAuth2 integration is covered with a good-quality test suite. Since your integration involves authentication, authorization, and sensitive data, we need to be sure it's working correctly so we don't introduce any security vulnerabilities.

We'll use some of the techniques we learned in the previous chapter to test our integration and ensure it works as expected.

Preparing For Testing

Before writing any tests, we should create a few files to help make our testing easier. Having a fake service class to use as a test double will be helpful for this. We'll create a `SpotifyServiceFake` class in the `app/Services/Spotify` directory like so:

```php
namespace App\Services\Spotify;

use App\Collections\Spotify\ArtistCollection;
use App\DataTransferObjects\Spotify\AccessTokenDetails;
use App\DataTransferObjects\Spotify\AuthorizationCallbackDetails;
use App\DataTransferObjects\Spotify\AuthorizationRedirectDetails;
use App\Interfaces\Spotify;
use App\Models\User;

final class SpotifyServiceFake implements Spotify
{
    public function getAuthRedirectDetails(): AuthorizationRedirectDetails
    {
        throw new \Exception('Not implemented');
    }

    public function authorize(
        AuthorizationCallbackDetails $callbackDetails
    ): AccessTokenDetails {
        throw new \Exception('Not implemented');
    }

    public function getTopArtists(User $user): ArtistCollection
    {
        throw new \Exception('Not implemented');
    }
}
```

Just as we did in the previous chapter, we've added exceptions to each method to indicate which we need to implement. We'll be implementing these methods as we write our tests.

We should now create a new `InteractsWithSpotify` trait in the `tests/Traits` directory to make our tests easier to read:

```
namespace Tests\Traits;

use App\Interfaces\Spotify;
use App\Services\Spotify\SpotifyServiceFake;

trait InteractsWithSpotify
{
    private function fakeSpotify(): SpotifyServiceFake
    {
        $spotifyServiceFake = new SpotifyServiceFake();

        // Swap the implementation of the Spotify interface.
        $this->swap(Spotify::class, $spotifyServiceFake);

        return $spotifyServiceFake;
    }
}
```

Similar to our GitHub example in the previous chapter, we've added a `fakeSpotify` method we can call to swap the implementation of the `Spotify` interface with our fake service class. We can then use this method in our tests to ensure we use the fake service class instead of the real one.

Testing the Controllers

We can now start writing tests for our OAuth integration. Let's start by writing tests for our `App\Http\Controllers\OAuth\SpotifyController` controller.

Testing the `redirect` Method

To begin with, let's write some tests for the controller's `redirect` method. As we've seen, this method generates the URL the user will be redirected to when they begin the OAuth flow.

Let's write the test in a `tests/Feature/Controllers/OAuth/SpotifyController/RedirectTest.php` file and then discuss what we're doing:

```
namespace Tests\Feature\Controllers\OAuth\SpotifyAuthController;

use App\Models\User;
use Illuminate\Foundation\Testing\LazilyRefreshDatabase;
use PHPUnit\Framework\Attributes\Test;
use Tests\TestCase;
use Tests\Traits\InteractsWithSpotify;

final class RedirectTest extends TestCase
{
    use LazilyRefreshDatabase;
    use InteractsWithSpotify;

    #[Test]
    public function user_is_redirected_to_spotify(): void
```

```
    {
        $this->fakeSpotify()->buildAuthorizationUrlUsing(
            authorizationUrl: 'https://dummy-redirect-url.com',
            state: 'dummy-state',
            codeVerifier: 'dummy-code-verifier',
        );

        $this->actingAs(User::factory()->create())
            ->get(route('oauth.spotify.redirect'))
            ->assertRedirect('https://dummy-redirect-url.com')
            ->assertSessionHas('oauth_spotify_state', 'dummy-state')
            ->assertSessionHas(
                'oauth_spotify_code_verifier',
                'dummy-code-verifier'
            );
    }
}
```

In the test class, we use the `LazilyRefreshDatabase` trait that Laravel provides. Using this will migrate our test database before the first database call is made so we can access the `users` table. We're also using our `InteractsWithSpotify` trait we created earlier to access the `fakeSpotify` method.

In the test itself, as we did in our GitHub example in the previous chapter, we're faking the Spotify service class. We're calling a `buildAuthorizationUrlUsing` method (which we'll look at in a moment) on the `SpotifyServiceFake` that lets us define how to build the authorization URL. We're doing this to generate a predictable URL and state value that we can use to make assertions in our test.

Following this, we're then creating a new `User` using `User::factory()->create()` and authenticating as that user. This is needed because our `redirect` method is protected by the `auth` middleware, so we must be authenticated to access it. We're then making a `GET` request to the Spotify redirect route in our application and then asserting that we're redirected to the URL we defined in our fake service class. We also assert that the `oauth_spotify_state` and `oauth_spotify_code_verifier` session values are set to the values we defined in our fake service class.

Let's look at what the `buildAuthorizationUrlUsing` method is doing in our `SpotifyServiceFake` class:

```php
namespace App\Services\Spotify;

use App\Interfaces\Spotify;

final class SpotifyServiceFake implements Spotify
{
    public string $authorizationUrl;

    public string $state;

    public string $codeVerifier;

    // ...

    public function buildAuthorizationUrlUsing(
        string $authorizationUrl,
        string $state,
        string $codeVerifier
    ): self {
        $this->authorizationUrl = $authorizationUrl;
        $this->state = $state;
        $this->codeVerifier = $codeVerifier;

        return $this;
    }
}
```

In this method, we simply set the values we pass to the method on the class to access them in our test when calling the `getAuthRedirectDetails`. We're then returning the class instance so we can chain the method calls together in our test if needed.

Using this approach, we create predictable values to make assertions against in tests. This means our `getAuthRedirectDetails` method may look like this:

```
namespace App\Services\Spotify;

use App\DataTransferObjects\Spotify\AuthorizationRedirectDetails;
use App\Interfaces\Spotify;

final class SpotifyServiceFake implements Spotify
{
    // ...

    public function getAuthRedirectDetails(): AuthorizationRedirectDetails
    {
        return new AuthorizationRedirectDetails(
            authorizationUrl: $this->authorizationUrl,
            state: $this->state,
            codeVerifier: $this->codeVerifier,
        );
    }
}
```

Testing the "callback" Method

Now that we've tested the `redirect` method, let's test the `callback` method in our `SpotifyAuthController`. This method handles the callback from Spotify and exchanges the authorization code for an access token.

There are multiple scenarios that we want to test here:

- The user can complete the OAuth flow and save their tokens to the database.
- The user is redirected with an error message if the authorization code exchange fails.
- The user is redirected with an error message if they deny the authorization request.
- An error is returned if the request does not contain the `state` field.
- An error is returned if the request does not contain the `code` field.
- An error is returned if the user's session does not contain the `oauth_spotify_state` field.
- An error is returned if the user's session does not contain the `oauth_spotify_code_verifier` field.

Before we start writing these tests, we should prepare our `SpotifyServiceFake` class to handle the different scenarios. Let's take a look at what this class might look like with the changes:

```
use App\DataTransferObjects\Spotify\AccessTokenDetails;
use App\DataTransferObjects\Spotify\AuthorizationCallbackDetails;
use App\Exceptions\Integrations\Spotify\SpotifyException;
use App\Interfaces\Spotify;
use App\Models\User;

final class SpotifyServiceFake implements Spotify
{
    private SpotifyException $failureException;

    public function authorize(
        AuthorizationCallbackDetails $callbackDetails
    ): AccessTokenDetails {
        if (isset($this->failureException)) {
            throw $this->failureException;
        }
```

```php
        return new AccessTokenDetails(
            accessToken: 'access-token-here',
            refreshToken: 'refresh-token-here',
            expiresAt: now()->addWeek()->toDateTimeImmutable(),
        );
    }

    public function shouldFailWithException(SpotifyException $exception): self
    {
        $this->failureException = $exception;

        return $this;
    }
}
```

In the `authorize` method, we first check if the `failureException` property has been set. This property can be set via the `shouldFailWithException` method and will be used in our tests to simulate what would happen if the request to Spotify failed. If the property has been set, we throw the exception. If it hasn't, we'll return an `AccessTokenDetails` DTO with some dummy values.

Let's begin by testing the first scenario. We'll write the test in a `tests/Feature/Controllers/OAuth/SpotifyController/CallbackTest.php` file and then discuss what we're doing:

```php
namespace Tests\Feature\Controllers\OAuth\SpotifyAuthController;

use App\Models\User;
use Illuminate\Foundation\Testing\LazilyRefreshDatabase;
```

```php
use PHPUnit\Framework\Attributes\Test;
use Tests\TestCase;
use Tests\Traits\InteractsWithSpotify;

final class CallbackTest extends TestCase
{
    use LazilyRefreshDatabase;
    use InteractsWithSpotify;

    #[Test]
    public function user_can_complete_connection_to_spotify(): void
    {
        $this->freezeSecond();

        $this->fakeSpotify();

        $user = User::factory()->create();

        $this->actingAs($user)
            ->withSession([
                'oauth_spotify_state' => 'dummy-state',
                'oauth_spotify_code_verifier' => 'dummy-code-verifier',
            ])
            ->get(route('oauth.spotify.callback', [
                'code' => 'dummy-code',
                'state' => 'dummy-state',
            ]))
            ->assertRedirect(route('dashboard'))
            ->assertSessionHas(
                'success',
                'Spotify account connected successfully.'
```

```
        );

        $user->refresh();

        $this->assertEquals('access-token-here', $user->spotify_access_token);
        $this->assertEquals('refresh-token-here', $user->spotify_refresh_token);
        $this->assertTrue(now()->addWeek()->equalTo($user->spotify_expires_at));
    }
}
```

We start the test by pausing the time using `freezeSecond`. We do this because we will make assertions against the `spotify_expires_at` field on the `users` table, and we want to ensure that the value is the same as the one we're asserting against.

We then proceed to swap out the `App\Interfaces\Spotify` implementation for our fake implementation using the `fakeSpotify` method. After this, we create a new user and make a `GET` request acting as them. The request includes the `oauth_spotify_state` and `oauth_spotify_code_verifier` session values as well as the `code` and `state` query string parameters. We then assert the user is redirected to the dashboard and that the `success` session value is set to the correct value.

Finally, we assert the user's `spotify_access_token`, `spotify_refresh_token`, and `spotify_expires_at` fields are set to the values we expect.

We can now write another test that ensures we correctly redirect the user if a `SpotifyException` is thrown when trying to exchange the authorization code for the access token:

```
namespace Tests\Feature\Controllers\OAuth\SpotifyAuthController;
```

```php
use App\Exceptions\Integrations\Spotify\SpotifyException;
use App\Models\User;
use PHPUnit\Framework\Attributes\Test;
use Tests\TestCase;

final class CallbackTest extends TestCase
{
    // ...

    #[Test]
    public function error_is_returned_if_the_authorization_fails(): void
    {
        $this->fakeSpotify()->shouldFailWithException(
            new SpotifyException(),
        );

        $user = User::factory()->create();

        $this->actingAs($user)
            ->withSession([
                'oauth_spotify_state' => 'dummy-state',
                'oauth_spotify_code_verifier' => 'dummy-code-verifier',
            ])
            ->get(route('oauth.spotify.callback', [
                'code' => 'dummy-code',
                'state' => 'dummy-state',
            ]))
            ->assertRedirect(route('dashboard'))
            ->assertSessionHas('error', 'Failed to connect to Spotify account.');

        $this->assertUserWasNotUpdated($user->fresh());
```

```
    }

    private function assertUserWasNotUpdated(User $user): void
    {
        $this->assertNull($user->spotify_access_token);
        $this->assertNull($user->spotify_refresh_token);
        $this->assertNull($user->spotify_expires_at);
    }
}
```

This test is very similar to our previous test, except we use the `shouldFailWithException` method on the `SpotifyServiceFake` class to tell it to throw a `SpotifyException` when the `authorize` method is called. We then assert that the user is redirected to the dashboard and that the `error` session value is set to the correct value. Finally, we use an `assertUserWasNotUpdated` helper method to assert that we didn't update any of the OAuth fields on the user.

We can then write a test to ensure that the user is redirected to the dashboard correctly if the user denies the authorization request:

```
namespace Tests\Feature\Controllers\OAuth\SpotifyAuthController;

use App\Models\User;
use PHPUnit\Framework\Attributes\Test;
use Tests\TestCase;

final class CallbackTest extends TestCase
{
    // ...
```

```php
    #[Test]
    public function error_is_returned_if_user_denies_the_connection_to_spotify()
    {
        $this->fakeSpotify();

        $user = User::factory()->create();

        $this->actingAs($user)
            ->withSession([
                'oauth_spotify_state' => 'dummy-state',
                'oauth_spotify_code_verifier' => 'dummy-code-verifier',
            ])
            ->get(route('oauth.spotify.callback', [
                'error' => 'access_denied',
            ]))
            ->assertRedirect(route('dashboard'))
            ->assertSessionHas('error', 'Spotify account connection denied.');

        $this->assertUserWasNotUpdated($user->fresh());
    }
}
```

This test is similar to our previous tests, except that we pass `['error' => 'access_denied']` as a query parameter in the URL. We then assert that the user is redirected to the correct page and that the `error` session value is set to the correct value. Finally, we use the `assertUserWasNotUpdated` helper method to assert that we didn't update any of the OAuth fields on the user.

Finally, we can add four more tests for the `authorize` method in our controller that ensure an error is returned if the request does not contain all the required query string parameters or the required session values are not set. These tests will all be very similar, with only one or two lines being different. For this reason, we'll only show one of the tests. This particular test will ensure that an error is returned if the code query string parameter is not set:

```
use App\Models\User;
use PHPUnit\Framework\Attributes\Test;
use Tests\TestCase;

final class CallbackTest extends TestCase
{
    #[Test]
    public function error_is_returned_if_the_code_is_missing_from_the_request()
    {
        $this->fakeSpotify();

        $user = User::factory()->create();

        $this->actingAs($user)
            ->withSession([
                'oauth_spotify_state' => 'dummy-state',
                'oauth_spotify_code_verifier' => 'dummy-code-verifier',
            ])
            ->get(route('oauth.spotify.callback', [
                'state' => 'dummy-state',
            ]))
            ->assertBadRequest();

        $this->assertUserWasNotUpdated($user);
    }
}
```

In this test, we are making the request to the callback URL. However, we have not passed the `code` query parameter. We then assert that the response is an HTTP `400 Bad Request` and that the user was not updated.

Testing the Service Class

So far, we've tested that our `SpotifyAuthController` is correctly using the input and output of the `Spotify` interface. However, we've not yet tested the `SpotifyService` class itself, so we need to do this to ensure that we're making the correct requests to the Spotify API.

Testing the "getAuthRedirectDetails" Method

We'll start testing our `SpotifyService` class by testing the `getAuthRedirectDetails` method first. We'll do this by creating a new `GetAuthRedirectDetailsTest` test class in the `tests/Features/Services/Spotify/SpotifyService` directory. Let's write the test, and then we'll explain what we're doing:

```
namespace Tests\Feature\Services\Spotify\SpotifyService;

use App\Services\Spotify\SpotifyService;
use Illuminate\Support\Str;
use PHPUnit\Framework\Attributes\Test;
use Tests\TestCase;

final class GetAuthRedirectDetailsTest extends TestCase
{
    #[Test]
    public function auth_redirect_details_can_be_returned(): void
    {
```

```php
// Define how random strings are built so that we can assert against
// them.
Str::createRandomStringsUsing(fn(): string => 'random-string-here');

config([
    'services.spotify.client_id' => 'client-id-here',
]);

$authDetails = (new SpotifyService())->getAuthRedirectDetails();

// Get the query parameters from the authorization URL.
$queryParameters = [];

parse_str(
    parse_url(
        $authDetails->authorizationUrl, PHP_URL_QUERY
    ),
    $queryParameters,
);

// Assert the authorization URL has the expected query parameters.
$this->assertCount(7, $queryParameters);

$this->assertEquals(
    '6XubkmX33mCpz3mcaXhGHtsewBFJsCQPCW5bff_tDac',
    $queryParameters['code_challenge']
);
$this->assertEquals('S256', $queryParameters['code_challenge_method']);

// Assert the state and code challenge are both returned.
$this->assertEquals($queryParameters['state'], $authDetails->state);
```

```
        $this->assertEquals('random-string-here', $authDetails->codeVerifier);
    }
}
```

There are many ways to test this method, as it involves creating random strings and building a URL. However, we've opted to start the test by using the `Str::createRandomStringsUsing` method to define how Laravel should generate random strings using the `Illuminate\Support\Str` class. This means when we try to build a random string for the `code_verifier` field, Laravel will run the callback we've provided and thus return `"random-string-here"` as the random string. We've also hardcoded the `services.spotify.client_id` config field so we can assert against it later.

Following this, we created a new instance of the `SpotifyService` class and call the `getAuthRedirectDetails` method. We then extracted the query parameters from the URL to assert that the correct ones have been added to the URL. We expect the URL to have seven query parameters, but we'll only test the two we manually add ourselves: `code_challenge` and `code_challenge_method`. You could add assertions for the other five query parameters, but it's not necessary as Saloon adds them, so we'd be testing Saloon's functionality rather than our own. So, in our test, we're only testing that the `code_challenge_method` is correct and that `code_challenge` is the hashed and base64-encoded version of our `code_verifier` field. We have hardcoded this field because that is what we expect it to be when the `code_verifier` field is equal to `"random-string-here"`.

We also added assertions to ensure that the `state` and `code_verifier` fields are returned in the `AuthRedirectDetails` object. We asserted that the `state` field is equal to the `state` query parameter and that the `code_verifier` field is equal to `"random-string-here"`.

Testing the `authorize` Method

Let's now test the `authorize` method of the `SpotifyService` class. This method is responsible for exchanging the authorization code for an access token and refresh token. We'll do this by creating a new `AuthorizeTest` test class in the `tests/Features/Services/Spotify/SpotifyService` directory. We'll write the test and then explain what we're doing:

```
namespace Tests\Feature\Services\Spotify\SpotifyService;

use App\DataTransferObjects\Spotify\AuthorizationCallbackDetails;
use App\Http\Integrations\Spotify\Requests\GetAccessTokenRequest;
use App\Services\Spotify\SpotifyService;
use PHPUnit\Framework\Attributes\Test;
use Saloon\Http\Faking\MockResponse;
use Saloon\Laravel\Facades\Saloon;
use Tests\TestCase;

final class AuthorizeTest extends TestCase
{
    #[Test]
    public function access_details_are_returned(): void
    {
        $this->freezeSecond();

        config([
            'services.spotify.client_id' => 'client-id-here',
            'services.spotify.client_secret' => 'client-secret-here',
        ]);

        Saloon::fake([
            MockResponse::make([
                'access_token' => 'access-token-here',
```

```
            'refresh_token' => 'refresh-token-here',
            'expires_in' => 3600,
        ])
    ]);

    $callbackDetails = new AuthorizationCallbackDetails(
        authorizationCode: 'dummy-code',
        expectedState: 'dummy-state',
        state: 'dummy-state',
        codeVerifier: 'dummy-code-verifier',
    );

    $spotifyService = new SpotifyService();

    $authDetails = $spotifyService->authorize($callbackDetails);

    $this->assertEquals('access-token-here', $authDetails->accessToken);
    $this->assertEquals('refresh-token-here', $authDetails->refreshToken);
    $this->assertEquals(
        now()->addHour()->format('U'),
        $authDetails->expiresAt->format('U')
    );

    // Assert our request was sent with the correct code verifier.
    Saloon::assertSent(static function (GetAccessTokenRequest $request) {
        return $request->resolveEndpoint() ===
                'https://accounts.spotify.com/api/token'
            && $request->body()->all() === [
                'grant_type' => 'authorization_code',
                'code' => 'dummy-code',
                'redirect_uri' =>
```

```
'https://consuming-apis-in-laravel-code-examples.test/oauth/spotify/callback',
                    'code_verifier' => 'dummy-code-verifier'
                ];
            });
        }
    }
```

We begin the test by freezing the time so we can assert against the access token's expiry time later in the test. We then set the `services.spotify.client_id` and `services.spotify.client_secret` config values.

Following this, we use the `Saloon::fake()` method covered in the previous chapter to mock a successful response for the API request.

We then create an instance of the `AuthorizationCallbackDetails`, typically created by the `SpotifyController` class. Next, we create a new instance of the `SpotifyService` class and call the `authorize` method. We then assert that the `accessToken`, `refreshToken`, and `expiresAt` fields equal the expected values specified in the mock response.

Finally, we use `Saloon::assertSent` to inspect the request made to Spotify. We assert that the request is being sent to the correct endpoint and that the request body is correct.

Testing the "getTopArtists" Method

We can now write a test for the `getTopArtists` method in the `SpotifyService` class that uses the access token to fetch the user's top artists from Spotify. We want to test the following scenarios:

- The user's top artists can be returned if the user has a valid access token.
- The user's top artists can be returned if the user has an expired access token and a valid

refresh token.

- An exception is thrown if the user is not connected to Spotify.

Let's start by writing a test for the first scenario. We'll create a `GetTopArtistsTest.php` file in the `tests/Features/Services/Spotify/SpotifyService` directory and write the test:

```
namespace Tests\Feature\Services\Spotify\SpotifyService;

use App\DataTransferObjects\Spotify\Artist;
use App\Http\Integrations\Spotify\Requests\GetRefreshTokenRequest;
use App\Http\Integrations\Spotify\Requests\UserTopArtists;
use App\Models\User;
use App\Services\Spotify\SpotifyService;
use PHPUnit\Framework\Attributes\Test;
use Saloon\Http\Faking\MockResponse;
use Saloon\Laravel\Facades\Saloon;
use Tests\TestCase;

final class GetTopArtistsTest extends TestCase
{
    // ...

    #[Test]
    public function top_artists_can_be_returned(): void
    {
        Saloon::fake([
            UserTopArtists::class => MockResponse::fixture(
                'Spotify/Top-Artists'
            ),
        ]);
```

```php
        $user = User::factory()
            ->create([
                'spotify_access_token' => 'access-token-here',
                'spotify_refresh_token' => 'refresh-token-here',
                'spotify_expires_at' => now()->addWeek(),
            ]);

        $artists = (new SpotifyService())->getTopArtists($user);

        $artists->ensure(Artist::class);
        $this->assertCount(20, $artists);

        Saloon::assertNotSent(GetRefreshTokenRequest::class);
    }
}
```

In this test, we use the `Saloon::fake()` method to mock a successful response for the `UserTopArtists` request. A recorded response is used from `tests/Fixtures/Saloon/Spotify/Top-Artists.json`.

We then create a new user and set the access token, refresh token, and expiry date for them. Following this, we call the `getTopArtists` method the `SpotifyService`, which will be responsible for making the request to the Spotify API.

We're performing some simple assertions on the artists returned to ensure all the items in the `ArtistCollection` are instances of `App\DataTransferObjects\Spotify\Artist` and that there are 20 items in the collection.

Finally, we use `Saloon::assertNotSent` to assert that the `GetRefreshTokenRequest` request was not sent. The user has a valid access token, so we don't need to refresh it.

You can also add assertions to this test to ensure the request being sent is correct, but we'll skip that in this example.

We can then add another test that simulates what would happen in the scenario that the user's access token has expired and we need to refresh it:

```
namespace Tests\Feature\Services\Spotify\SpotifyService;

use App\DataTransferObjects\Spotify\Artist;
use App\Http\Integrations\Spotify\Requests\GetRefreshTokenRequest;
use App\Http\Integrations\Spotify\Requests\UserTopArtists;
use App\Models\User;
use App\Services\Spotify\SpotifyService;
use PHPUnit\Framework\Attributes\Test;
use Saloon\Http\Faking\MockResponse;
use Saloon\Laravel\Facades\Saloon;
use Tests\TestCase;

final class GetTopArtistsTest extends TestCase
{
    #[Test]
    public function top_artists_can_be_returned_if_the_access_token_has_expired()
    {
        $this->freezeSecond();

        Saloon::fake([
            GetRefreshTokenRequest::class => MockResponse::make([
                'access_token' => 'new-access-token-here',
                'refresh_token' => 'new-refresh-token-here',
                'expires_in' => 3600,
            ]),
```

```
            UserTopArtists::class => MockResponse::fixture(
                'Spotify/Top-Artists'
            ),
        ]);

        $user = User::factory()
            ->create([
                'spotify_access_token' => 'access-token-here',
                'spotify_refresh_token' => 'refresh-token-here',
                'spotify_expires_at' => now()->subWeek(),
            ]);

        $artists = (new SpotifyService())->getTopArtists($user);

        $artists->ensure(Artist::class);
        $this->assertCount(20, $artists);

        Saloon::assertSent(GetRefreshTokenRequest::class);

        $user->refresh();

        $this->assertEquals(
            'new-access-token-here', $user->spotify_access_token
        );
        $this->assertEquals(
            'new-refresh-token-here', $user->spotify_refresh_token
        );

        $this->assertTrue(now()->addHour()->equalTo($user->spotify_expires_at));
    }
}
```

This test is very similar to our previous one, except that we're also mocking a successful response to the `GetRefreshTokenRequest` request. We're also using the `freezeSecond()` method to freeze the current time to assert that the access token's expiry date is correct.

We're then creating the user and attempting to get their top artists, then asserting that the intended results were returned. We're also asserting that the `GetRefreshTokenRequest` request was sent.

Finally, we're asserting that the user's access token, refresh token, and expiry date have been updated to the new values returned from the `GetRefreshTokenRequest` request.

If you prefer more strict tests, you may add assertions to ensure the `Artist` DTOs are instantiated correctly and the `GetRefreshTokenRequest` is correct.

We can now add our final test that simulates what would happen in the scenario that the `getTopArtists` method is called for a user that hasn't connected to Spotify yet:

```php
use App\Exceptions\Integrations\Spotify\SpotifyException;
use App\Models\User;
use App\Services\Spotify\SpotifyService;
use PHPUnit\Framework\Attributes\Test;
use Tests\TestCase;

final class GetTopArtistsTest extends TestCase
{
    #[Test]
    public function exception_is_thrown_if_user_has_not_connected_to_spotify()
    {
        Saloon::fake();

        $this->expectException(SpotifyException::class);
        $this->expectExceptionMessage('User is not connected to Spotify.');

        (new SpotifyService())->getTopArtists(User::factory()->create());

        Saloon::assertNothingSent();
    }
}
```

In this test, we're instructing PHPUnit to expect a `SpotifyException` to be thrown with the message "User is not connected to Spotify" when the `getTopArtists` method is called for a user who hasn't connected to Spotify yet. We're also using `Saloon::fake()` to ensure no requests are sent. This isn't necessary, but if a bug in your code leads to a request being sent, faking Saloon like this will ensure that the request isn't actually sent and that the test will fail.

Conclusion

This chapter examined what OAuth is and how it works. We looked at terminology you'll come across, use cases, the different flows, and the benefits and drawbacks. We delved into using the Authorization Code flow in Saloon to authenticate a user with Spotify, then finished by looking at how to test our OAuth integrations.

Using what you've learned in this chapter, you should now understand how OAuth works well enough to use it in your applications with confidence.

In the next chapter, we'll shift the focus. Instead of sending API requests to third-party services, we'll cover receiving requests from third-party services — also known as webhooks.

Webhooks

Webhooks form an important part of API integrations. They allow you to receive data from an external application when something happens, such as the successful delivery of an email or the placement of a new order. Your application can use webhooks to react to events asynchronously and perform actions based on them.

Depending on the API service you're interacting with, webhooks may sometimes be required to complete your applications' features and API integration. For example, when using a payment gateway such as Stripe, your application must accept webhooks sent from Stripe to be notified of successful and failed payments.

In this section, we will look at what webhooks are, how they work, and how to handle them securely in your Laravel application. We'll also look at real-life examples of how you might want to use webhooks. After this, we'll look at how you can test that your application can handle webhooks securely and robustly.

What Are Webhooks?

In their simplest form, webhooks are a way for an application to send an HTTP request to another application when something happens.

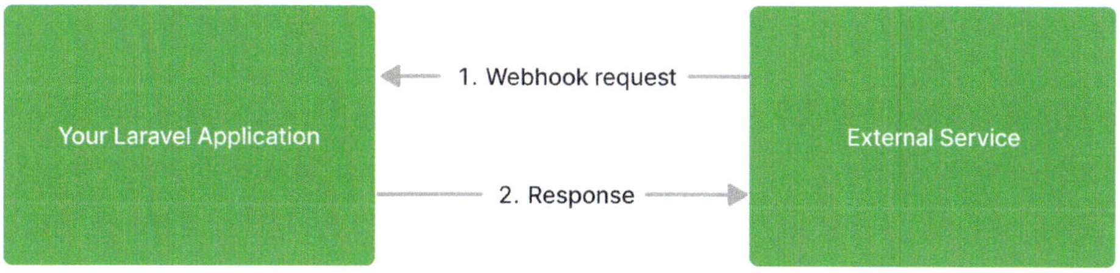

For example, say you are using Mailgun (a service that sends and receives emails) to send emails from your Laravel application. To do this, you would typically send an HTTP request to Mailgun to send the email, and they would reply with a response to let you know they've accepted the email and will attempt to send it. But this doesn't necessarily mean Mailgun sent the email successfully; it just means that Mailgun has acknowledged that you want to send it.

So how would you know if the email was delivered?

This situation is where webhooks come in. If you enable webhooks in Mailgun, they will send a request back to your application for different events, such as the email being delivered.

In fact, Mailgun offers different types of webhooks to give you a lot of visibility into what's happening with your emails. They provide the following webhooks:

- `clicked`
- `complained`
- `delivered`
- `opened`
- `permanent_fail`
- `temporary_fail`
- `unsubscribed`

You can imagine that this type of data can be very useful for your application. You can use it to send notifications to your users or update the email status in your database.

It's important to note that webhooks aren't necessarily triggered by an action you've taken. In our example above, we've triggered the webhook by sending an email. But webhooks can also be triggered by other actions, such as a new user signing up to the external application.

The Advantages of Webhooks

Webhooks can provide tremendous value and functionality to your application. Let's take a look at the different advantages that webhooks can provide:

Real-Time Updates

Webhooks allow web applications to receive real-time updates about events that occur in other applications or systems. This means your application can immediately react to changes or updates rather than relying on a user or another system to trigger an action.

Going back to our example about sending emails, let's imagine that your web application records the status of emails (e.g., pending, sent, delivered, opened, clicked) in a database. You could also record a reason for the email failing to send, such as a hard bounce or a spam complaint.

Without webhooks, you'd need to periodically send an API request to your mail provider to get the latest status. This technique of sending periodic requests is known as "polling". For instance, you could check this status every hour, but then you have to wait up to an hour to get the latest status of the email. Imagine you're building a newsletter application. You'd want to know when the emails were delivered as soon as possible.

With webhooks, you can receive feedback from the mail provider and update the email status in the database as soon as the events occur. Thus, you can provide your users with a better experience, as they can see the status of their emails without a long delay.

Reduced Load on Your Application

As mentioned previously, webhooks can reduce the need for polling third-party services. Continuing with our example of sending emails, if you were to use webhooks, you'd only need to send a request to Mailgun when you send an email. But if you were to use polling, you'd also need to send a request to Mailgun every hour or so to check the status of the emails.

Thus, with each poll, you'd query your database and add additional load to your servers — especially if you're sending many emails, as you'd run these queries every hour for every email you send. Sometimes, these queries retrieve fresh data, but they might also retrieve data you already have in your database. So a lot of unnecessary queries could run.

Using webhooks, you may only need to make queries related to the emails if you were handling a webhook that contained new data. This means that you can reduce the load on your servers and improve the performance of your application. It's important, however, to remember that using webhooks doesn't automatically improve your system's performance. You still need to ensure you're handling the webhooks efficiently and avoiding issues such as unnecessary database queries or unoptimized code.

Seamless Integrations With Your Application

Suppose your web application allows users to configure and send webhooks to other applications. In that case, you can improve the value of your product by allowing users to integrate your application with other services they use.

For example, say you are building an e-commerce website and want to allow the site's administrators to send webhooks to other applications. You could allow them to configure a URL to which an API request is sent whenever a new order is placed.

As a result, the value of your product improves because your users can automate part of their workflow to integrate with other applications they're already using.

The Disadvantages of Webhooks

Although webhooks can provide a lot of value to your application, there are also disadvantages to be aware of. Let's look at the drawbacks of using webhooks in your application:

Increased Complexity

Although webhooks are a great way to receive real-time updates from other applications, they can add complexity and maintenance overhead to your application.

You'll need to add the basics (such as the routes and controllers) to handle the webhooks, but you may also need to add jobs, middleware, service classes, data transfer objects, enums, and other pieces of code.

As is the case when adding any code to your projects, this will require writing tests to ensure that the code runs as expected. The more code you add, the more tests you'll need to write and maintain, which can be a lot of work when using many webhooks from different services.

Increased Security Risks

As mentioned, to accept a webhook request, you must add a new API route to your Laravel application to handle the request. By adding a new route to your application, you're also adding a new attack vector for malicious users to try and exploit.

Of course, a robust security strategy for verifying the requests (such as checking request signatures and using secret keys) reduces the risk of such attacks, but you must be aware of these risks. So when building the route, it's essential to ask, "Could someone use this route to do something malicious?".

Later in this section, we'll look at how you can securely handle webhooks.

Fire and Forget

One issue when using webhooks is that you can't always see whether the webhook request was successful. Some platforms, such as Mailgun, provide a dashboard showing the webhook requests' status. They also provide the ability to retry failed requests. But not all platforms offer such functionality.

For many services, webhooks are simply sent to your application and then forgotten. Thus, if the webhook request fails (for example, due to a bug in your code), you will only know about it if logging is set up. This can be a problem if you rely on the webhook to perform an important action, such as updating a user's subscription.

One way to mitigate this issue is to use a queue to handle the webhooks in your application. If there are any problems with the webhook, you can attempt to handle it again later (for example, after you have deployed a fix).

Defining Webhooks Routes

When building a web application that receives webhooks, you must define the routes to which the external application can send the webhook. These routes will then handle the webhook and perform any required actions.

Every system you work with will have its own way of defining webhook routes. You can usually find information about how to set up webhooks in their documentation.

Let's look at a few examples of how you may define webhook routes for different applications.

Defining Webhook Routes in the External Application's Dashboard

Some web applications, such as Mailgun, only allow you to define your webhook routes in their dashboard. Usually, this means you can't use a dynamic URL, such as one containing a parameter. For example, you may add an `/api/webhooks/mailgun` route to your application, but you can't necessarily add a route such as `/api/webhooks/mailgun/{email}`.

These applications may allow you to define individual webhook routes for each event that you want to receive. Using Mailgun as an example, you may wish to receive webhooks for the following events:

- `clicked`
- `complained`
- `delivered`

In your Laravel app, you could define three separate routes (one for each event):

- `/api/webhooks/mailgun/clicked`

- /api/webhooks/mailgun/complained
- /api/webhooks/mailgun/delivered

On the other hand, you may want to receive all the events in a single route (such as /api/webhooks/mailgun or by using /api/webhooks/mailgun/{event}). These are both valid approaches — the best method for your application and API integration is up to you.

Some applications don't allow you to define separate webhook routes for each event. In this case, you must define a single route that handles all the events.

Defining Webhook Routes at Runtime

Some web applications, such as Twilio, allow you to define the webhook routes at runtime. For example, take the following code you could use to send an SMS message from your Laravel application using Twilio:

```
use Twilio\Rest\Client;

$twilio = new Client(
    config('services.twilio.sid'),
    config('services.twilio.token'),
);

$twilio->messages
    ->create('+1234567890', [
        'body' => 'Example SMS body here',
        'from' => '+0987654321',
        'statusCallback' => 'https://myapp.com/api/webhooks/twilio/sms'
    ]);
```

You may have noticed that the `statusCallback` parameter is set to a URL defined in our application. This means that Twilio will send a request to this URL when the SMS message is sent, delivered, or failed to send.

Being able to define the webhook route at runtime opens up the possibility for us to use things like route model binding in our webhook routes. As an example, instead of using an `/api/webhooks/twilio/sms` route, we could use the following route:

```
use Illuminate\Support\Facades\Route;
use App\Http\Controllers\TwilioSmsWebhookController;

Route::post(
    '/api/webhooks/twilio/sms/{message}',
    TwilioSmsWebhookController::class
);
```

This route may point to a controller method that looks like this:

```
use App\Models\Message;
use Illuminate\Http\Request;

class TwilioSmsWebhookController
{
    public function __invoke(Request $request, Message $message)
    {
        // Handle the webhook request here...
    }
}
```

As we can see in the example above, we've type-hinted the `$message` parameter. As a result,

Laravel will attempt to resolve the model from the database when calling this controller method. For example, imagine we have a `Message` model stored in the database with an ID of `1`. If Twilio sent the webhook request to `/api/webhooks/twilio/sms/1`, Laravel would resolve the `Message` model with an ID of `1` and pass it to the controller method. If the message doesn't exist, Laravel will throw an `Illuminate\Database\Eloquent\ModelNotFoundException`, sending an HTTP 404 response back to Twilio.

So you'll need to choose your webhook route structure depending on where and how the third-party application allows you to define your webhook routes. You may not need to use route model binding in your webhook routes, but it can be helpful if your webhooks are sent to a dynamic URL and relate directly to a model in your database.

Building Webhook Routes

Now that we have a brief understanding of what webhooks are and how they can be used, let's look at how we can build a webhook route in a Laravel application.

We'll build a webhook route that handles an API request sent from Mailgun when an email is delivered. First, we'll focus on getting the webhook route working. Then we'll look at securing it to prevent malicious users from sending fake requests to our application.

Imagine the workflow for sending an email is as follows:

1. The user performs an action, such as submitting a form, that triggers an email to be sent.
2. A new row in an `email_logs` table is created with the status of `pending`.
3. Your application sends an API request to Mailgun to send the email, passing the ID of the row in the `email_logs` table as a "user variable" (we'll cover this in more depth later).
4. Mailgun handles sending the email to the correct recipient.
5. Mailgun sends an HTTP request to your application's webhook route, passing the ID of the row in the `email_logs` table as a "user variable".
6. Your application updates the email status in the `email_logs` table to `delivered`.

For this section, assume steps 1-4 are completed. We'll solely focus on steps 5 and 6, which involve building the webhook route.

What Will Be Sent

Before we touch any code, let's look at an example payload Mailgun will send to our webhook route. This will help us understand how to implement the code in the controller, service class, and middleware:

```
{
  "signature": {
    "token": "92e79f1325dc7f63b091cf4765e893937932f9faaf3fa35b2e",
    "timestamp": "1679932336",
    "signature": "541346f2701f6ab19b21e6ba7719be29c95bf95b605a643e3b139934581d0"
  },
  "event-data": {
    "id": "CPgfbmQMTCKtHW6uIWtuVe",
    "timestamp": 1521472262.908181,
    "log-level": "info",
    "event": "delivered",
    // ...
    "message": {
      "headers": {
        "to": "Alice <alice@example.com>",
        "message-id": "20130503182626.18666.16540@example.com",
        "from": "Bob <bob@example.com>",
        "subject": "Test delivered webhook"
      },
      "attachments": [],
      "size": 111
    },
    "recipient": "alice@example.com",
    "recipient-domain": "example.com",
    "user-variables": {
      "email_id": "123"
    }
  }
}
```

For this book, I've removed some of the information in this webhook as the payload contains a lot of information, and it's doubtful you'll need all of it. In this case, we'll only need:

- The `event` key, which tells us what type of event has occurred (e.g., `delivered`).
- The `user-variables` key, containing user variables we passed to Mailgun. For this example, we have the `email_id` key, containing the ID of the row in the `email_logs` table.
- The `signature` key, containing the signature needed to verify the request was actually sent from Mailgun. We'll cover this later.

Creating the Route

To start building our webhook route, we'll need to create a new route in our Laravel application that Mailgun can send requests to when an email is delivered. We'll add this to our `routes/api.php` file:

```
use App\Http\Controllers\Api\Webhooks\MailgunController;
use Illuminate\Support\Facades\Route;

Route::post(
    '/webhooks/mailgun/{status}',
    MailgunController::class
)->name('webhooks.mailgun');
```

As we can see, we've created a new `/api/webhooks/mailgun/{status}` route for our application. We will create an `EmailStatus` enum class containing all the possible values for the `{status}` parameter. As a result of using an enum, Laravel will be able to automatically resolve the enum class when a request is made to the route. This means we can reject requests that don't contain a valid status value and only accept requests for events we have explicitly defined. We'll cover the enum class in more depth further on.

It's important to note that the `/api` prefix for the route was automatically prepended for us because we added the route to the `routes/api.php` file. This behaviour is defined in the `boot` method of the `app/Providers/RouteServiceProvider` class that ships with Laravel. The provider may look like so:

```php
use Illuminate\Foundation\Support\Providers\RouteServiceProvider as
ServiceProvider;
use Illuminate\Support\Facades\Route;

class RouteServiceProvider extends ServiceProvider
{
    // ...

    /**
     * Define your route model bindings, pattern filters, and
     * other route configuration.
     */
    public function boot(): void
    {
        // ...

        $this->routes(function () {
            Route::middleware('api')
                ->prefix('api')
                ->as('api.')
                ->group(base_path('routes/api.php'));

            // ...
        });
    }
}
```

It's worth noting that we have also manually added the `as('api.')` line. This will automatically prepend all the route names in our `api.php` file with `api.`. Although you'll likely never be interacting with the API routes in your own application using the route names, you can use this feature for testing purposes. For example, in our tests, we can call `route('api.webhooks.mailgun')` rather than `/api/webhooks/mailgun`. However, this is purely personal preference and not something you have to do.

Creating the Enum

As mentioned above, we will create an `EmailStatus` enum that contains all possible values for the `{status}` parameter. This will allow us to reject requests that don't contain a valid status and only accept requests for events that we have explicitly defined.

We can also use the `EmailStatus` enum in the `EmailLog` model we'll create next. This will allow us to improve the accuracy and type safety of our `EmailLog` model.

Let's create a new `app/Enums/EmailStatus.php` file that will contain our `EmailStatus` enum:

```
namespace App\Enums;

enum EmailStatus: string
{
    case Pending = 'pending';

    case Delivered = 'delivered';

    case TemporaryFail = 'temporary_fail';

    case PermanentFail = 'permanent_fail';
}
```

As a result of creating these enum values, we can now make requests to the following variations of our `/api/webhooks/mailgun/{status}` route:

- `/api/webhooks/mailgun/pending`
- `/api/webhooks/mailgun/delivered`
- `/api/webhooks/mailgun/temporary_fail`
- `/api/webhooks/mailgun/permanent_fail`

Typically, you could now enter these URLs in your Mailgun dashboard to configure webhooks to send to these routes. For example, you could configure a webhook to be sent to `/api/webhooks/mailgun/delivered` whenever an email is delivered. Note that we won't set up a webhook to send to the `/api/webhooks/mailgun/pending` route because the emails would be automatically set as `pending` when first created in the `EmailLog` model.

Creating the Model

We must now create our `EmailLog` model that can be used to interact with the `email_logs` table in the database. For this chapter, assume we have already created the table and added any columns we want.

To improve the accuracy and type safety of our `EmailLog` model, we'll use the `EmailStatus` enum containing possible values of the `status` column in the `email_logs` table.

We can then update our `EmailLog` model to use the `EmailStatus` enum cast for the `status` column:

```php
declare(strict_types=1);

namespace App\Models;

use App\Enums\EmailStatus;
use Illuminate\Database\Eloquent\Factories\HasFactory;
use Illuminate\Database\Eloquent\Model;

final class EmailLog extends Model
{
    use HasFactory;

    protected $casts = [
        'status' => EmailStatus::class
    ];
}
```

As a result of this, we can write things like `$emailLog->status = EmailStatus::Delivered` and `$emailLog->status === EmailStatus::Pending` so we can interact with the enum in our application's code. But Laravel will take care of the casting to store it in the database as a string (such as `delivered`).

Creating the Controller

We can now create the new `MailgunController` we referenced in the route. We can do this by running the following Artisan command in our project's root:

```
php artisan make:controller Api/Webhooks/MailgunController -i
```

You may have noticed we used the `-i` option when running the command. This option creates a new controller with only a single method, the `__invoke` method. This is different from the default behaviour of the `make:controller` command, which creates a controller with all the CRUD methods (such as `index`, `create`, `store`, `show`, `edit`, `update`, `destroy`). I use this approach because I prefer my webhook controllers to have only one method. This helps ensure a controller is only responsible for handling a single webhook request. I usually create a new controller for each webhook I need to handle.

Now that we have the outline of the controller created, we can add the code to handle the webhook request. We'll keep all the code to handle the webhook inside the controller for brevity. But you may want to extract the logic from the controller into a service or action class. Your code may look something like this:

```php
declare(strict_types=1);

namespace App\Http\Controllers\Api\Webhooks;

use App\Enums\EmailStatus;
use App\Http\Controllers\Controller;
use App\Models\EmailLog;
use Illuminate\Http\JsonResponse;
use Illuminate\Http\Request;

final class MailgunController extends Controller
{
    public function __invoke(Request $request, EmailStatus $status): JsonResponse
    {
        // Grab the data we need from the request.
        $emailId = $request->input('event-data.user-variables.email_id');

        // Update the email log with the new status.
        EmailLog::query()
            ->whereKey($emailId)
            ->update([
                'status' => $status,
            ]);

        // Return a successful response.
        return response()->json(['success' => true]);
    }
}
```

In our controller above, we've added the logic to handle the webhook request if a `delivered`, `temporary_fail`, or `permanent_fail` event is received. As we've already mentioned, if an invalid `status` is passed to the controller that cannot be resolved to an `EmailStatus` enum value, Laravel will automatically return a 404 response. This gives us some extra peace of mind that we won't be handling webhook events we don't expect. We then update the `email_status` field in the database with the new status. Finally, we return a successful JSON response to the webhook provider (in this case, Mailgun). This is important as it lets the webhook provider know we've received the webhook and handled it successfully.

The controller in the example above doesn't extensively track the email. For instance, we're not logging the time the email status was updated or tracking previous statuses. You may want to add this, but we have kept the code simple to focus on handling webhooks.

Even though we haven't configured any webhooks to be sent to the `pending` variation of the route, you may also want to add a check to your controller to reject any requests to `/api/webhooks/mailgun/pending` for improved safety.

A handy point to remember is that many third-party services use similar payloads for each webhook they send. For example, the payload sent by Mailgun for the `delivered` event has the same structure as all the other event payloads (such as `temporary_fail`, `permanent_fail`, etc.). As mentioned previously, this means you can sometimes reuse the same controller for all the webhooks you're receiving from Mailgun if it's written in a way that can handle all the different events (such as the controller in the example). This isn't the case with every service, so you must check the documentation for each service to see how they handle their webhooks.

It's important to return a suitable response if an error occurs. Some third-party systems allow you to return specific error codes instructing them to keep retrying to deliver the webhook. For example, Mailgun states the following in their documentation:

- If Mailgun receives an HTTP 200 (success) response code from your webhook route, it will determine that the webhook request was successful and not retry.
- If Mailgun receives an HTTP 406 (not acceptable) response code from your webhook route, it will determine that the webhook request was rejected and will not retry the request

again.

- If Mailgun receives any other status code (e.g. 500, 400, 403, etc.), it will determine that the webhook request failed and will retry the request again using the following schedule: 10 minutes, 10 minutes, 15 minutes, 30 minutes, 1 hour, 2 hours, and 4 hours.

It is strongly advised to read the documentation for the webhook provider you're using to see how they handle errors and what response codes they expect you to return. The ability to retry the webhooks can be useful if your webhook-handling code currently has any errors or bugs, as you may be able to fix the issue, and the webhook provider will automatically retry the webhook request.

Webhook Security

As with any part of your application, it's crucial to handle webhooks securely. This is especially important when using webhooks to trigger actions like sending emails or notifications. If you have insufficient security measures, anyone could send a request to your webhook route and trigger the action.

A typical way to ensure a webhook was sent from the expected third-party service (not a malicious user) is by verifying a signature or token sent in the payload. Services may implement this in different ways. For example, some providers pass a signature in the payload and expect you to build a signature using the same algorithm and compare the two. Others pass a secret token in the payload to compare to a secret token stored in your application's `.env` file.

Verifying the requests generally involves having a secret token or key in your application's `.env` that no one else should know about apart from the third-party service. Thus, if someone else sent a request to your webhook route, they wouldn't have the secret token or key, so the request would be rejected.

Why You Must Secure Your Webhooks

To understand why securing webhook routes is necessary, let's look at an example of how someone could exploit an unsecured webhook route.

Imagine you're building a software-as-a-service (SaaS) web application that requires payment to access certain features. Assume you're using Stripe as your payment provider and you've set up a webhook route that will be triggered whenever a user makes a payment. When the payment is successful, you want to upgrade your user's account so they can access the premium features. The workflow may look like this:

1. A user signs up for your application.

2. The user is granted access to the free features.
3. The user upgrades their account to a paid plan.
4. A payment is taken via Stripe.
5. Stripe sends a webhook request to your application to confirm the successful payment.
6. Your application receives the webhook and upgrades the user's account to the paid plan.

Since Stripe is a popular payment provider, it's relatively straightforward to go online and find the structure of a payload sent in a webhook request. If a malicious user figured out your application's webhook route (perhaps something like `/api/webhooks/stripe`), they could try sending requests to the route with a payload.

When building your webhook route and controller, you might assume the data will always be sent from Stripe. Thus, you may have written the code only to handle a valid payload where the payment is always successful.

In this case, if a malicious user sends a request to your webhook route with a payload that your application expects, they could access premium features for free. This is a big security issue you must take steps to prevent.

One way of doing this is using a middleware to verify the webhook is coming from who you expect. Usually, this is done by checking the validity of a unique code sent by the third-party service. This code — a signature, key, or token — should be a secret only your app or the third-party service knows or can create.

We will review code examples validating that the request is from a third-party service.

Validating a Mailgun Webhook

Let's see how to validate that a webhook request was sent from Mailgun. To verify that a webhook request is valid, Mailgun provides a `signature` field in the webhook request body. This `signature` field looks like so:

```json
{
  "signature": {
    "token": "92e79f1325dc7f63b123454765e893937932f9f12345a35b2e",
    "timestamp": "1679932336",
    "signature": "541346f212345ab19b21e6ba7719be29c95bf9512345643e3b139934581fa"
  }
}
```

The following instructions are provided in the Mailgun documentation to determine whether a webhook request is valid:

- Concatenate the `timestamp` and `token` values from the outer `signature` field together.
- Hash the concatenated string using the HMAC SHA256 algorithm and your Mailgun "webhook signing key" as the key. You can find this in your Mailgun dashboard. It'll be stored in your `.env` file like so: `MAILGUN_SECRET=your-mailgun-webhook-signing-key`. This allows us to access it in our application using `config('services.mailgun.secret')`.
- Compare the generated hash with the `signature` value from the `signature` field in the webhook request body.
- If the two hashes match, the webhook request is valid.
- If the two hashes don't match, the webhook request is invalid and wasn't sent from Mailgun.

Mailgun also advises you to check the `timestamp` value from the `signature` field to ensure the request isn't too old. If the request is older than an amount of time (such as 1 minute), it is likely invalid. This could be a "replay attack" where a malicious actor attempts to send a request to your webhook route using a previously sent payload. If you'd prefer not to check against an expiry time, Mailgun suggests storing the `token` value in the `signature` field in your cache. As the `token` is unique to each request, you can check if it has been used by storing it in your cache. If it has, then the request is invalid and should be rejected.

For this guide, we will check the timestamp to ensure that the request isn't older than 1 minute. If it is, we'll reject the request.

You can change this threshold depending on the type of application you're building. Reducing the threshold to a lower time can improve the security of the webhook route by reducing the timeframe in which a request could be captured and replayed in an attack. However, making the threshold too small could cause valid requests to be rejected, so it's important to balance security and usability. To help you decide on a suitable time threshold, consider the following:

- **Network latency** - If your Laravel app experiences high latency, the requests can take longer to send. You may want to increase the threshold to account for this.
- **Risk tolerance** - Consider the severity of the consequences if a malicious user could exploit your webhook route. If there is potential for harm, you may want to reduce the threshold to reduce the risk of this happening.

It's also important to ensure your server's clock is correct. If not, the request could be rejected even if it's valid because the timestamp in the `signature` field will be too different from the timestamp on your server. A computer's clock can "drift" over time, as they usually don't run at precisely the correct speed. Over time, this causes the system time to become less accurate. This may go unnoticed until time-based activities (such as checking the signature of an incoming webhook request) fail. To keep your server's clock in sync, you can use NTP (network time protocol) to sync it with an external authoritative system's time. We won't be covering how to keep your server's clock in sync in this guide, but it's an essential part of configuring a robust server.

To start with verifying that the request has been sent from Mailgun, create a new middleware using the following command:

```
php artisan make:middleware VerifyMailgunWebhook
```

You should now have a new `app/Http/Middleware/VerifyMailgunWebhook.php` file. Let's apply this middleware to our `MailgunController` route that will handle the webhook requests. We can do this by using the `middleware` method like so:

```
use App\Http\Controllers\Api\Webhooks\MailgunController;
use App\Http\Middleware\VerifyMailgunWebhook;
use Illuminate\Support\Facades\Route;

Route::post('/webhooks/mailgun', MailgunController::class)
    ->name('webhooks.mailgun')
    ->middleware(VerifyMailgunWebhook::class);
```

We can now update our `VerifyMailgunWebhook` class. It may look like so:

```
declare(strict_types=1);

namespace App\Http\Middleware;

use Carbon\Carbon;
use Closure;
use Illuminate\Http\Request;
use Symfony\Component\HttpFoundation\Response;

final readonly class VerifyMailgunWebhook
{
    public function handle(Request $request, Closure $next): Response
    {
        if (!$this->verify($request)) {
            abort(Response::HTTP_FORBIDDEN, 'Invalid signature.');
        }
```

```
        return $next($request);
    }

    private function verify(Request $request): bool
    {
        return $this->signatureIsValid($request)
            && $this->timestampIsRecent($request);
    }

    private function signatureIsValid(Request $request): bool
    {
        $expectedSignature = $request->input('signature.signature');

        return $this->buildSignature($request) === $expectedSignature;
    }

    private function buildSignature(Request $request): string
    {
        $token = $request->input('signature.token');
        $timestamp = $request->input('signature.timestamp');

        return hash_hmac(
            algo: 'sha256',
            data: $timestamp.$token,
            key: config('services.mailgun.secret'),
        );
    }

    /**
     * Ensure the timestamp is within 1 minute of the current time.
```

```
     */
    private function timestampIsRecent(Request $request): bool
    {
        $timestamp = $request->input('signature.timestamp');

        return now()->isBefore(
            Carbon::createFromTimestamp($timestamp)->addMinute()
        );
    }
}
```

Our `VerifyMailgunWebhook` middleware class is now responsible for verifying that the request is from Mailgun and was sent less than a minute ago. If the request is invalid, we'll return a 403 (forbidden) response. Otherwise, we'll continue with the request as normal. We can now safely assume that if the request makes it to our `MailgunController` route, it's a valid request from Mailgun.

Testing Webhook Routes

As with any other part of your API integration, it's important to ensure you have automated tests for your webhooks. These tests increase your confidence that your webhooks are secure and working as expected.

Let's write tests for the webhook route created in the previous section for handling Mailgun events. Before we write any tests, let's break down what we want to test:

1. The webhook route returns an error if the request is not sent from Mailgun.
2. The webhook route returns an error if the request is for a webhook event we do not support.
3. The webhook route returns an error if the request was sent over 1 minute ago.
4. The `EmailLog` model can be updated to `delivered` when the `delivered` event is received.
5. The `EmailLog` model can be updated to `temporary_fail` when the `temporary_fail` event is received.
6. The `EmailLog` model can be updated to `permanent_fail` when the `permanent_fail` event is received.

As you might have noticed, tests 4, 5, and 6 are similar. For this reason, we can likely use data providers (as covered previously in this book) to reduce the amount of code we must write.

We will pass payloads from JSON files to simulate the webhook request as much as possible. These payloads will contain the same request structure Mailgun sends when triggering a webhook event. Some third-party services, such as Mailgun, allow you to generate dummy payloads for these purposes. We assume we have generated four payloads and stored them in the following directories:

- **delivered** - `tests/Fixtures/Webhooks/Mailgun/delivered.json`
- **temporary_fail** - `tests/Fixtures/Webhooks/Mailgun/temporary_fail.json`
- **permanent_fail** - `tests/Fixtures/Webhooks/Mailgun/permanent_fail.json`

- **clicked** - `tests/Fixtures/Webhooks/Mailgun/clicked.json`

A benefit of using JSON files to define the test payloads is that it can help de-clutter test files to make them easier to maintain and read. It also means we can reuse the same payloads in multiple tests if needed.

The tests class may look something like this:

```
declare(strict_types=1);

namespace Tests\Feature\Controllers\Api\Webhooks;

use PHPUnit\Framework\Attributes\DataProvider;
use PHPUnit\Framework\Attributes\Test;
use App\Enums\EmailStatus;
use App\Models\EmailLog;
use Carbon\Carbon;
use Illuminate\Foundation\Testing\LazilyRefreshDatabase;
use Illuminate\Support\Facades\File;
use Tests\TestCase;

final class MailgunControllerTest extends TestCase
{
    use LazilyRefreshDatabase;

    protected function setUp(): void
    {
        parent::setUp();

        // Fix the time to the date and time included in the fixture JSON files.
        $this->travelTo(Carbon::parse('2023-03-27 15:52:16.0'));
```

```php
    }

    #[Test]
    #[DataProvider('validWebhookEventsProvider')]
    public function email_log_status_can_be_updated(
        string $jsonFixturePath,
        EmailStatus $status
    ): void {
        // Create the email log that should be updated. The ID is hardcoded in
        // the fixture JSON file, so we also set it here to ensure it matches.
        $emailLog = EmailLog::factory()->create(['id' => 123]);

        $postBody = File::json(
            path: base_path($jsonFixturePath),
            flags: JSON_THROW_ON_ERROR,
        );

        $this->post(route('api.webhooks.mailgun', $status), $postBody)
            ->assertOk()
            ->assertExactJson(['success' => true]);

        $this->assertSame(
            expected: $status,
            actual: $emailLog->fresh()->status,
        );
    }

    #[Test]
    public function error_is_returned_if_the_webhook_event_is_not_supported()
    {
        $postBody = File::json(
```

```php
        path: base_path('tests/Fixtures/Webhooks/Mailgun/clicked.json'),
        flags: JSON_THROW_ON_ERROR
    );

    $this->post(route('api.webhooks.mailgun', 'clicked'), $postBody)
        ->assertNotFound();
}

#[Test]
public function error_is_returned_if_the_request_was_not_sent_from_mailgun()
{
    $this->post(route('api.webhooks.mailgun', EmailStatus::Delivered), [
        'invalid_key' => 'invalid_value',
    ])
        ->assertForbidden();
}

#[Test]
public function error_is_returned_if_the_timestamp_is_not_recent(): void
{
    // Travel to 1 minute and 1 second after the JSON fixture's "timestamp"
    // field. This is outside the 1-minute threshold, so the request
    // should be rejected.
    $this->travelTo(Carbon::parse('2023-03-27 15:53:17.0'));

    $postBody = File::json(
        path: base_path('tests/Fixtures/Webhooks/Mailgun/clicked.json'),
        flags: JSON_THROW_ON_ERROR,
    );

    $this->post(
```

```
            route('api.webhooks.mailgun', EmailStatus::Delivered), $postBody
        )
            ->assertForbidden();
    }

    public static function validWebhookEventsProvider(): array
    {
        return [
            'delivered' => [
                'tests/Fixtures/Webhooks/Mailgun/delivered.json',
                EmailStatus::Delivered,
            ],
            'temporary_fail' => [
                'tests/Fixtures/Webhooks/Mailgun/temporary_fail.json',
                EmailStatus::TemporaryFail,
            ],
            'permanent_fail' => [
                'tests/Fixtures/Webhooks/Mailgun/permanent_fail.json',
                EmailStatus::PermanentFail,
            ],
        ];
    }
}
```

As a result of writing these tests, we have greater confidence that our webhook route is working as expected. If we were to make changes to the webhook route, we could run our tests to ensure we haven't broken existing functionality. Likewise, it also makes adding new webhook events (e.g., `clicked`) much easier as we can write the tests first and then write the code to make the tests pass.

Using Queues to Process Webhooks

Now that we understand how to receive and handle webhooks in our Laravel applications, let's see how we can take this further.

In the examples we've covered so far, we've only been performing a simple "update" statement to record the delivery status of an email. However, some webhooks may require more complex logic to be performed that may take longer to complete.

For example, your application might receive a webhook indicating a successful payment. In this case, you may create new rows in the database, email the customer, and notify your team on Slack that you have a new sale — this could take longer to run than a simple "update" statement.

For these reasons, handling the webhook request using a queued job can be useful. Doing this allows you to asynchronously process the webhook request without forcing the external service to wait for your application to complete all these tasks. This means you can quickly respond to the webhook request while processing the job in the background.

Benefits of Processing Webhooks Using Queues

Processing webhooks using queued jobs can provide many benefits. Let's look at some of these benefits in more detail.

Rate Limiting

By using Laravel's queue system to process webhooks, you can access the rate-limiting features the framework provides. This lets you limit the number of jobs processed within a given time frame.

Limiting the number of webhooks processed at once can help reduce the load on your application's database.

For example, say you send 10,000 emails from your Laravel application using Mailgun and you've configured Mailgun to send you a webhook for each email. Doing this would likely result in your application receiving 10,000 webhook requests in a short time. Depending on your infrastructure and how well-optimized your code is, your application may be able to handle these synchronously all at once (as covered in our previous code examples).

However, it's likely receiving all the webhooks at once (partnered with the usual traffic and activity your application receives) could strain your application's infrastructure — especially your database. This could result in your app running slowly or even crashing if connections to the database timeout because of the load (something I've witnessed many times on projects I've worked on). This may frustrate your users and result in a loss of revenue if it happens often.

Let's look at a basic example of how you could add rate limiting to a job responsible for processing a webhook request.

In this example, we will limit the number of jobs processed to 100 per minute. This is an arbitrary number chosen for this example. You should choose a limit appropriate for your application and available resources. You should refer to your application's logs and usage metrics to help you fine-tune this number and find a good balance between speed and limiting load on your infrastructure.

To get started, define a rate limit in your `app/Providers/AppServiceProvider`'s `boot` method by using the `RateLimiter` facade:

```php
declare(strict_types=1);

namespace App\Providers;

use Illuminate\Cache\RateLimiting\Limit;
use Illuminate\Support\Facades\RateLimiter;
use Illuminate\Support\ServiceProvider;

class AppServiceProvider extends ServiceProvider
{
    // ...

    public function boot(): void
    {
        RateLimiter::for(
            name: 'mailgun-webhooks',
            callback: static fn ($job) => Limit::perMinute(100)
        );
    }
}
```

In the code above, we defined a rate limiter called `mailgun-webhooks` that we will use to ensure we only process a maximum of 100 jobs per minute.

We can use this rate limiter in our job using the `RateLimited` middleware. Assume we have a `ProcessEmailStatusWebhook` job responsible for handling the webhook request. We can add the `RateLimited` middleware to the job's `middleware` method like so:

```php
declare(strict_types=1);

namespace App\Jobs\Webhooks\Mailgun;

use Illuminate\Bus\Queueable;
use Illuminate\Contracts\Queue\ShouldQueue;
use Illuminate\Foundation\Bus\Dispatchable;
use Illuminate\Queue\InteractsWithQueue;
use Illuminate\Queue\Middleware\RateLimited;
use Illuminate\Queue\SerializesModels;

final class ProcessEmailStatusWebhook implements ShouldQueue
{
    use Dispatchable;
    use InteractsWithQueue;
    use Queueable;
    use SerializesModels;

    // ...

    public function middleware(): array
    {
        return [new RateLimited('mailgun-webhooks')];
    }
}
```

Retry Without Waiting for the External Service

Another benefit of processing webhooks using the queue is that we can retry the job if it fails. As mentioned, some services, such as Mailgun, can resend webhooks if they fail to receive a successful response from your application. However, not all services provide this functionality.

If your application fails to process the webhook when it's first sent (for example, because of a bug in your code), you may not receive the webhook again. This can be problematic if it's crucial to process the webhook.

By processing the webhook using a queued job, you can rely on Laravel to retry the job if it fails. This removes the need to wait for the external service to resend the webhook.

It also means that if any webhooks fail to process, you can easily retry them using the `queue:retry` Artisan command. You may do this if you've fixed a bug in your code that was causing the webhook to fail.

Creating a New Job Class

Let's look at how to update our previous code examples to process the webhook using a queued job. To get started, we'll need to create a new job class. We can do this by running the following `make:job` Artisan command:

```
php artisan make:job Webhooks/Mailgun/ProcessEmailStatusWebhook
```

This should create a new `app/Jobs/Webhooks/Mailgun/ProcessEmailStatus.php` job class for us. We'll move the logic (that updated the row in the database) from our controller and into this job class. The job class should look something like this:

```php
namespace App\Jobs\Webhooks\Mailgun;

use App\Enums\EmailStatus;
use App\Models\EmailLog;
use Illuminate\Bus\Queueable;
use Illuminate\Contracts\Queue\ShouldQueue;
use Illuminate\Foundation\Bus\Dispatchable;
use Illuminate\Queue\InteractsWithQueue;
use Illuminate\Queue\SerializesModels;

final class ProcessEmailStatusWebhook implements ShouldQueue
{
    use Dispatchable;
    use InteractsWithQueue;
    use Queueable;
    use SerializesModels;

    public function __construct(
        public readonly int $emailId,
        public readonly EmailStatus $emailStatus,
    ) {
        //
    }

    public function handle(): void
    {
        // Update the email log with the new status.
        EmailLog::query()
            ->whereKey($this->emailId)
            ->update([
```

```
                'status' => $this->emailStatus,
            ]);
    }
}
```

We haven't included any rate limiting or retry logic in this job class, but this may be something that you want to add.

You may have noticed in our job's constructor that we're only accepting the email ID and the email status. We're not accepting the actual webhook data or request object. This means we'll be responsible for parsing the data we need for this job from the request in our controller.

An advantage of this approach is that we can keep our job class simple and focused on doing one thing. We'll only pass it the information needed to do its job. It also means this job class can be reused in other places in our application because it's decoupled from an HTTP request, although this is unlikely if it's a bespoke job only for processing a specific type of webhook. As we'll see later, this approach also makes it easier to test our job class because we can easily mock the data that we must pass to it.

A disadvantage of only passing the bare minimum number of parameters and not the request object is that this can limit the usefulness of retrying the job if it fails. For example, imagine we have a bug in our controller and pass the `log-level` field from the JSON payload to the job class instead of passing the `email` field. If this leads to the job failing, there wouldn't be much benefit in retrying the job because it would fail again (due to the incorrect data being passed to it). Therefore, it's essential to be aware that bugs outside the job class can prevent the job from being retried successfully because the job class will not know about the request object.

You'll need to decide which of these approaches you prefer: passing the request object to the job class or only passing the data it needs. There's no right or wrong approach here, and it will depend on your application's requirements.

Generally, I opt towards only passing the needed data directly (as parameters) or in the form of a data transfer object. This encourages me to keep the job class lean and focused on doing one thing while ensuring that my controller is only used for parsing data from the request, dispatching the job, and returning an HTTP response. To reduce the likelihood of bugs in my controller, I also write tests for it (which we'll see later) that ensure the job is dispatched with the correct data.

Updating the Controller

Now that we have created our job class to process the webhook, we can update our controller to dispatch the job. We can do this by updating our controller like so:

```php
declare(strict_types=1);

namespace App\Http\Controllers\Api\Webhooks;

use App\Enums\EmailStatus;
use App\Http\Controllers\Controller;
use App\Jobs\Webhooks\Mailgun\ProcessEmailStatusWebhook;
use Illuminate\Http\JsonResponse;
use Illuminate\Http\Request;

final class MailgunController extends Controller
{
    public function __invoke(Request $request, EmailStatus $status): JsonResponse
    {
        // Grab the data we need from the request.
        $emailId = $request->input('event-data.user-variables.email_id');

        ProcessEmailStatusWebhook::dispatch(
            emailId: $emailId,
            emailStatus: $status,
        );

        // Return a successful response.
        return response()->json(['success' => true]);
    }
}
```

As you can see, we've replaced the logic that updated the row in the database with `ProcessEmailStatusWebhook::dispatch()`. This will dispatch the job to the queue with the

ID of the email that we want to update and the new email status.

That's it. We've now updated our controller to asynchronously process the webhook using a queued job.

Updating the Tests

Now that our application code has been updated, let's update our tests. We'll start by updating our `MailgunControllerTest`.

We want to update our tests so they no longer assert that the `$emailLog` model has been updated. Instead, we want to assert that the `ProcessEmailStatusWebhook` job has been dispatched with the correct data.

To assert whether the job has been dispatched, we can first use the `Queue::fake()` method in our `setUp` method to fake the `ProcessEmailStatusWebhook` job. This will prevent the job from being dispatched and run in each of the tests while allowing us to assert that the correct data was passed to it by using the `Queue::assertPushed` method.

We can do this by updating our tests like so:

```
declare(strict_types=1);

namespace Tests\Feature\Controllers\Api\Webhooks;

use App\Jobs\Webhooks\Mailgun\ProcessEmailStatusWebhook;
use Illuminate\Support\Facades\Queue;
use PHPUnit\Framework\Attributes\DataProvider;
use PHPUnit\Framework\Attributes\Test;
use App\Enums\EmailStatus;
```

```php
use App\Models\EmailLog;
use Carbon\Carbon;
use Illuminate\Foundation\Testing\LazilyRefreshDatabase;
use Illuminate\Support\Facades\File;
use Tests\TestCase;

final class MailgunControllerTest extends TestCase
{
    use LazilyRefreshDatabase;

    protected function setUp(): void
    {
        parent::setUp();

        // Fix the time to the date and time included in the fixture JSON files.
        $this->travelTo(Carbon::parse('2023-03-27 15:52:16.0'));

        Queue::fake([ProcessEmailStatusWebhook::class]);
    }

    #[Test]
    #[DataProvider('validWebhookEventsProvider')]
    public function email_log_status_can_be_updated(
        string $jsonFixturePath,
        EmailStatus $status
    ): void {
        // Create the email log that should be updated. The ID is hardcoded in
        // the fixture JSON file, so we also set it here to ensure it matches.
        $emailLog = EmailLog::factory()->create(['id' => 123]);

        $postBody = File::json(
```

```
        path: base_path($jsonFixturePath),
        flags: JSON_THROW_ON_ERROR,
    );

    $this->post(
        route('api.webhooks.mailgun.queued',$status),
        $postBody
    )
        ->assertOk()
        ->assertExactJson(['success' => true]);

    Queue::assertPushed(
        job: ProcessEmailStatusWebhook::class,
        callback: static fn (ProcessEmailStatusWebhook $job): bool =>
            $job->emailId === $emailLog->id
            && $job->emailStatus === $status
    );
}

#[Test]
public function error_is_returned_if_the_webhook_event_is_not_supported()
{
    $postBody = File::json(
        path: base_path('tests/Fixtures/Webhooks/Mailgun/clicked.json'),
        flags: JSON_THROW_ON_ERROR
    );

    $this->post(route('api.webhooks.mailgun.queued', 'clicked'), $postBody)
        ->assertNotFound();

    Queue::assertNothingPushed();
```

```
    }

    #[Test]
    public function error_is_returned_if_the_request_was_not_sent_from_mailgun()
    {
        $this->post(
            route('api.webhooks.mailgun.queued', EmailStatus::Delivered), [
                'invalid_key' => 'invalid_value',
            ]
        )
            ->assertForbidden();

        Queue::assertNothingPushed();
    }

    #[Test]
    public function error_is_returned_if_the_timestamp_is_not_recent(): void
    {
        // Travel to 1 minute and 1 second after the JSON fixture's "timestamp"
        // field. This is outside the 1-minute threshold, so the request
        // should be rejected.
        $this->travelTo(Carbon::parse('2023-03-27 15:53:17.0'));

        $postBody = File::json(
            path: base_path('tests/Fixtures/Webhooks/Mailgun/clicked.json'),
            flags: JSON_THROW_ON_ERROR,
        );

        $this->post(
            route('api.webhooks.mailgun.queued', EmailStatus::Delivered),
            $postBody
```

```
        )
            ->assertForbidden();

        Queue::assertNothingPushed();
    }

    public static function validWebhookEventsProvider(): array
    {
        return [
            'delivered' => [
                'tests/Fixtures/Webhooks/Mailgun/delivered.json',
                EmailStatus::Delivered,
            ],
            'temporary_fail' => [
                'tests/Fixtures/Webhooks/Mailgun/temporary_fail.json',
                EmailStatus::TemporaryFail,
            ],
            'permanent_fail' => [
                'tests/Fixtures/Webhooks/Mailgun/permanent_fail.json',
                EmailStatus::PermanentFail,
            ],
        ];
    }
}
```

Since our controller tests no longer check that the row in the database is updated, we'll need to add some tests for our `ProcessEmailStatusWebhook` job.

We can create a simple test that uses a data provider to accept every type of valid email status. We'll then test that our job correctly updates the email log with the correct status.

The test class may look something like so:

```php
declare(strict_types=1);

namespace Tests\Feature\Jobs\Webhooks\Mailgun;

use App\Jobs\Webhooks\Mailgun\ProcessEmailStatusWebhook;
use PHPUnit\Framework\Attributes\DataProvider;
use PHPUnit\Framework\Attributes\Test;
use App\Enums\EmailStatus;
use App\Models\EmailLog;
use Illuminate\Foundation\Testing\LazilyRefreshDatabase;
use Tests\TestCase;

final class ProcessEmailStatusWebhookTest extends TestCase
{
    use LazilyRefreshDatabase;

    #[Test]
    #[DataProvider('validEmailStatusProvider')]
    public function email_log_status_can_be_updated(EmailStatus $status): void
    {
        // Create the email log that should be updated. The ID is hardcoded in
        // the fixture JSON file, so we also set it here to ensure it matches.
        $emailLog = EmailLog::factory()->create(['id' => 123]);

        $job = new ProcessEmailStatusWebhook(
            emailId: $emailLog->id,
            emailStatus: $status,
        );
```

```php
        $job->handle();

        $this->assertSame(
            expected: $status,
            actual: $emailLog->fresh()->status,
        );
    }

    public static function validEmailStatusProvider(): array
    {
        return array_map(
            callback: static fn($status): array => [$status],
            array: EmailStatus::cases()
        );
    }
}
```

By doing all of the above, we've been able to test our webhook integration and ensure that our Mailgun webhooks are processed asynchronously.

Conclusion

In this chapter, we've reviewed what webhooks are, why you would use them, and the integration and secure handling of them in Laravel applications. We learned how to use middleware to secure webhook requests, ensuring they originate from the proper source and are timely. We also delved into writing tests to fortify our confidence in our webhooks' secure and effective operation. Additionally, the chapter explained the use of queues for asynchronous processing, granting us the benefits of rate-limiting and robust retry mechanisms. By coupling these elements with good practices, we're well-poised to develop scalable and resilient Laravel applications that can seamlessly interface with webhooks.

Final Words

That's it. All done!

I hope you enjoyed reading *Consuming APIs in Laravel* as much as I enjoyed writing it. I really do hope you've learned some new things and that you feel more confident as a web developer. Hopefully, you now feel confident enough to build awesome API integrations that add cool features to your Laravel applications.

I want to give a huge thank you to Jess Allen (jesspickup.co.uk) for creating the amazing front cover for the book and the artwork for the website!

I also want to thank some other people who have played huge roles in getting this book to release:

- Sam Carré for actually creating the amazing Saloon package and giving me constant feedback.
- JD Lien for all his help with proofreading and removing my silly mistakes.
- Jon Purvis for the feedback and support in each chapter.
- API Insights for sponsoring the book.
- Everyone else that has given me feedback and support along the way. You know who you are!

I appreciate every single one of you and I couldn't have done it without you!

If you enjoyed this book, you might also be interested in checking out my other book: *Battle Ready Laravel*. It's a guide to auditing, testing, fixing, and improving your Laravel applications. You can find out more about it at battle-ready-laravel.com.

If you have any feedback on the book, feel free to reach out to me:

- Website - ashallendesign.co.uk
- Email - mail@ashallendesign.co.uk
- GitHub - github.com/ash-jc-allen
- Twitter/X - twitter.com/AshAllenDesign
- LinkedIn - linkedin.com/in/ashleyjcallen

Keep on building awesome stuff!

Printed in Great Britain
by Amazon

30203339R00304